Building Stakeholder Relations and Corporate Social Responsibility

'Contemporary post-capitalist society is the society of organizations and the knowledge society, as Peter F. Drucker characterized the social context of the present economy and business. It calls for new relations between all parties engaged. Their stakes (tangible and intangible) should be identified and the stakeholders, both internal and external, get involved in the process of social contract formulation. An organization, whether company, corporation, or enterprise, is a dynamic system composed of stakeholder groups (subsystems) between which, and the organization as a whole, exist necessary contradictions, but aims of particular subsystems (return of the stakes) may be reached as a consequence of achieving the goal of the organization as a whole only. The fundamental structural fact of an organization is the solidarity of aims taken for granted in the structure of the organization; this is why a sense-making perspective is so important for mutual relations between stakeholders of any organization. This very idea is presented by Dr Barbara Fryzel, a scholar of the Jagellonian University, Krakow, Poland, in an excellent manner. Her book – addressed to leaders and managers, business ethicists, and corporate citizenship activists – offers the innovative approach to corporate social responsibility strategy planning and practice.'

Professor Wojciech W. Gasparski, *Dr. Sc., Director, Business Ethics Center, a joint unit of the Kozminski University and the Polish Academy of Sciences, Warsaw, Poland; Member of the Academy of Management; Society for Business Ethics; and the International Society of Business, Economics and Ethics*

Reviewers of the book were:

Professor Peter Abell, London School of Economics and Political Science, UK; and Copenhagen Business School, Denmark

Professor Lidia Zbiegień-Maciąg, AGH University of Science and Technology, Krakow, Poland

Also by Barbara Fryzel and published by Palgrave Macmillan

THE ROLE OF LARGE ENTERPRISES IN DEMOCRACY AND SOCIETY
(co-editor with Paul H. Dembinski)

Building Stakeholder Relations and Corporate Social Responsibility

Barbara Fryzel

First published 2011 by
PALGRAVE MACMILLAN

Palgrave Macmillan in the UK is an imprint of Macmillan Publishers Limited, registered in England, company number 785998, of Houndmills, Basingstoke, Hampshire RG21 6XS.

Palgrave Macmillan in the US is a division of St Martin's Press LLC, 175 Fifth Avenue, New York, NY 10010.

Palgrave Macmillan is the global academic imprint of the above companies and has companies and representatives throughout the world.

Palgrave® and Macmillan® are registered trademarks in the United States, the United Kingdom, Europe and other countries.

ISBN 978–0–230–27325–2

This book is printed on paper suitable for recycling and made from fully managed and sustained forest sources. Logging, pulping and manufacturing processes are expected to conform to the environmental regulations of the country of origin.

A catalogue record for this book is available from the British Library.

A catalog record for this book is available from the Library of Congress.

10   9   8   7   6   5   4   3   2   1
20   19   18   17   16   15   14   13   12   11

Printed and bound in Great Britain by
CPI Antony Rowe, Chippenham and Eastbourne

Contents

v

List of Tables and Figures

Tables

Figures

Acknowledgments

I would like to thank the reviewers of this book, Professor Lidia Zbiegień-Maciag of the University of Science and Technology, Krakow, and Professor Peter Abell of the London School of Economics and Copenhagen Business School. The comments of Professor Zbiegień-Maciag helped me to improve the final text and the presentation of the conclusions. My special thanks go as well to Professor Peter Abell for his suggestions regarding new potential areas of further investigation derived as a consequence of the research results presented in the book. I also thank Professor Wojciech Gasparski for sharing his insights on CSR, specifically in its regional-embedded context.

The project was financed by the Polish Ministry of Science and Higher Education as part of the research grant no. NN115 5513 38.

BARBARA FRYZEL

Introduction

The definition of corporate social responsibility used in this book, assumes that it is an approach to management where the enterprise needs to find a balance between the interests of all the stakeholders in a way which not only maximizes the value of the company but also contributes to the wellbeing of a society and the generation of common good, including wealth. The concept of corporate social responsibility (CSR) postulates exceeding a standard compliance with law and as such it becomes an expectation that companies will actively engage in fulfilling their duties towards the stakeholders. It is an expectation that corporate codes of conduct will be backed up by more profound strategic deeds.

Such a definition counters Friedman's statement that 'the business of business is business'. In fact, generating value in the economic sense and contributing to the wellbeing of a society are both at the core of the business activity, specifically given the postulation of the social legitimization of the business, according to which only those companies which are useful – that is, generate needed and useful outcomes – are legitimate. A contradiction between economic and social goals is artificial and unjustified.

Such a definition of CSR also points towards a broader discourse about the role of business at large in a society, the role inevitably changing in parallel to how the borders between private and public sphere evolve, how the activities traditionally inherent to the public sphere are gradually taken over by the private sphere, while the mutual relations between private and public are becoming increasingly interlocked (WBCSD, 2006).

These can be seen most explicitly in the privatization processes in Central and Eastern Europe, especially in the sectors traditionally public such as education, health and communication infrastructure, where more and more projects are being realized in public–private partnership (PPP) structures.

Apart from the fact that a discussion about CSR significantly evolved from the initial concept of corporate citizenship, whereby the enterprise would treat equally individual members of the society as far as obligations towards other societal actors were concerned, the concept of CSR is also subject to organic development, as it keeps incorporating various operational complexities into its basic dogma.

First, there is a clear polarization of the character of CSR, depending on the organizational form of an enterprise. Private and public enterprises enjoy different possibilities as far as decisions about utilizing the assets are concerned. In private enterprises, where ownership is often merged with the management and control functions, they are more flexible, while in public enterprises, where the manager is considered an agent for the capital provider, responsible for the most effective allocation of that capital and all the resources financed by that capital, including time, a business case is needed to justify the engagement in corporate social responsibility activities. The fact that entities where the ownership and management functions are separated build business cases justifying involvement in CSR is not, therefore, a proof of the instrumentality with which they treat an issue of business responsibility; in fact, it is proof of the responsible treatment of the resources they manage and which belong to someone else. For that reason CSR involvement in private companies and in public ones should be assessed from different perspectives.

Second, transnational corporations (TNCs) present a different case with regard to responsibility, which usually gets analyzed from the perspective of their patriotic obligations towards their own country (Jones, 2005), which are ignored when a company extensively outsources its operations to low-cost countries, thus, at the same time, depriving its own country from the economic growth opportunities afforded, with no consideration of the structural and organizational consequences of such a strategy. TNCs managed to convert themselves into coordination centres, controlling the vast supply networks in the supply chains, but formally not having a legal and direct responsibility for a great deal of operational risk. Additionally, a deep work specialization in the supply network and often their total economic dependency upon a key customer, exercising its purchasing power, destabilizes the whole sector, when the supplier loses the client but does not have the capacity to subsidize the loss by converting immediately to other production and other potential customers. One of the questions which comes to mind as a natural consequence of this process is whether we will be confronted with a necessity to split TNCs by law (Dembinski, 2010). The question is not completely unjustified if the discourse about the new economy is considered, whereby the assumptions of the classical economic theory are questioned, the suggestion being that they are not valid any more (Fryzel, 2009).

Third, there are significant changes in the internal environment of organizations which emanate to the external environment, mainly influencing the structure of the labor market. A fundamental change in the dynamics of relations between the manager and the employee can be noticed, whereby a manager executing a linear relation with the team members based on a simple exchange of pay for work is now expected to exercise a much more complex network of employee relations based on the multiplicity of managerial roles. Instead of being simply an executor of the work quality and a check as to whether the work was done as agreed, a manager becomes a mentor, a coach, a leader, caring also for the development of professional career of his people and as well for their work–life balance. A manager is expected to understand the cultural aspects and subtleties of the international environment he manages and, moreover, he is often stigmatized where this environment does not meet the social expectations in terms of its ethical and moral quality – falling into the category of 'McJobs', whereby the benefits of the behavioral evolution of management science are compromised for the sake of its effectiveness and cost-optimization, thus leading to a certain 'taylorization'.

A paradigm of optimizing the labor cost and giving the companies more flexibility to maneuver with its workforce capacity, which is particularly useful in times of crisis, has led also to significant changes of the forms of labor contracts, which give potentially dangerous social results.

Flexible employment forms, based on civil law contracts instead of labor law, on the one hand make it easier for the company to reduce the workforce, thus diminishing the strength of corporate obligations towards the employee, who suddenly gets converted into a 'supplier' of certain services. On the other hand, they break the bond of a long-term loyalty of employee towards the employer built on the basis of the psychological contract without offering any serious substitute. The contractual obligations related to handling sensitive information belonging to a client can hardly be sufficient from the point of view of the enterprises who now deal with contractual suppliers, usually working on multiple contracts to secure their living.

Enterprises operating with more flexibility are more exposed to the risks of losing intellectual property or compromising their know-how, not to mention that, although contractual arrangements might be more effective in short term, in the long term they may affect negatively knowledge-building capacity as well as the intellectual and social capital of the company. Given that we are talking about intangible assets such as knowledge, as a key success factor of the company in the knowledge-based economy, the question emerges as to whether outsourcing of employment should become subject to risk management procedures as the company outsources its core asset.

On a macro scale, it is also possible to imagine a scenario, in which the mass-scale outsourcing of employment stimulated by the increasing pressures on cost-efficiency and flexibility of corporate resources, leads to the polarization of the labor market between the minority of fully employed managers responsible for the complex business processes which will always be retained in-house and the majority of the workforce specialized in basic business processes which are likely to be outsourced. Will this lead to a further polarization of the labor market between highly remunerated directors, well embedded on the market, and low-paid contractual employees navigating between temporary job contracts and always dealing with a permanent uncertainty? Since, for the majority of people, enforcing temporary contracts is distressing, should this be seen as an attack against employees, undermining any sense of worker allegiance?

A natural consequence of these processes is an observable loss of the traditionally understood loyalty between employer and the employee, for which the market does not seem to be offering an alternative. The practical question emerges: what should become a basis for managing employees' attitudes, if not long-term employment based loyalty? Perhaps value systems should be reconsidered in management education?

More importantly, current formal corporate social responsibility programs do not offer the answer to these deep dilemmas, since their implementation does not seem to relate explicitly to reducing the risk of unethical behavior in the workplace. What does reduce such wrong-doings as fraud, corruption or use of corporate assets for private purposes is investment in employees (training, education, benefit systems), as this creates the only situation in which wrong-doing does not pay off (Turek, 2010).

Fourth, there is a risk of marginalizing real value CSR engagements, in those cases where enterprises attempt to build dialogical relations with stakeholders and make it a foundation for strategic CSR, as acclaimed by Porter and Kramer in their HBR text (Porter and Kramer, 2006), through attempts to control the public sphere instrumentally for the sake of gaining public consensus. Excessive use and wrong interpretation of public relations can often become an instrumental tool of such control. On the one hand, there is increasing communication and promotional activity in the private sector, combined with financialization of the CSR concept (eco buildings, various forms of cause-related marketing thriving on a niche segment of ethical consumerism). On the other hand, excessive reporting as well as the normalization and standardization trends open the gates for creating significant financial flows using the social sentiment but offering dubious returns (for example, 'good food' – a trade mark recently promoted in Poland, supposedly guaranteeing that no additives are used and the product is well balanced, but treated with a great deal of suspicion by the public; the same applies to the certification of CSR standards such as SA8000 or AA1000, which are perceived specifically by the SME sector as a dubious way of making money by consultants).

This is not a political science book, where the main theme would be focused on discussion about political systems and their interactions with the fabric of society at large. Neither is this a book about the philosophy of society and ontology of notions such as common good, attempting to verify how can it be defined and whether it exists at all.[1]

This is a management book written from the perspective of the observer and researcher, which situates the observed phenomena in the context of the profound social and organizational changes we are witnessing – changes whose evolutionary or revolutionary character is yet to be determined. Nevertheless it is a book standing in between all the interdisciplinary shifts and perspectives inherent to the area of management. Having said that, any analytical asymmetry manifesting itself through the preferential treatment of a selected perspective, be it sociological, economical, political or other, however well it might fulfill the paradigms of academic research, will not return an accurate and heuristic view on the reality analyzed, which, by definition, spans a variety of intellectual lines of thought, as management activity in reality spans various areas of human activity, requesting from managers that they are good technocrats as well as psychologists and sometimes even politicians. Inevitably, discussing and analyzing the world of management becomes increasingly squeezed between explanatory limits of traditional research techniques (and what is deemed to be a sound academic approach) and the overwhelming complexity of the environment in which enterprises function, influencing its shape at the same time in a very dynamic manner.

Not only are analysts and observers of everyday organizational life confronted with the traditional polarizations between descriptive and explanatory, qualitative and quantitative, static and dynamic; today's challenge is, also, more about intellectualizing about directions of causality and patterns of interlocks between spheres of life, which so far have remained visibly different if not distant – for example, public and private spheres, politics and business, social policies and governmental duties to care for citizens versus economic policies and government duties to provide a proper environment for business operations.[2]

The goal of the book is, therefore, to look into the organizational world, specifically into enterprises, which, on the one hand, became powerful entities, whose influence on all aspects of human life has been commented upon and analyzed over the last few decades and which, on the other hand, have experienced quite dramatic evolution and change within their own framework of operations.

Enterprises, out of the rich variety of organizational entities, became one of the key players on the market. Motivated by financial gain and subject to greed, they can potentially do more harm than any other entity. They accumulate a disturbing amount of power over the spheres which used to be public – examples include health services and education. On the other hand, specifically in those countries with post-communist experience, asymmetrically positioned enterprises are exposed, paradoxically, through the activities of non-profit organizations, who not only become significant stakeholders in corporations while they try to channel social problems and expectations and accommodate them via a nexus of fundraising, but also become a substitute or perhaps even a new form of public sphere in Habermas's sense, as they develop towards stronger civil society. Thus, we have an operational setting in which CSR becomes an intervening construct between business and society, thus accommodating one more dichotomy of for-profit versus not-for-profit operations.

Using Balmer and Soenen's (1999) approach, this book researches selectively communicated identities,[3] specifically corporate reputations among stakeholders (four cases) and corporate communications using the method of analysis of media coverage (a sample of 150 enterprises).

The book starts by showing the overall context of this evolution – which is the source of today's discussion about the place enterprises occupy in the world, their role in society and their ontological status with all the deriving consequences, specifically their responsibilities. I discuss, the corporate social responsibility concept as a result of power asymmetry embedded in the globalization process.

While it is a strategic aspect of responsibility on its corporate level, which becomes a key focus of the book, minimizing the issue of individual ethics, it does not mean that the latter is less important; however, not being a psychologist, one needs to admit that the individual aspect of CSR – that is ethics – is also a construct which needs to be managed to ensure coherence between individual and corporate goals. In that sense we shall, rather, concentrate on the cultural aspect of organization which intermediates between individual human nature, which is untamable at organizational level, and the operational goal of organization, thus providing a value-based tool for managing teams.

However, the goal is also to look into organizational practices which happen at the interface between organizations and their direct communities, however seamless it might seem, and to understand how the organizations function in the dynamic and fluid environment of relations they create with various constituencies – the relations which, by their very nature, destabilize the technocratically determined concept of the organization as a separated entity with closed-end processes subjected to managerial engineering.[4] Enterprises are social constructs of relations upon which their existence depends. Construction of those relations, naturally embedded in the interpretations of the world around us, converts them into a consensus of meaning between the parties involved.

I continue, in the second chapter, introducing, thus, a sensemaking perspective of CSR and concentrating specifically on the meaning-related spheres of organizational life, such as identity creation, which, being a metaphor in itself, becomes the key meaning creation platform through which the organization negotiates its position among its constituencies. A discussion about the communication processes follows, which helps to transpose corporate identity to its operational environment.

The third chapter presents what is, hopefully, a complex and heuristic view of stakeholder relations. Polish enterprises build and operate in their local environments and generally on the market. The relations are intermediated by the concept of corporate identity and negotiated through the process of communication, along the lines of the theoretical background presented in the second chapter.

The combination of qualitative and quantitative methods, presented in the third chapter, follows, first deconstructing and verifying the macro-scale assumptions about potential causal relations between identity and the communication strategies; second, presenting specific trends within local environments; and, third, building the heuristic portraits of four organizational cases, showing the processes of their identity construction at length, positioned within the context of their local environments.[5]

The book is based on a research method designed on the basis of previously defined theoretical framework. Although methodologically I tried to observe academic rigor, I also try to present the results of the investigation, as well as the conclusions and intellectual speculations, in a narrative manner, addressed to practitioners, managers and business people – all those involved in operational management – who may find some of the conclusions presented here useful in planning strategies for building their relational network.

The approach used in the presented study is embedded in epistemological dualism, typical, it seems, in social sciences (Sułkowski, 2006). The issue of corporate communication with the environment is treated as part of a larger discourse upon relations between business and society at large. The questions which come to mind are, specifically:

- Are enterprises using local communities as the medium to take over control of public spheres to be able simply to better manage the risk?

- Can an increased engagement of local communities in dialogue with enterprises become a counterbalance for lack of a traditional public sphere and can it become a platform for discourse regarding common, public good?

1

Corporate Social Responsibility: A Response to Growing Corporate Power

Globalization and evolving forms of enterprises

Sources of pressure on businesses

Contemplation of the concept of corporate social responsibility as a derivative of certain conditions markets create, thus determining the nature of relations between various market players, positions it in the context of major forces in today's economic and social changes. Those changes include the processes of globalization and, as a result of corporate adjustment, structural changes in the way the companies operate. Contemporary enterprises do not resemble much the businesses of past eras, even more recent decades, in anything more than that profit and wealth generation remains their main driving force. Apart from the obvious external determinants of this evolution – for example, the mentioned globalization – there are some endogenous changes influencing the look of contemporary businesses, such as:

- the changing role of employees,
- the nature of work itself, with its processes becoming increasingly complex,
- different and new competencies replacing the old ones, as is the case with the sectors specifically prone to technological advancement, where traditionally understood meta-competencies responsible for the complex process of understanding the surrounding world and solving the problems it creates are being replaced by narrowly defined technical ones, creating as a result a new elite of workers, composed of those who are capable of understanding

11

the new systems and as such control, in a sense, the information flow in organizations.

The latter also is a form of contemporary power in organizations. Apart from the profound shifts in internal power structures, there is a significant asymmetry of power spread among the market players, with big enterprises clearly in a privileged position as they accumulate formal power, either economic (deriving from the control of resources) or economies of scale or scope or accumulation of capital, or as they accumulate informal power, often politically embedded as is the case of monopolies or oligopolies in the non-liberalized sectors. Moreover, these changes are wrapped in the phenomena of diluting borders between the private sphere and public sphere, which increasingly tend to overlap, thus contributing to uncertainty and lack of clarity as far as solving of moral dilemmas is concerned.

Observing the interplay between those grand social and economical forces, unleashed, it seems, by the changing political setting of the past few decades (mainly underlined by the liberalization policies), two major lines of adjustment become visible. On the one hand, enterprises adjust to the evolving markets by changing their organizational structures and, on the other hand, societies adjust to the changing conditions, trying to make sense of the new influence setting, whereby global problems emerge, to which nation states and governments cannot offer a reasonable solution. Thus we have an interplay between the private sector, thriving on the new opportunities offered by the market and accumulating power, and societies trying to cope with emerging problems and the uncertainty as to who should be liable for dealing with them.

In such circumstances a growing corporate influence meets with a growing social expectation that businesses should participate accordingly in sustaining the collapsing environment, which ultimately provides its operational scene, where the wellbeing of communities becomes a background for the spending power of consumers in the end. Companies are pressurized through activities aimed at voicing social expectations, either through the network of watchdog organizations or directly through various forms of stakeholders' activism – which in a sense becomes a surrogate for the traditional public sphere, apparently currently in descent. Having said that, it is not impossible that a kind of downgrading observable even in those countries where the public sphere was linked to the institutions of civil society (mature markets and traditionally liberal economies as opposed to countries with the centrally planned economy tradition) is partly due to the growing conviction that various public sphere platforms, such as chambers of commerce, think tanks or research institutes, for example, increasingly serve as mediation platforms for business contacts with politicians rather than platforms of independent and free thought.

The direct results globalization brings to both the spheres mentioned, in some cases beneficial in some cases not, seem to justify such a view. While business seems to be benefiting from the possibilities to invest, produce and sell globally – soaring profits of enterprises may serve as a proof[1] –individual consumers continue losing a range of services aimed at guaranteeing state attention (public health services, for example) and become more exposed to market forces without being equipped, however, with parallel dynamics of their personal incomes. Given the accuracy of the information provided by the dynamics of the Gini coefficient, depicting the growing social stratification and polarization of economic status within societies, the fact that there is only a very limited number of individual beneficiaries of globalization does not seem to be easily deniable. While cultural benefits of globalization for individuals are difficult to contest, as people can enjoy freedom of movement, travel and information flow, economic benefits, show uneven distribution patterns, although it is significant that, while global wealth is ever increasing, societies are left ever more polarized.[2]

Given the described background, the social and economic basis for intellectual turmoil around the idea of untamed wealth and power of enterprises, as opposed to their responsibilities towards other market members, is strong enough to create a significant market force to be dealt with by companies. Thus, irrespective of whether analysts tend to link socially responsible actions to the individual, moral qualities of managers or to their Machiavellic urge to exploit the naivety of social activists and to turn it into new marketing potential, corporate social responsibility is another factor in managerial guidebooks, a phenomenon with the potential single-handedly to generate deadly operational risks; as such it requires equal attention to other strategic aspects of general management.

First, enterprises' operational policies are embedded in phenomena of economic globalization which drive and enforce the interdependence of enterprises and other actors. As the scale and scope of the negative impact of potential corporate wrong-doings on the lives of ever greater numbers of individuals grow, globalization encourages the discussion of new possibilities of governing and controlling businesses, preferably with the participation of a generally defined public.

Second, enterprises that are under strong market pressure to improve their transparency often fight against doing so, consequently resulting in a negative perception of the business sector at large, which may result in a downgrading of the individual image of a given company. The company might, therefore, be tempted to build their competitive strategies on the basis of social responsibility and corporate involvement in the issues important for their social environment.

Strategies of corporate social responsibility become legitimized if they are provable as genuinely implemented actions and deeds, adjusted to stakeholders' expectations and based on the accurate understanding of their actual needs. The importance of such legitimacy grows in parallel to the increasing criticism of social responsibility reports, often regarded skeptically as yet another public relations tool used to manipulate the social perception of corporate image. It seems that the key to an accurate understanding of stakeholders' needs and the tool to ensure a positive perception of corporate activities is an effective relation-building strategy. The latter has become recently strongly associated with proposals to involve stakeholders in regular dialogue with the company.

Increasing pressure on businesses, to include social goals in their actions, questions the traditional model of an enterprise, which prioritizes gain creation over other potential goals of the company. The reflection of such diversity of views on what the company is, who it should be serving and how, is expressed in the public discourse around corporate responsibility, which distinguishes the 'after profit' and 'before profit' model, acknowledging or denying the priority of shareholders against other groups of interest, respectively.

Evolution of operational forms

One of the most fundamental changes in the operational forms of enterprises was initiated by the split of ownership and managerial functions. This is not only the change in the formal structure of the decision-making process; much more importantly this change draws a division line between what used to be personal morality and ethical reasoning as the direct basis for dilemma solving, in the case of the owner of a family enterprise, and what now becomes complex and multidimensional accountability towards stakeholders, in the case of the paid manager who becomes the agent for the shareholder, being, at the same time, the steward of the capital she manages. With this change the concept of responsibility stopped being linear, in a sense, as it previously involved a possible bi-dimensional conflict between the owner managing his resources and operating in his environment and became non-linear with the agent/manager being an intermediary between owner and stakeholders and, thus, not only having to exercise his or her own moral rationale but also being responsible for aligning the moral sensitivities of the parties he is tied to through the employment contract or through other interdependencies, respectively.

The classic work of Berle and Means comes to mind, with its focus on the phenomenon of the power of managerial discretion, which had its roots in the Great Depression in the USA. Rising managerialism showed itself as a potential threat to democracy. Berle and Means were concerned not only with the classic problem of agency, as we would call it today, but also with a general accountability of managers towards society at large. Separation of ownership and control was obviously contributing to the growth of a discretion power of managers, mainly through decomposition of capital after 1920, as some sociologists would argue (Hilferding, 1981; Roe, 1994; Riesman, 1953). Capitalist leaders no longer run politics and, in consequence, there was a break-up of a ruling class. While Berle and Means were pointing at the dangers of managerial discretion, sociologists were praising new shareholder capitalism as an advancement of democracy. Interlocks were seen as a tool by which to exercise power dispersed among leading capitalists in the early 1920s. However, as they reduce competition and drive prices up, interlocks can also pose a threat to the very efficiency of the market economy. They also are a threat to democracy, as they intermediate the relations between 'formally' independent players, thus concentrating the power.[3] The latter is clearly related to control functions located in the non-executive board members elected, usually under the condition of their independency. However, it is not clear what interlocks mean; they are best explained as the understanding of the boards themselves – the role of independent directors and a balance of power between boards and the CEOs and the rest of executive management.

Some evidence points to the friendship patterns the interlocks may reflect (Mizruchi, 2004) or resource dependence (Pfeffer and Salancik, 2003), but there is no evidence that they reflect the political or control mechanisms. The latter can be treated as a hypothesis only, since the power exercise requires intentionality – therefore, interlocks can be treated as a structure (grid) for exercise of power; however, they do not guarantee it as such. The role of boards of directors (passive vs active) is a counter-factor for the significance of interlocks in their potential to enable exercise of power.

The theory of managerialism did not gain much attention from economists, on the grounds of the assumption that a firm is a unit, which responds to market forces – therefore, who controls it internally is irrelevant (*ibid.*). The assumption is not completely invalid, as there is empirical evidence that there is a very small difference in profits between owner-controlled and manager-controlled firms (*ibid.*). However, in later studies, the theory of managerialism gained attention from transaction cost economics and agency theory, with new empirical evidence, which acknowledged the behavioral aspect of managerial discretion. Agency theory is focused around difficulties of monitoring with dispersed ownership, while transaction cost was based upon an assumption of management discretion.

Another important change influencing the business operations is related to the structure of the financing business receives. The possibilities to extend sources of financing beyond the private capital holder or, alternatively, the banking system, with its traditional crediting function, created, in effect, new categories of shareholders. Instead of being a small and elite type of group, the shareholders now represent a mass society – thanks to technological advancement, which made investing easy, cheap and quick. At the same time, however, shareholders have also became very fragmented and usually geographically dispersed, holding individually relatively small amounts of stock. Such a shareholder not only is anonymous but also relatively weak individually in terms of the influence he can exercise over corporate decisions. To such a dispersed group of shareholders, a manager becomes a personalized face of the 'entity', giving it a certain identity and, thus, replacing the role previously played by the identifiable owner of the company.

The net result of dispersed and fragmented ownership is that both the company and the shareholders become anonymous to each other, thus changing substantially the conditions in which creating a healthy psychological contract between them would be possible. While the shareholders are looking for some kind of personalized contact with the company and personal assurance about the manner in which their investment is being managed, the manager dealing with a 'faceless' ownership base might be tempted to abuse their relatively diminished influence over corporate actions. Assuring the equal treatment of all shareholders, including minority ones, and observation of their rights irrespective of the stock holding-related power they have, contributes to the complexity of corporate responsibility the managers need to deal with.

Opening up financing opportunities and enabling companies to seek capital in the non-banking market created also an institutional shareholder, whose power to influence the company is incomparable to that of individual shareholders, given the share of stock they usually hold; but, more importantly, it introduces another intermediary into the game, as institutional shareholders are usually funds managing the capital of other people as well. The psychological contract to be built between the company and its investors is, in this case, the contract between two agents, hired by someone to manage the capital.

Mizruchi (2004) notes that a center of power shifted towards institutional stockholders and, as their holdings become bigger and bigger but also more difficult to dispose off in the event of dissatisfaction, they attempt to get more involved in influencing corporate policies and decisions; however, there is no evidence that this is a cohesive and unified group, although some of them would be well connected and powerful institutions (Citigroup, for example). The conclusion is that this particular group remains strongly interrelated within professional networks but not within the class. Mizruchi also claims that there is no more an identifiable and homogeneous group which would control business or state (as banks did at some point in the early twentieth century). Market-originated pressures are addressed towards all the other actors. The consequence is that pressures are now amorphous and anonymous.

In view of increasing globalization and internationalization of capital markets, national governments cannot control their business communities any more; dispersion of the managerial workforce, therefore, and, as a result, the whole community, may in effect lead to the disappearance of the corporate elites.[4] Furthermore Mizruchi argues that individual businesses, on the whole, are able to pursue their own goals even on the edge of legal activities, while the business community as such is less able to act coherently. This situation is a result of a unified attack by business communities (in the 1970s and later) on the interventionist state, mainly based on accusations regarding high inflation and on unions being blamed for low productivity. The aggression was seemingly triggered by the energy crisis, resulting in high unemployment and inflation at the same time and capital shortages which contributed to the growing power of banks. Such were the roots of Reagan's and Thatcher's neo-liberal economics. The business community, in effect, lost the unifying institutions which would focus it on a long-term perspective, as neither the state nor the labor markets were accurate in this function any more and the role of banks in this context started to decline from the 1980s.

In fact, these were the neo-liberal paradigms promoted by the politics of Reagan and Thatcher which became the foundations for the massive processes of privatization, later copied all over the world from the model examples provided by the UK (such as the almost legendary privatization of BT).[5] Due to the ownership transfer on a massive scale, which privatization initiated, business responsibilities started to be discussed also from the perspective of public and private ownership. A property rights approach to public and private ownership emphasizes that, although each form of ownership presents agency problems, private ownership ensures the better use of resources because it is market transferable and therefore it can be assessed through the market mechanism. As Martin and Parker say (1999), 'monitoring by residual claimants is more efficient than monitoring through the political process'. The firm is a nexus of contracts between management, suppliers and other stakeholders; its boundaries are defined by relative costs of transacting for inputs in the market against the employment within the firm, considering information asymmetry, inability to write complete contracts and the costs of monitoring the contracts. To design the proper monitoring system and ensure proper teamwork, with the 'free rider' problem non-existent, management needs incentives, which in property rights literature are mostly related to profit. Incentives in the incomplete information situation lead to different behaviors. Completeness of the contracts would make the ownership insignificant because a contract could prevent any discretion in the managers' behavior, while incomplete contracts lead to the problem of adverse selection, because of hidden information and the problem of moral hazard resulting from hidden action.

Another change of the form in which companies operate relates to the shift in the growth patterns of companies from organic growth to inorganic, mainly based on extensive mergers and acquisitions, usually in distant locations, thus providing global business coverage. This, combined with organizational engineering such as outsourcing and off-shoring, converted the big enterprises into coordination centers exercising big influence on their subcontractors and effectively controlling vast resources, but, in reality, not being formally and directly responsible for their actions as they are all separate entities. For example, a company might formally have as few as 300 people on the payroll, but, due to its complex subcontractor base, providing anything from base materials, parts of production or services like accounting and HR, the company might effectively control thousands of people. Apart from the generic implication of such a setting, that power execution is imbalanced with the responsibility stance, such organization of the work process also has the potential to disadvantage the smaller subcontractors in a market sense, as the interdependence between the client and the subcontractors in the case of big enterprises is strongly asymmetrical. Subcontractors are usually highly specialized in the tailor-made production they provide for a few key clients, and face substantial market risks when the client decides to change its business model or simply shifts the orders somewhere else.

In summary, the evolution of organization which spreads from splitting the functions of management, control and ownership, through the public appearance of the companies seeking the capital beyond the banking system, to the internationalization of operations combined with internal engineering, consisting of outsourcing the business processes and off-shoring certain operations, leads to a set of responsibility dilemmas extending significantly beyond the honesty and ethicality of individual business owners.

Corporate power

Untamed market trends

In parallel to the changing market scenery, both in the political context with liberalization postulates and in the economic context with the increasing difficulty in competing as the markets are becoming gradually saturated with new businesses, managers are put under growing pressure to deliver better profits, driving managerial efforts to improve productivity and reduce corporate costs to the limits.

Certain aspects of economical globalization carry a significant emotional charge. For example, at the beginning of the second millennium, the 100 largest multinationals controlled about 20 per cent of global foreign assets. Sales of General Motors and Ford were bigger than the GDP of the whole of Sub-Saharan Africa and the revenues of Wal-Mart exceeded most of the GDPs of Central and Eastern European economies, including Poland, the Czech Republic, Hungary, Slovakia and Romania. The number of mergers increased globally. In the USA alone the figure grew by 142 per cent between 1991 and 1997, from a reported 1,529 to 3,702. In early 2000 alone, 5,000 mergers were reported, with the most spectacular ones being Vodafone and Mannesmann, SmithKline Beecham and Glaxo Wellcome and AOL and Time Warner. Mergers result usually in massive lay—offs, which immediately allow the boosting of the share price. Information about American company ConAgra about planned lay-offs of 6,500 people resulted in such a massive share price increase that market capitalization of the company increased by US$500 million within 24 hours (Hertz, 2001a).

Such a type of narrative in the business and economics literature created the emotionally polarized discourse about the role business plays in the world and about the right balance between using resources to maximize its own profits and returning a fair share to society and the local economy, which sustain business entities.

Together with the changing form of organization, a scientific and analytic focus of corporate power is evolving. From being concentrated on the individual power of a person, it shifts its attention to the power groups within organizations, with separated ownership and management, and power of concentrated private entities over their environment. One of the simplest definitions of the notion of power is that it is a capacity to affect organizational outcomes

(Mintzberg, 1983). It is also one of those notions that is easily and naturally perceived by various actors, irrespective of whether a proper, academic definition of the term is provided (Pfeffer, 1992). A more classical definition by R. Dahl (1957) states that A has a power over B to the extent that he can get B to do something that B would not otherwise do. In a similar manner Weber (1978) defines power as 'a possibility of imposing one's will upon behaviour of other persons'. Power is also defined as an interpersonal relation and a feature of the system (Parsons, 1963), showing all the features of a network (Foucault, 1998), used by societies to achieve their goals or by corporations as a management tool (Pfeffer, 1972). It is a capacity to influence external events – that is, legislative processes, policy decisions, customer behavior (Hindess, 1999) – as well as to use resources – for example, wealth, status or expert knowledge, to affect others (Hickson and McCullogh, 1980). Its key measures are people having access to the key positions. Perceiving power as a tool to achieve society's goals encourages the legitimization of its asymmetry, even if it is treated as a voluntary obedience based on common interests or a legal legitimization (Weber, 2002).

The relational aspect of corporate power relates, first of all, to the interlocks which facilitate the exercise of power, but also to the fact that the ties between actors transmit the consequences of actions and it is through these ties that influence happens. There are two basic perspectives in the analysis of organizational power: one looks into internal power manifestations and one analyzes its external expressions. Examples of the internal context include: research on boards and CEOs (Bigley and Wiersema, 2002; Westphal and Zajac, 1995; Golden and Zajac, 2001; Stiles 2001),[6] studies on departmental power (Pfeffer and Salancik, 1974; Enz, 1988) based on the assumption that power (influence) is shaped by social beliefs,[7] studies of ownership concentration, voting rights and coalition forming (Schleifer and Vishny, 1997; Napel and Widgren, 2003) and studies of power as the ties between the actors (Krackhardt, 1990) focusing on a structural aspect of these relations.

Examples of a broader, external aspect of power include:

- research on interlocking directorates, treated as a widely used environmental management strategy (Bazerman and Schoorman, 1983);

- study of corporations influencing the state and policies in the context of globalization and accumulation of capital (Carroll, 2004; Farnsworth, 2004; Herman, 1981; Parkinson, 1993),
- study of relations among organizations and the flow of resources through them (Stinchcombe, 1989) and its influence on key policy domains (Laumann and Knoke, 1989);
- study of manipulating market value using symbolic actions to oppose governance pressures (Westphal and Zajac, 1998);
- study of stakeholder influence strategies (Frooman, 1999) based on a theory of systems and networks (Rowley, 1997).

Usually studies on power are done on various levels independently, including individual, organizational or societal, which deprives the research of the richness of acknowledging mutual relations and can make the results one-dimensional. In reality the notion of power operates on various dimensions simultaneously.

Each power process has entities (individuals, groups, communities or societies). Individuals enter the environment with the key variables (expectations, status) which affect the outcomes (role structure, societal laws and norms). Any artificial structure, be it an organization, a department or a society, constrains people. People experiencing such a structure shape it simultaneously. From the perspective of a larger system, corporations influence society through economic, social, cultural, educational and political spheres (Epstein, 1973; Kemelgor, 1976). Kemelgor argues that those levels are linked. Power processes and power relationships in organizations mirror the expectations and propensities derived from a society at large. At the same time, organizational power reinforces the society base by shaping attitudes and behaviors.

From the single feature, described psychologically and measured as a skill of particular individuals, power becomes plural and a multiple characteristic difficult to measure directly as it does not belong any more to a particular actor. Instead, it becomes a feature of the links and relations between them. In its most visible contexts it is analyzed as a feature of societies,[8] organizations, individuals and as a network feature of relations between public and private sphere. On a corporate level manipulative power is best visible in persuasive power, based on strong brands, reputation, promise of new experiences to customers and lifestyles people want to identify themselves with.

Corporate power seems to be more of an abstract; however, it is intermediated – among other things – by personal networks and interlocks. Power can be treated as an interpersonal relation of a network character and a structure of activities and deeds (Foucault, 1998). The ontological question fundamental for power measurement is whether its total amount is fixed or non-fixed in a given environment. In other words, is it possible to increase one's power without depriving others of it (non-zero sum game) or does the increase of one's power mean automatically that others loose some of it (zero-sum game)? This seems to depend on the culture of the company and, while it is obvious that in the conflict-based firms power will be a zero-sum game, it is not obvious any more in the case of the companies which enjoy a culture of trust and non-competitive cooperation. The argument against the theory of power as a zero-sum game lies in the theory of conflict. Since conflicts cannot be predetermined, the implication is that we discuss the consequences of power in conditions which do not depend on us.

In summary, in analysis of corporate power, observation of the following issues should be undertaken:

- its interdisciplinary character implies the acknowledgment of various perspectives such as philosophy, sociology, psychology, anthropology and politics, which legitimizes the use of complex and interdisciplinary methodology;
- as organizations function as a part of the system, their internal processes are interdependent with what is happening in the environment; therefore, both internal and external power perspectives should be analyzed in conjunction;
- external perspectives relate to the mutual influence of organizations and environment, which positions an organization within a broader structure of relationships; it links to the question of how and if organizations can shape their external environment;
- internal perspectives relate to power structures within an organization and link to the question of how power structures interfere with boards doing their jobs properly;
- considering that two main functions of the boards are to act as a resource function (bringing the resources into organizations) and asset management function, the conclusion comes to mind that the internal and external aspects of power are linked through

the very structure of the boards; this is also reflected in existing research, where one of the key characteristics of the board is its diversity and external interlocks. (Buck *et al.*, 1998)

Concentration of global business leads to mighty power networks, which extend beyond the formal authority of local and even state governments and control vast capital resources, able to influence politics and economy. Through relational interlocks (i.e.,directorship interlocks) corporate power reaches its societal level, where it influences not only other corporations but customers, societies and national states. Carroll (2004) claims the imbalance of power caused by globalization of capital promoted the goals of profitability, degrading those of the communities as a result.

As organizations, in a similar manner to governments, have broad access to power sources and instruments, property and organization in particular, they seek alliance with each other, naturally assuming that disorganized local communities are much weaker in the game. Corporate–governmental alliance appears attractive for its promise of future gains – a situation which Galbraith defines as a compensatory power (Galbraith, 1985). In anticipation that governments can overrule local communities, the option to involve the latter in any discourse appears an unnecessary cost – an observation not unimportant from the perspective of developing CSR discourse.

Concerns about power are neither local nor restricted to any particular region (i.e.,developing countries). *Business Week's* polls (*Business Week*, 2000) showed that three-quarters of Americans think that business has gained too much power over too many aspects of their lives and only 47 per cent think that what is good for business is also good for Americans, while 66 per cent believe that large profits are more important for big companies than safety, quality and reliability of their products. As *Business Week* states, 'part of this problem is that no one's reining the business anymore. Most of the institutions that historically served as a counterweight to corporate power – big government and strong unions – have lost clout' (*ibid.*). Richard Grossmann says: 'Giant corporations govern. ... they are delegated no authority to make our laws and define our culture. Corporations have no constitutions, no bills of rights. So when corporations govern, democracy flies out the door' (www.zmag.org/intgrossman. htm). And he continues: 'In terms of having this fundamental authority to shape our society, to make the real decisions, to control investment, to control production, to control our work, they have been able to get the law to reflect their position, which is that this is private property of these private entities' (*ibid.*). As Grossman argues, the problem is that:

> corporate CEOs continue to make the wrong decisions primarily because they make them in private, based on their own values and on immediate return. What do we have now? Poisoning of our food supply, our air, our water, the warming and poisoning of the whole planet, an incredible increasing gap between rich and poor and CEO salaries which are a billion times higher than workers' salaries. You have the center of the society imploding because of decisions made by a few people.[9]

A Galbraithian concept of power

To all those who question a study of power as a legitimate discipline of science or would like to call it an esoteric knowledge, Galbraith offers an argument, quoting Adolf Berle:

> subject is not a remote or esoteric thing. No one should venture into it with a feeling that it is a mystery that only the privileged can penetrate. There is a form of scholarship that seeks not to extend knowledge but to exclude the unknowing. One should not surrender to it and certainly not on a subject of such great practical importance as this. All conclusions on power can be tested against generally acceptable historical evidence and most of them against everyday observation and uncomplicated common sense. (Galbraith, 1985)

Galbraith speaks of three instruments in the exercise of power: condign, compensatory and conditioned. The first two have a common feature, that those being the subject of such power are aware of it, as opposed to the conditioned power, where the submission is unconscious and subliminal. Those who submit to conditioned power are hardly aware of it, being usually convinced that they are pursuing their own beliefs.[10] On the other hand, such perception is legitimate if one can agree that the very substance of conditioned power is to make people internalize the imposed values and beliefs. There is, however, a very strong motive for submission, which is that it reflects socially acceptable and reputable forms of behavior (*ibid.*).

Further to the three types of power, there are three sources of it: property, personality and organization. In contemporary societies personality, similar to organization, is most obviously associated with conditioned power, while property is more associated with compensatory power (the ability to purchase submission) (*ibid.*). Condign power is loosing its place in modern societies, at least in its most obvious forms (death penalty, condemnation of a physical abuse of other people, abolition of slavery). Galbraith notes that the position of a free worker working for the benefits of a compensatory power is much higher than that of a slave in fear of a condign power being exercised over him. However, economic conditions of the market can alter this one-dimensional perception and introduce a great deal of relativity to the balance between compensatory and condign power. A question remains as to which of those instruments prevails if there is permanent threat of unemployment, which motivates employees to fight for underpaid jobs. The influence of economy on the instruments of power is unquestionable.

Specifically political power, being an attribute of both the internal and external environment of organizations (corporate relations with public sphere), is believed to be conditioned power – it is a 'product of continuum from objective, visible persuasion to what an individual in a social context has been brought to believe is inherently correct' (*ibid.*). There is a distinction to be made though, between explicit and implicit conditioning (advertising and obtrusive forms of winning belief versus an imposed subordination, taken for granted presented in the form of education, which, as Galbraith says, is a far more reputable way of winning beliefs).

Sources of power are associated with certain enforcement instruments:

- Organization with conditioned power; the decline of property-originated power is related to the rise of organization-related conditioned power. This serves as an illustration of the evolving form of organization from the owner-manager model to joint stock companies with separate ownership and management and with a new category of managers remunerated to look after other people's capital.

- Property with a compensatory power; the role of property is significantly declining in modern society, according to Galbraith. It was once very strong, as the examples of J. D. Rockefeller and J. P. Morgan show (*ibid.*). Although the social consciousness of the former was very poor quality, because it came from the richest man in the USA it attracted attention in relation to issues like benignity of wealth or improvement of race by social Darwinism (Bergman, 2001). A similar situation prevailed with Morgan, who convinced the congressional committee of the greater importance of character than assets when lending money. The views of the both these men were reflected in legislation.[11]
- Personality was originally associated with condign power; however, with society evolving towards condemnation of this form of power, personality now associates more obviously with conditioned power. In modern societies, Galbraith speaks of a synthetic (created) personality, which appeals more to the instinct and perception of people due to its past connotation with archaic forms of power exercise – those related to physical strength; as a result, personality is attributed to heads of organizations and this 'imagery' is cultivated both by professionals and by and through media. However, political rituals like meetings, conventions, speeches etc. (organizational as well – AGMs, board meetings, presentations for media or analysts) can misrepresent an individual's power, as he or she speaks to an already-conditioned crowd; furthermore, he or she adjusts the speech to meet the audience's beliefs (in politics it may be the case, however, that a politician may be perceived as not genuine enough and may face a risk of being called a demagogue; in organizations the case is not straightforward, although a degree of manipulation may be involved – more so with AGMs, not so much with industrial analysts, rather with employees).

Organization is associated naturally with property and to a lesser extent with personality, although a perspective of corporate identity opens a gate for discussion whether it could be seen as a surrogate or even a synonym of personality. It seeks external subordination, conditioning its customers to purchase products; it seeks external subordination of the state to its goals (Galbraith, 1985), often using the argumentation of its economic value for the state and economy. Organization can have access to all three instruments of power, but the degree of its success on external subordination depends, to a great extent, on a degree of internal power (no sabotage practices tolerated, no criticizing of colleagues of same profession, corporate groups lobbying). The degree of internal subordination depends on the scale of goals and their range – the more diverse the goals, the more difficult it is to win internal integrity on subordination as it requires a bigger toolkit to exercise power effectively. This is the reason why political parties are usually less powerful than lobby groups who focus on very narrow issues (such as abortion, immigration law, environmental pollution). Galbraith characterizes organization as a source of power with three characteristics (*ibid.*):

- bimodal symmetry (external submission follows only as much as the internal one is won); Galbraith argues that internal submission is less critical of lower ranks, but it becomes crucial in top management,
- diversity of purposes,
- effective access to all instruments of power; here Galbraith gives the example of the success of National Socialist Germany, as a result of the personality of Hitler, the property of a Third Reich, effecting Prussian-originated beaurocracy combined with punishment of dissidents, compensation flowing from public works (jobs, orders, military manufacture) and Goebbels' propaganda and social conditioning.

As much as people and organizations try to extend their power with the use of all available sources and instruments, resistance to submission fights against this tide using the same toolkit. Therefore, following this thought by Galbraith, I tend to think that it is a balance of accessibility of all sources and instruments which determines who wins in the game. The solution to governing power should, therefore, be sought in limitations to access to sources and instruments of power, which is a paradox; the majority if these matters could not be regulated in a free, democratic society. This is what I call a paradox of power.

Corporate power is mainly a result of capital accumulation. It is natural, therefore, that TNCs become its direct manifestation. Top executives who have access to the main types of economic power[12] (operational, strategic, allocative) become capitalists thanks to their influence on organizations and all other actors involved. Social relations extending beyond organizations create a network between corporations, a form of corporate society. The social organization of big business reflects, therefore, the structure of power in a society.

Herman (1981) argues that corporate power depends not only on resources and market control of individual firms, but also on the extent to which companies coordinate their activities and behavior. Structural ties, which help coordination and mutual business dependence with minimal personal contact, form two extremes of power. What is important is that between them lies a wide spectrum of linkages (interlocking directorates, common membership in trade associations, government advisory boards, public affairs groups and personal connections). The channels through which supra-corporate linkages can influence corporate behavior may be classed under the headings of command, communication and community of interest.

Economic power grows with sales volume, profits, shareholder value and market capitalization. Economic power needs a space to grow. From a societal perspective, power is intermediated by norms and, eventually, by laws, which have a reciprocal relation with individual values, thus connecting to personal perspective. At the same time, norms and laws influence organizational roles within organizational structure, authority and individual attitudes, needs and perceptions. Within Kemelgor's (1976) model, social norms and laws are the most vital element in the whole structure of power. They are influenced only by individual values and it is a question of direction of causality between attitudes, perceptions and values which determines to what extent social norms can have a manipulative character. Ability of social norms to influence individual needs potentially diminishes the role of individual values in shaping social order.

The external aspect of power relates to economic strength and is mainly understood as a result of a capital accumulation. It is interpreted as the external influence of corporations on the environment (mainly regulators). It can be circumscribed by the conflicts arising between TNCs and nation (host) states (Negandhi, 1984). Carroll (2004) compares corporate power to that based on Marx's class society, where systemic inequalities result in a certain class of people having access to capital and ownership, thus constructing the class of capitalists, who are backed up by organic intellectuals. The latter is represented by various professions, such as academics, economists, consultants and lobbyists.

There is a relation between internal power structure and external links. For example, a state-owned services company, which has a single source of supply, a fixed customer base defined by the government and fixed, centrally controlled prices is totally dependent on the power of other organizations; therefore, it is itself completely paralyzed (Hickson and McCullogh, 1980). Similarly universities, which are much less constrained by external powers but have more internal politicking among their units, become restrained internally and not able to exercise their potential external freedom.

First, organizations try to secure their future by negotiating their environment (for example, a company concerned about being supplied by only one supplier can seek to sign a long-term contract with him or to diversify the supply base). Greater external dependence is correlated with greater centralization internally – if there is a key contract on which the whole organization depends, it is more likely to be managed by the key management positions.

Second, if the power can be derived from uncertainties coming from the environment, then any change in uncertainties changes the internal power structure as well – for example, if there are fluctuations in the market then the sales department managing to get income is more powerful; if the fluctuations dissipate then the sales department becomes less powerful as the future of the organization is less dependent on it. The variables of such internal power are: immediacy (if the given unit fails the whole organization feels it immediately) and pervasiveness (the flow of work connects a given department to all other units in the organization, so it stays within a focus of what is happening instead of being on the fringe of activities).

Structured relations as a response towards corporate power

Governance[13]

Since the scandals of Enron, Ahold or Parmalat exposed the scale of loss to individual people that corporate wrong-doing might cause, claims regarding increasing the transparency of business operations increased. However, the idea was opposed by business for a long time. It seems to have disturbed multinational corporations to such an extent that they lobbied very strongly against the European Transparency Initiative proposed in the late 1990s.[14] The idea was to ensure mandatory lobbying disclosure legislation, which would provide fully researchable data on how lobbying companies are financed and whom they work for. The European Public Affairs Consultancies' Association claimed that a voluntary approach was sufficient. This proved to be wrong when the case of C4C came to light. C4C – a group set up to lobby MEPs over the Software Patents Directive and claiming to represent musicians, artists, engineers and all those who make a living out of their creativity – was an offspring of a professional London-based PR agency representing software multinationals, including Microsoft.[15]

Corporate governance is an institution which deals with the conflicts of interests, designs the ways to prevent corporate misconduct and aligns interests of shareholders using the incentive mechanism (Schleifer and Vishny, 1997). A governance structure is built mainly of rules, regulations and institutions, as well as statutory, common and elective laws establishing the processes of control. They mostly relate to matters like disclosure of information, audit, holding and conduct of the shareholders meetings, the liability rules restricting management discretion and imposing the standards on their dealings, laws determining who has the standards to impose those rules on others (Parkinson, 1993). Most importantly, however, the governance system defines a relational mode in the organization.

Gourevitch and Shinn (2005) understand corporate governance as the authority structure of the firm. They distinguish between corporate governance laws, which are composed of the obligations of the board, and securities laws, which deal with the shareholding processes. Authority structure in the firm is shaped by outside processes:

- labor market regulation shape employees' job protection and therefore gives them substantial influence over how the firm is being run (more job protection more influence),
- rules shaping firms' connections to suppliers and distributors define the claims and obligations of each,
- rules on antitrust, banking and finance and competition (domestic and international).

The main areas of governance procedures, according to the OECD Principles of Corporate Governance (2004), are:

- the rights of shareholders and their equivalent treatment,
- the role of stakeholders,

- transparency and disclosure,
- the role of the board.

From a firm-level perspective governance is not only about compliance but also about creating the value (Nestor, 2002), which, in the case of governance procedures, is trust generated in the stakeholder environment, manifesting itself directly, for example, in the lower cost of capital. Value-adding governance is, therefore, much about the mode of cooperating between the boards and the management – a trustworthy, strategically contributing, loyal and sustainable board generates trust, which stimulates management to provide the directors with the proper information. It is an iterative process of building a capacity to create a common platform of experience and knowledge sharing. The evidence for the link between governance and performance is that those firms in the top governance quartile across 25 markets have an average of 33 per cent on their return on capital employed (ROCE), while those in the bottom quartile have only 15 per cent (Gill, 2003). Nestor (2005) suggests that inter-corporate effort for best practice corporate governance is much more important than a normative environment.

Out of the many corporate governance checkpoints, independence of the board creates, often, many controversies, which hide in the interpretation of what it means to be independent and what guarantees such a status quo.[16] The issue is not unimportant, given that boards constitute the core of any governance system (Fama, 1980; Fama and Jensen, 1983; Walsh and Seward, 1990). It is boards who can actually alleviate two main potential abusers: the government – keeping the controlling shareholding and wanting to politicize the publicly owned enterprises and seeking private benefits on the expense of the minority shareholders – and poorly monitored managers. The condition for the board, however, to actually perform this alleviation function, is that it needs to be independent. The key factor of ensuring the independence of the board is the quality and mode of the nomination process.

In France, where the industrial representation view was adopted, a number of board members are appointed by the majority shareholder, the rest by the workers and other shareholders at the AGM – this mode still operates in Netherlands, Portugal and Spain. In Italy it is mandatory for privatized companies to elect their directors through cumulative voting, while in Sweden minority shareholders participate in a nominating committee (Nestor, 2005).

However, it remains to be discussed to what extent 'industrial democracy' boards can be effective, since it is impossible to avoid the conflict of interests between groups on the boards, therefore the value added of such boards, as far as strategy setting is concerned, is questionable – they may also experience difficulties in committing themselves to the goals of the company, other than those of their particular representation groups.

The monitoring role of the boards increases in technology-intensive industries undergoing substantial evolution, where they need to balance the need for an entrepreneurial and risk-taking CEO and increased market risks.

Apart from the legal instruments, which would discipline the companies through various formal regulations, their anticipated efficiency to be considered and discussed, the majority of attempts to scrutinize managers and organizations focuses around the modes of internal operations in the companies, touching upon issues like leadership and governance. Given all the technical capacities governance systems have to structure relations inside and outside of the organization, its key objective becomes to provide a certain level of ethical comfort, both to capital holders (be they banks, institutional investors or individual shareholders) and to societies, that no privileged group abuses the morally accepted equilibrium to progress own interests.

Leadership, transparency and management by objectives and participation

Paradoxically, being an omnipresent aspect of the organizational world in one or other form and as such serving also as the behavioral artifact through which the culture of the organization can be defined, power is considered as well as a management tool. As such it relates to leadership and the management hierarchy.

When power derives from leadership it becomes a hegemony with its two key aspects: cohesion (a well-integrated business network becomes a business community) and reach into the public sphere (business leaders often transfer to politics and retired politicians often become members of the business community through membership in the supervisory boards, for example; a phenomena referred to as 'revolving doors'). Cohesion is based on solidarity, and private contacts facilitated by memberships in private clubs. Although hegemony has its source in the internal environment, its features help it to expand effectively, affecting external relations with society as well. Hegemony and the political aspect of organizations are key to understanding how power conditions governance and why consent of the subordinates is such a critical part of this process. Reach into the public sphere is managed through privatization of public institutions like health care, social security, education and housing. Business influences social policy and takes over the functions originally attributed to the state. Farnsworth (2004) suggests that all decisions on social policy are made under the influence of 'business'. As examples, he points at the following changes, which could be observed in social policy:

- business requires an educated but relatively inexpensive and productive workforce, as well as access to the markets; therefore, business pushes for a reduction of the 'unproductive state' (decrease of taxation and spending on social protection and health care) and expansion of the 'productive state' (more spending on education and training services);
- the only sphere excluded from discussions on cutting state spending seems to be education (not in all countries, however; for example, in Poland government spending on education and research was one of the lowest in European countries. Discussions about reversing this dangerous trend have started relatively recently) and resulted in a substantial reform of higher education and science funding introduced in 2011.
- business prevents international discussions on minimum social standards.

Corporate hegemony rules through persuasion and with the negotiated consent of those governed. A negotiation of consent attempts to seal existing power structure, by enhancing its current imbalance towards those already empowered, mostly through a managerial hierarchy and the structure of responsibility.

It is understandable that, because no one empowered is interested in losing his/her power, there are attempts to seal the status quo and hegemony as a perfect tool for this. Power is disguised under a veil of voluntary consent, thus giving the false impression that power is not being exercised. Consent is a balance point at which a type of power is decided. It legitimizes it: autocracy through formal hierarchy, hegemony through voluntary subordination. Existing structures of power and consent negotiating are linked by reciprocal causality.

Hegemonized organizations, dominated by political correctness and illusionary empowerment, in effect develop a culture, which I call externally as opposed to internally driven, because it derives from imposed conditioning of conforming to the transparency requirements (thus imposing more norms and procedures), instead of coming from internalized core values, which eventually could become a normative basis at a later stage. Such an organization becomes an incidental gathering of people driven by conformity rather than by a deep belief in a necessity of additional control, especially given that this control sometimes does not include high management.

Both hegemony and consent negotiation are embedded in a political context of organizational life. Organizations are political systems in the sense that the chances of the employee satisfying their needs and goals (career, pay, status, etc.) depend on their position within the organization's hierarchy, which is a most common medium reflecting the power structures within organizations. The firms are also part of the political system functioning in a society and they influence the interest relationships between larger social groups. Whose interests will prevail in such context is defined by the policies, which are a bridge between external and internal power.

Policies are a political phenomena; however, their political nature is disguised by the neutral, legal and rational idioms in which they are portrayed. Masking the political character under the key of neutrality is a key feature of modern power (Shore and Wright, 1997). As Shore and Wright argue, techniques involving self-regulating capacities of the subjects, internalized though powers of expertise, become a basis for modern forms of government and establish the conditions for governing in a liberal and democratic way. Subjects, in order to be governable, need to be self-activating and free (self-activation happens when the procedures are internalized and adopted by people who believe in the expertise of those who define the procedures). Therefore, the idea of freedom acts as an instrument of government control by creating new subjects of power and intermediaries who intervene in social structures (*ibid.*). Durkheim highlighted that, while institutions bear down upon people, people cling to them; they place constraints upon individuals, and yet they find satisfaction in the way institutions function, in that very constraint (Durkheim, 1982): 'External norms may indeed constrain us, nevertheless they are likely to be experienced, constitutive and liberating' (Shore and Wright, 1997). Having observed management structures for many years, I believe that the same idea of freedom (to choose how you prove that you are efficient and needed) contributes to what is sometimes a very depressing and power-oriented organizational climate. Internal procedures of control, similar to external policies, mask their power-oriented character under neutrality and the expertise of those who design them.

Is participation a democracy?[17]

Hegemony as deriving from leadership is complementary to economic power. Hegemony makes sure that economic power rules. It rules through persuasion and with the consent of those governed. Consent, however, does not mean democracy. Democratic procedures are namely those based on self-governance, while corporate capital organizes the consent of subordinate groups through their dependency. One can see the truth of these words as the tendency to centralize governance proceeds (i.e., the centralized control over law professions excludes self-governance mechanisms of the profession). Consent, in general, can be reached either via negotiations with governments and states or via influence on citizens and societies.[18] Lobbying is one of the most obvious ways of influencing.

On the whole, argumentation about balancing the two standpoints of corporate power are dominant: one puts pressure on governance mechanisms; another sees the control procedure being related to the participation of various constituencies in the management process. Democracy in organizations relates to participation (Clegg, 1983). Task-centered participation relates to the organization of work and leadership style issues, such as giving employees more discretion in structuring their work, in agreeing targets and defining ways to achieve them. It is argued that, by using these tools, organization increases job satisfaction and therefore contributes to improvements of productivity. However, although such actions have some democratic potential it is questionable for whom their value is bigger. Clegg suggests that it is much greater for the management, with their already-concentrated power, minimizing the risk of strikes and the costs of control as it imposes the responsibility and self-governance on the employees. The view that participation can lead to a bigger power differentiation (as a contradiction of the view of power equalization obtained through increased participation) is also expressed by others (Strauss and Rosenstein, 1970; Strauss, 1982). Furthermore, through task-centered participation, employees become more self-actualized and, as such, more harmonious and cooperative. Cooperation, especially, is a purely managerial concept – a subtle way to control by consent by which management again secures hegemony (Clegg, 1983).

There are two faulty assumptions about task-centered participation: first, the assumption that the corporation has the prerogative to know what people need and is the only body with the capacity to satisfy the needs; second, that the initiative comes from upwards instead of downwards from the workforce itself (the whole movement of work humanization came as a result of McGregor and Herzberg's ideas). This is how the paradox is developed: a policy with democratizing potential becomes anti-democratic.

Clegg argues, further, that job restructurization comes always as a result of certain economic situations; he cites, as an example, the economically expansive period of the 1890s, when the scientific management of F. Taylor enabled business to acquire a new work-force (simplified, routinized and deskilled work processes allowed the hiring of women and even children), and continued simplification of work enabled the extention of the unskilled workforce to offices in a post-war period (which then helped to increase the efficiency of capital in the inter-war times).

Problems with controlling the labor process at the level of the particular enterprises in a fully employed war economy and post-war boom introduced the concepts of E. Mayo. Finally, with a continuing full-employment economy, division in control techniques was introduced, which depended on a position within a class structure of occupations. The jobs peripheral to the work process, the less skilled and easily replaceable, were controlled more technologically, while those central to the labor process enjoyed the control, based on social regulative interventions (Clegg, 1983).

On the other hand, the illusion of democracy, based on the structural representation of employees, stems from the fact that employee directors are often prevented from effective communication with other employees, largely due to the confidentiality of all board-level decisions and actions; therefore, putting an employee representative on the board seems to be a manipulation designed to invalidate complaints by the staff. It gives a formal voice on a decision-making body, but without a real possibility to mediate.

Another paradox, which substantially limits the concept of democracy, is its circular and cumulative causality and path dependency. Citizens learn how to participate by becoming active in various social institutions; therefore, the pattern of participation is socially structured (Pateman, 1983).

The evidence shows that those who are less likely to participate are also less likely to have an opportunity to learn how to do so and therefore are also less likely to develop any characteristics needed for citizenship or participation (Pateman, 1983). So-called 'participation', which allows management to obtain the collaboration of employees, especially when there is a need to introduce the changes, but leaves the power structure intact, is not real participation (*ibid.*).

A weakening state and withdrawal of the public sector[19]

Shrinking markets – expanding markets

To understand the background of corporate pressure on government bodies and the pressures the corporations are exposed to themselves, one must consider global economic conditions. The paradigm of maximizing profits and shareholder value situates Western European and American corporations within the limits of matured western markets. In the market where the gap between rich and poor is widening dramatically and where more and more people can afford less every day, corporations need to look for alternatives in order to sustain their growth. The alternative is to expand to new markets.

Following subtle suggestions in various publications, it is not entirely impossible that this might have been the motivation for business attempts to bring Africa and Central and Eastern Europe into the market economy zone, with as much trade liberalization and standardization of the rules as possible.[20] No wonder that strong lobbying groups occupied with African aid, such as the Corporate Council on Africa (see www.africacncl.org), involve major multinational corporations like Halliburton, Exxon Mobil, General Motors, Coca-Cola, Microsoft and Boeing. It is no surprise, either, that when an aid fund is created, like the US$500 million of Business Action for Africa, it is managed and controlled by the private sector, in spite of being financed almost entirely by public money (the UK foreign budget, G8 and the World Bank). The fund, which aimed to create an investment-friendly climate, was managed by a former Unilever chief executive and representative of its business in formerly apartheid South Africa.

The US African Growth and Opportunity Act, 2000 (see www.agoa. gov), which combined philanthropy with self-interest says 'African countries must bring about a market economy that protects private property rights ... the elimination of barriers to United States trade and investment and a conducive environment for foreign policy interests.' In return, they will be allowed 'preferential treatment' for some of their products in the USA. Specifically, clothing factories in Africa will be allowed to sell their products to the USA, but only if they use fabrics fully formed and cut in the USA or if they do not compete directly with US firms. This is only one example of an imbalance of interests, where an economically strong market, thriving on increased profits for their multinationals, uses the 'aid' card in order to open access to new markets. The above agreement was, indeed, classified as foreign aid. The World Business Council for Sustainable Development promoted the philosophy of 'Sustainability Through the Market', which backs up the idea that trade and investment liberalization benefits poor people.

There are more examples of multinational businesses getting involved in 'aid' actions or becoming 'concerned' with ethics and environment. Examples are the US Council for International Business, which involves over 300 multinational corporations, where Procter & Gamble (P&G) directors chaired the Environment Committee and the National Government Relations Committee, or the World Business Council for Sustainable Development set up to respond to business challenges arising from Earth Summits and chaired by a former chairman of Royal Dutch Shell.

The enlargement of the EU allowed an opening of markets and also provided a new solution for expansion-seeking corporations, as was revealed in the document 'The East–West Win–Win Business Experience', produced in 1999 by the European Round Table of Industrialists (see www.ert.be) – a powerful lobby group. Part of the problem solving was to force new member states to reduce their taxes, speed up the privatization process and remove the restrictions on land purchase by foreign companies. The creation of a single market with harmonized trade rules was a fulfillment of corporate dreams for businesses struggling in the face of Chinese and Asian competition. Journalist George Monbiot (www.monbiot .com/2001/06/20/stealing-europe) states that:

> in 1983 the chief executive of Volvo brought together the heads of 15 other corporations including ICI, Unilever, Nestlé, Fiat to see if they could find a way of harmonising trade rules in Western Europe, which would allow their companies to reach the scale necessary to resist pressure from non-European competitors. The ERT presented a proposal the same year to the European Commission and two months later a white paper was produced which later became the basis for the Single European Act [1986].

As admitted by Jacques Delors, the ERT was one of the main driving forces behind the Single Market. There were other contributors as well: the OECD promoted business-centered approaches to employment markets; the World Bank, IMF and WTO worked on developing the policies to reduce restrictions on capital mobility and to privatize the welfare services; the EU Council Summit in 1997 promoted global competitiveness through a skilled and adaptable workforce responsive to economic change (training and lifelong learning); the EU Lisbon Summit in 2000 promoted improvement on training and education; and, last but not least, the EU backed the introduction of GATS, which seriously undermined the future of welfare services.

In a world where the majority of countries hold democracy very dear, economic power cannot rule autocratically. It needs public consent for its actions, a consent, which is negotiated and persuaded.

Corporate face lift

One of the roles of lobbying groups is to build a corporate image, which, while helping in a positive perception among customers, will allow pursuance of profit-driven interests. Lobbying techniques apply to all levels of relationships: national, international and global. An example is EuropaBio (see www.europabio.org). This organization, set up in 1996, unites over 600 major industrial firms, including pharmaceuticals, which lobby effectively for a stronger role for biotechnology in the EU's economy. The group promotes commercialization of GM food in Europe and even more patent protections for big corporations. Other groups, like the International Chamber of Commerce, Transatlantic Business Dialogue, the Davos Group, the Bilderberg Group or UN Global Compact (the CSR framework, criticized for being used as a UN approval seal for corporations which did not change their behavior but just improved their public image) are typical examples of business–politics exchange platforms.

Business and politics interlocks are performed on various informal and formal platforms, the Centre for European Policy Studies being another example. It claims to be free of external influences, but enjoys the presence of corporate members like P&G. The Centre also hosts corporate breakfast meetings, which provide a platform of direct contact between business and members of the European Commission, the European Parliament and the European Council, who usually are invited as speakers. Activities of many similar organizations, be they think tanks or research institutes, which build their management structures on the basis of thought and experience exchange between business people, politicians and other decision-makers, are often considered as being important sources of influence in establishing the policies and rules of the market game.

Hegemony consent is also negotiated by addressing directly citizens and communities, either to claim leadership through influence on education and research or to build a positive brand perception among consumers. Building a brand and managing a corporate image became a business by itself. Corporations hire professional PR agencies to help them design their 'customer perception'. The most famous PR agency specializing in 'perception management' is Burson-Marsteller. Their list of clients includes companies who failed miserably to sustain a responsible image – for example, Monsanto, involved in the production and promotion of genetically modified food.

Intensified involvement of private business in 'meaning management', either directly or through lobbying, can be seen as an example of consent negotiation, thus becoming an exercise in hegemonic power. In a sense, it reaches into the public sphere as it attempts to shape the commonly generated interpretation of the facts. Another, much more explicit channel of reach into the public sphere is private business involvement in the areas traditionally managed by the state – I call it a social expansion.

The majority of multinationals get involved in educational campaigns, often backed up by governments. P&G seems to be particularly active in this area, producing teaching materials for students. Although the logo of the sponsor was minimal in these materials, all the product cases in the book happened to be P&G products, so the booklet became, effectively, the P&G product catalogue (for details, see the 1998 report 'Captive Kids' by the Consumers Union at www.consumersunion.org).

In the Czech Republic, in the early 1990s, the initiative 'School and Computer – the Basis of Life' caused an outrage. For a school to enter the competition to win Apple computers, each student had to collect at least ten coupons from P&G products. P&G could gain as much as 3 billion Kc (600 times the value of the computers), which, by the way, were so obscure that most software found them incompatible. Another interesting P&G action was an educational package called 'Decision Earth', distributed widely in the USA in 1997. It contained controversial material on waste disposal, mining and forestry issues. For example, it described clear-cut forestry practices as mimicking natural processes, creating new habitat for wildlife and opening the forest floor to sunshine to stimulate growth and provide food for animals.

Other major multinationals getting involved in education and research include Unilever (UNEP/UNESCO Partnership on Youth and Life Styles: The Youth and Sustainable Consumption Research Project, Unilever Nelson Mandela Scholarships, Unilever – Cambridge University Partnership for Science) and Bayer (Makes Science Make Sense Project, Bayer's Institute for Health Care Communication, Bayer's Patient Education Center, Bayer's School of Natural and Environmental Studies, Berkeley Biotechnology Education Inc.). Although the initiatives seem to be very positive, they immediately bring to mind the question of the independent character of future research. For example, Berkeley Biotechnology Education Inc. was the program designed by Bayer in partnership with Berkeley High School and resulted in developing a curriculum that trains students in skills necessary for employment in the biotechnology industry.

The problem with corporations getting involved in research and education is that they wish to contribute not only to knowledge creation in general but also to a knowledge creation framework and workforce suited to their own corporate, profit-driven needs. It endangers the independent nature of research and education needed to benefit the development of the whole of society. The problem was apparently addressed by academic society in 2001, in protests by the world's 13 largest medical journals against rich drug companies, who were accused of distorting the results of scientific research for the sake of profits.[21]

Stakeholders' rights abuse

Using power to the benefit of certain groups of people must result in some evidence of disadvantages of other stakeholders. The evidence is provided by the cases of direct rights abuse, be it the rights of consumers, employees, society or state. On the inter-corporate level these are usually manipulations of the power balance within corporations, like abusing fiduciary rights by the directorate through issuing new shares to destroy the current balance of power between shareholders (for example, to get more support). Sometimes the misuse of power affects employees. Infamously, Wal-Mart not only seems to be paying lower wages as compared to the average in the sector, but it was also accused of donating US$500,000 to the campaign in 2004 to oppose Proposition 72,[22] which stipulated that employers were required to provide basic health insurance for their employees.

On a state and government level there are allegations that corporations give huge money donations to political parties, sponsor election campaigns or party congresses and meetings. However, there are other examples, where whole societies and states suffer from abuses. Noreena Hertz (2002) states that Rupert Murdoch's News Corporation pays only 6 per cent tax worldwide and in the UK, up to 1998, it paid no British net corporate tax, in spite of generating a profit of £1.4 billion since 1987. Business avoiding taxes not only exposes the state to direct budget losses but also affects citizens with a stake in the welfare. An even bigger scale of abuse can occur with industrial espionage. Hertz gives an example: in 1947 British, American, Canadian, New Zealand and Australian spy agencies agreed to share security information in order to renew the alliance which helped to defeat the Nazis so successfully. The system was operated under codename Echelon and was justified by the existence of the communist Soviet Union, considered to be a threat to Western Europe. There would be nothing strange or condemnable about this fact, except that it stayed fully operational after the Berlin Wall came down and the whole Soviet Union together with it. The key element of the system was a listening station at Menwith Hill in Yorkshire, which was apparently so powerful that it was capable of recording every single telephone call, fax or email transmitted over satellites anywhere in the world. Abuse of the system came to light in 2000, when documents of the American Defense Department were posted accidentally on the internet. Later allegations stated that the system helped in the theft of major contracts from Asian and European firms after confidential, commercial information was recorded and used to the advantage of US corporations (Airbus and Thomson CSF, NRC of Japan being named as some of the losers to the benefit of Boeing, AT&T).

Last, but certainly not least, citizens are abused, not only if they are deprived of their share in profits, but also when public money is used for corporate purposes, with the consent of governments. For example, Pfizer Business Park, known as Pfizer World, is supposed to be used to promote new drugs to the public. 'My only comment on the issue is that both the president and I support any endeavour to teach young people about capitalism ... wait ... I mean about health', Dick Cheney was reported as saying when he left the meeting at which Pfizer announced the building of the park. It looks like the myth of governments making decisions in the public interest is somewhat questionable.

Social activism and ethical and socially responsible behavior

The economist Noreena Hertz claims that contemporary consumers who have shifted from Sunday masses to shopping malls, become both ethically more conscious and politically less engaged. Ethical consumerism is expressed by customers buying more often the products of corporations which are perceived as ethical. As faith in politicians and governments, who fail miserably to care for citizens and society's interests and instead become corrupted agents of business, diminishes every year, people decide to take direct action. Consumers are capable of undertaking harmful and powerful boycotts of corporations whom they perceive as pursuing unethical activities. Consumer activist groups are taking over the role of governance institutions and address corporations with the same powerful weapon, which is so often used to manipulate corporate image – the media and public opinion. With the media often being engaged or even belonging to powerful corporations it is difficult; however, examples show that consumers are not always powerless (consider the De Beers and diamonds case, Shell and Brent Spar, BP and exploration of Arctic natural resources and, only recently, the BP and the Gulf of Mexico case). More effectively, corporations can be influenced from within (i.e. the Interfaith Centre on Corporate Responsibility in the USA – a shareholder advocacy organization).

Institutional consumers target the corporation and buy into it, influencing the decisions at shareholders' meetings. There is a growing tendency among institutional investors, especially pension funds who manage massive portfolios worldwide, to avoid investing in any business which is perceived as potentially exposed to unethical behavior (tobacco, alcohol, oil, weapons). One of the examples could be the Stewardship group of funds managed by F&C Asset Management.

There is, however, a downside. Even if customers are successful in their actions, the result is likely to be short term if it is not backed up by legislation. As the case of the European Transparency Initiative shows, the fact that legislation has been postponed for such a long time points to governmental dependency on business, with politicians intending to step aside from any conflict which involves big corporations. For the consumers to integrate and take action, they must be provided with independent and objective information, which increasingly becomes the issue of concern with the accumulation of power in broadcasting networks, and their alleged politicization in the CEE region.

Being private, not only can they remain guardians of private interests, but also, by making their living out of a flood of commercial adverts, they also remain dependent. Growing control over information is yet another example of the power network and a main obstacle to consumer-driven governance Perhaps excessive privatization of state-owned media did not fully benefit the states. Aidan Whilee of the International Federation of Journalists commented: 'We are now seeing the dominance of a handful of companies controlling information and how that information reaches people. ... we will have corporate gatekeepers to the flow of information who will define content to suit their market strategies' (Hertz, 2001b,). The question is to what extent the public attention focused on private companies and their growing influences becomes the determinant of the corporate involvement in socially responsible behavior.

One aspect of analyzing CSR relates to the reasons why companies get involved in the process. For example, research done in Hungary revealed that 70 per cent of managers perceive their moral obligations to be strictly related to the fact of being a member of society, but 60 per cent believe them to be related to the duty of profit creation as well (Fulop *et al.*, 2000). The research determined a few layers of social responsibility, including responsibility towards clients, employees and society at large. Specific measures of the latter category include sensitivity regarding social problems, legal compliance, fulfilling local needs, environment protection, effective resource management and genuine information (*ibid.*).

Interestingly enough, ethical decision-making occupies ninth place on the list of CSR elements determined in the study (*ibid.*).[23] According to the theory of moral maturity of organizations, the latter can be controlled in a number of ways. Pre-conventional ethics based solely on the mechanisms of prize and penalty seems insufficient as individual analysis of costs and benefits of given behavior can always result in actions escalating the risk of harming others. This approach can be slightly improved if it is based on analysis of what is broadly understood as one's own benefit, including also other interested groups. Nevertheless, it will prove insufficient as well if being ethical only proves to be economically attractive in the short term. Conventional ethics does not seem satisfactory as it relates solely to the norms commonly accepted in given societies, which opens the gate for justifying one's own deeds using the argumentation 'everyone does it'. In such circumstances, an individual sense of what is good and right might get significantly blurred.

In conclusion, ensuring good organizational behavior which benefits the larger spectrum of stakeholder groups requires higher standards, as assumed in post-conventional ethics (Falkenberg, 2004). This is based on the following:

- the rule of equality understood as equal access to resources and opportunities to act, not as equal distribution of goods;
- institutional genuineness, related to the golden rule of treating others the way one would like to be treated; this implies the necessity of being able to look at the situation from the perspective of others;
- corporate duty to ensure and protect human rights (Donaldson, 1989);[24]
- the rule of coherence related to countries where institutions are too weak to ensure the morality of business, where international organizations should define the standards and code of practices beyond local standards (De George, 1993);[25]
- responsibility coupled with capacity related to situations where there is no legal obligation to undertake or refrain from given action but the enterprise has a capacity to react to the negative consequences of its own deeds.

The circumstances for individual ethical behavior are embedded between the poles of individual moral philosophy – that is, relativism and idealism.

Relativism makes us reject any universal moral rules (Forsyth, 1980). Relativists are often tempted to consider the circumstances of the situation where the morally assessed activity took place (Axin *et al.*, 2004). Descriptive realism accepts the fact that standards and beliefs might be different for different people and societies, which means that people can differ significantly in terms of moral behavior, even though they might have similar codes of ethics. The influence of social environment is not insignificant. Descriptive realism defines the differences in individual or societal moral views, but it refrains from valuing any particular behavior. Specifically, relativists accept that the basic source of differences between perceptions of moral value of behaviors lies in the traditions and ethical environment of one's upbringing (cultural relativism) (Carson and Moser, 2001; Brandt, 2001). Equally tempting is the view that people internalize and consider obligatory those moral norms which are coherent with those accepted in the society one belongs to (normative relativism). Idealists, on the other hand, believe that adequate behavior can always guarantee foreseeable results. Such a standpoint relates to the profound belief that spiritual forces dominate material ones.

Relativism is not an opposite to idealism. The research performed with the use of PRESOR scale (perceived importance of ethics and social responsibility) showed that people from Asia, the USA and Europe differ significantly in their moral philosophies (Axinn *et al.*, 2004). Asian respondents scored higher both on relativism and individualism, which may suggest that they are more likely to behave 'unethically' if they are convinced that their actions will have a positive end result and the situation relates to higher values, such as saving others from harm. For example, one might not hesitate to tell lies if he or she believes that this will save someone from a potential threat or harm. Asian respondents proved to be situationists in this context.

Interestingly enough, relativism does not seem to be related in any way to the perception of corporate social responsibility.

From the individual perspective, however, apart from adopting the generic paradigm and being a relativist or a situationist, people use different motivations in their ethical reasoning. The most trivial approach is based on the avoidance of penalty and expresses a somewhat egoistic point of view, whereby one should be focusing on one's own existence and wellbeing. The decisions taken are assessed from the standpoint of potential formal or legal consequences and penalty avoidance becomes the key criteria of decisions, making people obedient to the law and formal hierarchy which has the power to enforce the rules.

Next comes the orientation towards the instrumentally defined goals and mutual benefits. Such an approach prevails in situations where one is motivated by narrowly defined self-interest, sometimes including also the interests of a direct circle of close family and cooperators. Being aware that other people also have their own interests, which might be in conflict with ours, makes people enter into negotiations and sign contracts as long as this facilitates the achievement of their own goals. Decisions and actions are assessed against the criteria of the equivalent exchange, equalized contribution and just distribution of the net receipts.

Orientation towards the values legitimizing the social contract assumes that the existing social order is a result of agreement over the aspirations of various groups with their own interests. This is, therefore, the order founded upon certain value sets, promoted by those groups – the value sets which are, therefore, relative. One accepts this social construct, first, because it is believed to be serving for the common good and, second, because it is known to be temporary and therefore subject to change, although some values such as life or freedom are understood to be of an absolute and universal character. In consequence, a further development of ethical reasoning orientations would involve the universal values composed in the sets every person defined individually and in an autonomic manner. Those should be the values serving the good of all the people, which can also be considered guides for behavior.

The more sophisticated reasoning is based upon orientation towards acceptance and interpersonal harmony, where the obligations of individuals are assessed from the perspective of the relations people have with each other. One should be focused on fulfilling the expectations of others, related to the role we have in the group and in society at large. The key values in such a role-oriented setting would be trust, respect and loyalty, as they help build strong relationships.

Last, but not least, reasoning based on social order and law takes social order, which becomes the unquestionable value in itself, as the foundation for the decisions people take and for the roles they play. The key obligation of individuals is a duty of respect towards institutions and society, leading them to act in a way which helps sustain those institutions.

One universal measuring tool, which can be easily adapted to the specifics of corporate social responsibility, is the balanced scorecard (van der Voerd and van den Brink, 2004).[26] A model of the CSR balanced scorecard is based, typically, on four dimensions: financial perspective, consumer perspective, internal processes perspective and learning and development perspective. They are adapted as follows:

- capital owners and lenders,
- customers and suppliers (distribution chain),
- internal processes,
- employees and learning processes,
- planet and safety.

Such design of RBS complies with the ideology of corporate social responsibility driven by commonwealth and synergy,[27] which means that ecological, social and economical goals can be aligned in the process of cooperation and engagement of stakeholders (*ibid.*).

There is a richness of research linking CSR behaviors with financial results of the company (Rodriguez *et al.*, 2000; Waddock and Graves, 1997; Wright and Ferris, 1997), introducing the notion of strategic CSR (Porter and Kramer, 2006) which might serve as a way of explaining the divergence in the above-mentioned research results, often pointing to positive, negative or lack of correlation between CSR and profit.

From the operational perspective, the key issue is to differentiate between managerial and social aspects of CSR (Hillman and Keim, 2001). The logical consequence of such an approach manifests itself in a debate on how to manage stakeholder relations, previously categorized against the criteria of importance, urgency and various other factors, as opposed to performing a dialogue with them and building relations based on common values (Dunham *et al.*, 2006; Hughes and Demetrious, 2006; Charan and Freeman, 1979).

The majority of research focusing on instrumental aspects of CSR (Jones and Wicks, 1999; Donaldson and Preston, 1995) seems to favor the context of managing external relations (Freeman, 1984), where stakeholder identification, stakeholder accommodation problems and goal alignment remain key operational questions. Attempts to approach stakeholder dialogue strategies from the operational perspective are still rare (Dunham *et al.*, 2006). For example, Dunham *et al.* promote the view that cooperation with stakeholders should be based on building common values, especially when the symbiosis with given stakeholder groups is significant. From an operational perspective, both approaches are justified although distinct in their ontological background.

A substantial part of existing research deals with the aspect of potential relations between corporate social responsibility and financial performance (as discussed at the Academy of Management Annual Meeting 2007: 'Doing well by doing good'). On top of an interest of prime academic and business circles in the subject, as the example of the Academy of Management shows, known research provides quite ambiguous results (Rodriguez *et al.*, 2006), which is probably a reason why Porter (2006) proposed a hypothesis, that such a positive relation between CSR strategy and financial results could happen only in the case where so-called strategic CSR is being practiced – that is, where the activities of the company addressed to stakeholders are coherent with its core business.

This is an attempt to explain why some of the available research shows a lack of relation between CSR and the financial bottom line (McWilliams and Siegel, 2000), and a positive correlation between the two (Waddock and Graves, 1997; Margolis and Walsh, 2001; Orlitzky *et al.*, 2003) as well as a negative one (Wright and Ferris, 1997).

Hillman and Keim (2001) introduced the split between social and managerial aspects of CSR into the contemporary management discourse. Its logical consequence is a debate on the form and tools for managing stakeholder relations in the context of categorizing and prioritizing them as opposed to inviting them to dialogue and co-defining of mutual values (Freeman, 1984; Hughes and Demetrious, 2006; Charan and Freeman, 1979). Hart (1995) and Russo and Fouts (1997) point to the relation between strategic CSR and competitiveness, basing this on the assumption that companies make decisions about engaging in CSR activities on the basis of cost analysis (McWilliams and Siegel, 2001).

Another new aspect of CSR discourse relates to the role of activists and other stakeholders in leveraging the asymmetry of information, which prevents consumers, who base their knowledge about the company only on CSR reports, from making an accurate assessment of the actual CSR involvement of the company (Fedderson and Gillian,

2001). Apart from the common postulate that companies use CSR as a PR tool to enhance their public image, some researchers also stress that it can be used as a political strategy tool, designed to increase the costs of competitors (Marvel, 1977; McWilliams *et al.*, 2002). Although there is a certain amount of application research dealing with the instrumental aspects of CSR (Jones and Wicks, 1999; Donaldson and Preston, 1995), it seems to concentrate on the issue of managing stakeholder relations (Freeman, 1984), where key questions evolve around identifying stakeholders, categorizing them or managing conflicting stakeholders' goals from the risk management perspective (stakeholder accommodation problem). An interesting line of thought points to the role of social leadership, defined as positively influencing and stimulating activities which may facilitate realization of common good goals (Lorenzi, 2004).[28]

One of the consequences of CSR theory, aimed at designing tools to enable its management, is the idea of corporate social performance (CSP). This is defined as the ability of the organization to manage its relations with the environment (Igalens and Gond, 2005). Among different CSP models (Carroll, 1979; Wartick and Cochran, 1985; Wood, 1991), the Clarkson model (1995) seems best suited to the dynamics of contemporary markets. Deriving from stakeholder theory, Clarkson proposes that, in each stakeholder group – that is, employees, shareholders, consumers, suppliers, government and state, competitors and others – problems characteristic for a given group should be defined. Three dimensions of CSP which build the overall picture of corporate engagement as far as CSR is concerned, include: the stakeholder taxonomy, normative taxonomy (i.e., organizational, institutional and individual rules and regulations) and management processes (i.e., environment analysis, stakeholder management, social consequences of organizational programs and policies) (Wood, 1991). Igalens and Gond (2005) suggest the following categories of CSP measures:

- measures based on annual reports,
- pollution indexes, e.g., toxic release inventory (TRI),
- perception measures defined on the basis of survey research, which include synthetic psychometric scales analyzing managers' attitudes towards CSR,
- indexes of corporate reputation based on survey research as well,
- measures designed by rating agencies, e.g., KLD or ARESE.

Interestingly enough, small entrepreneurs do not believe that they need any special systems or management tools simply to be good people, and, while they do engage in various activities related to common good and seem to be social entrepreneurs at the same time, they consider the majority of aspects of CSR to be irrelevant to their business.[29] Also, they seem to react negatively to suggestions that CSR can be treated as a practical management tool to enhance financial results: it is perceived as 'unethical' to use common good and socially sensitive arguments to create the market niche, even though this would benefit all stakeholders. It is almost as if they are claiming that CSR should be free from pragmatic philosophy, even if it might have a negative result on income maximization. It is more 'OK' to accept a lower income for the sake of sharing with somebody else, than to design CSR activities with the view to enhance one's own profit.

2
Creating Meanings:
A Sense-Making Perspective of
Corporate Social Responsibility

Sense-making and organizational identity

Identity construction as a sense-making exercise

Given, the increasing dynamics of the environment organizations operate in, I sympathize with the view that they are not structuralized objects available for analysis; they are rather a certain type of social contract based on the mutually defined goals and expectations wrapped in the ongoing flow of situational images carrying certain meanings and embedded in the cultural modus operandi. Those meanings are subject to individual interpretations as we all become participants in everyday life situations and, depending on how we interpret those meanings, we either reduce or enlarge (if we lack understanding of the surrounding reality) the degree of uncertainty around us. The detailed ontology of those meanings obviously resides largely in the psychological context of the organized activities people participate in; however, they seem to function on a subtle equilibrium between our own creative interpretations – that is, our own mental constructions imposed during the interpretative process – and the interpretations designed in the process of organizing – that is, how certain events are presented, situations orchestrated or analyzed, as in the case of the formal communication organizations produce. In other words, making sense of what surrounds us is an inherent part of any human activity, just as the uncertainty[1] level increases. Given that organizations express natural entropic tendencies, sense-making is part of organizational processes almost simultaneously.

Sense-making theory, introduced in organization studies by Karl Weick (1995), follows the postulate of anti-realism according to which the reality we observe does not exist independently of us, as an external set of objects and relations to analyze, but is constantly formed by all the actors in the process of building and reinterpreting their mutual relations. This way activities on an interpersonal level precede what we call hard structures – that is, the structures and procedures which structuralize our corporate activities.

In dealing with organizational issues, sense-making requires us to look for explanations and answers in terms of how people see things, rather than structures or systems. 'Sense-making suggests that organizational issues – "strategies", "breakdowns", "changes", "goals", "plans", "tasks", "teams", and so on are not things that one can find out in the world or that exist in the organization. Rather, their source is people's way of thinking' (Basu and Palazzo, 2008). The sense-making process should therefore be treated as a cognitive map of one's reality.

Sense-making as an attempt to create situational awareness and understanding of unclear situations is initialized as the ambiguity increases. 'It is a motivated, continuous effort to understand connections (which can be among people, places, and events) in order to anticipate their trajectories and act effectively' (Klein *et al.*, 2006a). Klein *et al.* also point to the fact that attempting to create a shared understanding out of individual sense-making and interpretation is a socio-cognitive activity. From the organizational perspective, such shared interpretation will be the result of not only direct management processes, such as leadership or motivation, but also equally, or even more importantly, the outcome of certain organizational culture. Key aspects which constitute sense-making are (Weick, 1995):

- it is grounded in identity, meaning that no sense-making activities can happen without a sense-maker;
- it is not an isolated process – rather, it is constituted by its host (a person or organization); sense-making hosts usually have multiple identities – for example, as an employee of the company which pollutes natural environment and as a citizen living in the direct neighborhood of its factories, which may imply different assessments of the situation, as opposed to being only an employee of the company and not affected directly by its wrong-doings;

on the organizational level, subcultures within the overall organizational values and meanings setting can be seen as equivalent to multiple identities;

- it is always retrospective, as if it was almost a measure of success and a check for the internal process of verification as to whether the interpretation worked out is successful; should the process fail to provide a balance between what is thought of as clear and understandable and what remains convoluted, it will most likely be repeated;
- it is enactive; as such it follows the logic that people in organizations usually create at least part of the environment they function in. However, as the balance between being independent and being manipulated is rather dynamic and unlikely to reach either of the extremums, sense-making serves as a tool to locate the meanings in between them;
- it is social, given that all activities people do depend on a nexus of influences from others, which implies that all social aspects of human behavior, like stereotypes, group thinking, etc. do count;
- it is focused on extracted cues, which means that it is limited by the psychologically related individual bias of every person – this might be related to selectiveness of our perception – we tend to notice cues which are convergent with our own interests or other focuses valid at the time, we are incapable of internalizing all data available, or performing an accurate analysis above the amount of data we can absorb;
- it is biased by the human tendency to accept the optimal solution as opposed to best solution – that is, when analyzing any ambiguous situations, people are satisfied with first available solution and do not feel inclined to continue further search.

Basu and Palazzo (2008) propose a process view of sense-making, distinguishing between its three basic dimensions: cognitive, linguistic and behavioral.

Cognitive dimension includes corporate identity paraphrased as 'what organizations think of themselves' and how they position themselves against other market players. They could express individualistic relations if the dominant mode of self-positioning in the environment relates to leadership, outplaying the competition and dominating the marketplace in a competitive fight. Other possibilities include relational identity if organization presents itself as a partner to various groups, like customers, employees or collectivistic identity, if the company relates to a broader category of social or even global problems in its role – for example, by attempting to eliminate social exclusion through the employment of people whose chances are seen as diminished by the current market and social setting. The best proxy for assessing corporate identity understood as a cognitive aspect of sense-making is an analysis of how people see the corporate mission, where companies express the perception of their own role. On top of corporate identity, the cognitive aspect of sense-making is complemented by the mode of legitimization built around getting social support for corporate activities.

The linguistic dimension includes all that organizations say about their activities. Most importantly – what kind of argumentation they use to justify what they do. For example, argumentation can be based on a law-related slogan, when it uses notions such as obligations, sanctions, compliance, code of conduct, etc. This is usually the language based on the company's own, internal system of language constructs. A science-supported argument can also be useful to build such justification, especially if backed up by various experts, as well as an economic argumentation, which might use statements like 'creation of job places' or 'supporting regional economic growth'. One of the important aspects of the linguistic dimension of sense-making is the transparency mode in which the company operates. It can be based on the ongoing process of communication, irrespective of the current market reaction, as opposed to the asymmetric mode, when the company only reacts to public criticism and bad publicity, without engaging in information policies at quiet times.

Last, but not least, both cognitive and linguistic dimensions find their final confirmation in what companies actually do. This depicts the behavioral dimension of a sense-making process, largely related to how an organization reacts to criticism – defensively, openly or with a hesitance and uncertainty.

Perception of a corporate identity as one of the dimensions of sense-making is in line with its definition proposed by Balmer (1998) as the distinguishing attribute of an organization, its central and enduring element which helps distinguish it from other organizations. As such, corporate identity can be interpreted as the perceptional lens, through which we perceive the 'surrounding world' (Konecki,

2002). It is a cognitive scheme provided for and by the members of organization.

Corporate identity, understood as the internal perception of organizational members, is different from image, defined as the external view of an organization perceived by the outside environment – in other words, identity interpreted by non-members of organization. It also differs from reputation, defined as the features attributed to an organization by outside observers who compare it with competition (*ibid.*).

Identity as a metaphor

In the long history of metaphors in organizational theory, two main lines of thought dominate. One of them, the reductionist view, says that metaphor is a literal proposition and as such is a deviant form of a literal meaning which depicts the objectively existing reality (Cornelissen, 2003). Such a standpoint, postulating that metaphor usefulness depends on the ability of individual person to actually see the reality as it is, would stand in opposition to the assumption that reality does not exist independently of us but is co-constructed by everyday interactions where our behavioral qualities precede formal structures of organization (Nijhoff and Jeurissen, 2006). Given the latter, metaphors gain much more of the cognitive value and from the organizational perspective can be seen as producing new meanings as well as providing variation to existing interpretations (Cornelissen, 2006) and that is coherent with a sense-making view of organizational reality.

'A metaphor depends upon ... perceived analogies of structure between two subjects belonging to different domains' (Ortony, 1979, after Cornelissen, 2003). Its key quality lies in its imagery (imaginative capacity), which should facilitate the process of hypothesizing about the subject studied (Cornelissen, 2003). Czarniawska (1995) refers to a dramatism in the organizational studies as introduced by Burke – to recover the balance between the stability of roles and the uncertain dynamics of an unfolding narrative (Goffman, 1981; Davies and Harre, 1991).

The use of metaphor in relation to corporate and organizational identity research is twofold. First, organizational identity can be examined as a metaphor itself (organization is identity); however, Cornelissen (2003), using his two criterion method,[2] shows that it has little heuristic value for researchers since neither notion, organization and identity, fulfills the criterion of similarity, being simply incomparable. Second, as metaphors seem an inherent tool in designing mission statements and other visionary corporate communication and, as such, belong to the linguistic dimension of the sense-making process, they seem an accurate measure to assess corporate identity (externally projected).

The concept of identity I refer to in this book, relates to the one crafted by Burke where people are 'symbol-makers, symbol-users and symbol mis-users' (Czarniawska-Joerges and Jacobsson, 1995). Corporate identity is considered a strategically important concept given that its effective management could lead to better investor and community relations, among other positive aspects contributing to organizational performance (He and Balmer, 2007). The confusion of various concepts of identity spans across three lines of thought, mainly related to the construct of social identity, organizational identity and corporate identity. Elaborating on the subtleties of overlapping conceptualizations of those three constructs, as well as on differences between them, Cornelissen *et al.* (2007) confirm that the primary definition of organizational identity is 'shared meaning in the organization which arises from its members', while corporate identity is 'the image communicated by the entity which helps structure public engagement with it'. Defined in this particular manner, both constructs seem coherent with the sense-making process perspective in its cognitive and linguistic dimensions (Basu and Palazzo, 2008). The latter becomes the assumption for the research perspective adopted in this study. When the respondents from the researched companies express their scale of approval to the generic mission statements, they express the perceptions of the organizational identity – the shared meaning as they see it. The meanings hidden in the formal communication such as the texts I analyze in this book depict corporate identity – the communicated picture. From the point of view of the symmetry of communication between the organization and its constituencies, a perfect alignment of those identities would be ideal. The lack of such alignment – that is, different organizational and corporate identities – may have multiple reasons, it seems: one relates to the misperception of the respondent, which could be a signal of incoherence of internal culture;[3] one relates to the exact divergence of the communicated image from the internal one, which could be either a signal of a faulty communication design or a signal of a purposeful action, thus pointing to the certain instrumentality of communication process and conscious meaning manipulation.

Given the placement of organizational identity in between internal (shared meaning) and external (basis for projected communication) focus, the research approach presented in this book is both cognitive and symbolic (Cornelissen *et al.*, 2007) when it looks at the linguistic artifacts represented in mission statements (in the case of the latter).

Although organizations are built of individual people with identities of their own (social identity) and although out of these identities a collective identity construct emerges, it is still distinct from the organizational identity which has a capacity to take on a life of its own and express its own dynamic (Cornelissen *et al.*, 2007). Such a line of thinking is deemed to have its origins in the biological metaphor of organizations looking at entities as if they are organisms (Cornelissen, 2002, 2005, 2006; Gioia, 1998; Hatch and Schultz, 2002, after Cornelissen *et al.*, 2007). A natural consequence of such a line of thinking would be to relate identity to a sense-making process in organizations, given that it serves as a cognitive frame for organizational members sharing meanings (Brickson, 2005; Dutton and Dukerich, 1991; Dutton *et al.*, 1994; Elsbach and Kramer, 1996; Scott and Lane, 2000), as well as perceptual lens assisting interpretative schemes (Dukerich *et al.*, 2002; Fiol, 2002; Gioia *et al.*, 2000; Gidia and Thomas, 1996; Labianca *et al.*, 2001). At the same time, being symbolically embedded, organizational identity expresses itself via language and other cultural patterns (Cornelissen *et al.*, 2007).

Irrespective of the numerous interpretative perspectives of the identity construct, there are some commonalities across them (*ibid.*). First, collective identities are dynamic and, as such, are resistant to fixing procedures – Gioia (1998) speaks of the 'adaptive instability' of organizational identity which enhances the capacity of an organization to adapt to dynamic circumstances, not compromising its capacity to communicate a coherent message on who it is to its members. Second, they provide a platform for shared meanings, with organizational identity serving as a perceptual lens and corporate identity being a determinant for stakeholder orientation towards the organization (Hatch and Schultz, 2001). Third, they can be strategically managed, as managers equipped with an arsenal of symbolic and culturally embedded activities design an identity promoting a certain behavioral response (Alvesson and Robertson, 2006), while, on the corporate level, they manage the external image to ensure a proper stakeholder response (Gray and Balmer, 1998).

In summary, two main schools of thought from which the identity research emerges are organizational theory (organizational identity) and marketing (corporate identity and communications). The differentiation between organizational identity (interpreted in the context of shared meanings) and corporate identity (as its projected and communicated image) falls logically in the cultural framework of Schein's basic assumptions, which, in the process of organizational sense-giving, manifests itself in cultural artifacts (Schein, 1985; Cornelissen and Elving, 2003). However, there does not seem to be any empirical evidence that corporate culture determines identity (Cornelissen and Elving, 2003).[4] Perception of the very concept itself depends on the perspective adopted, be it the functionalist one, which draws upon identity being a social construct, or an interpretative one, sympathizing with the view that identity is constructed together with all surrounding reality rather than given as a stand-alone subject for our analysis. Following this logic, postmodernists would argue that identity 'is not only enabled, but also produced, by the use of language ... at the collective level, identity is at best fiction, produced by power holders to serve their interests' (Soenen and Moingeon, 2002b).

An interesting line of thought is consider organizational identity in the context of the evolution of the form of enterprises. Firms evolved from family-owned enterprises, being a collective entity, where the identification of the firm was provided by the owner, who at the same time managed and controlled it, thus serving, as well, as the reference point for organizational accountability to stakeholders. They evolved towards entities with often fragmented and diffused ownership structure, managed by 'agents'[5] hired to take care of shareholders' capital and, as such, with much more diluted lines of responsibility. In such cases, managers serve as a human face to the whole organization, providing its interface with the market. The corporate identity concept, with its metaphorical qualities, is very handy in such circumstances, where personification of entities facilitates the notion of accountability and corporate responsibility. Firms got personalized and are now treated as an individual 'person with attendant rights and ... ascribed responsibilities' (Christensen and Cheney, 1994, after Cornelissen and Elving, 2003).

There seems to be a general consensus across corporate identity definitions (Melewar and Jenkins, 2002) that, among other areas of corporate reality, it mainly involves communications, as its main task is to present an organizational face to all stakeholder groups. As Balmer and Soenen (1998) define, it is 'the mind, soul and voice'. In such a widely defined 'identity mix', 'soul' includes values, both individual and organizational, while 'voice' includes internal and external communication. Such a standpoint makes organizational culture an integral part of the concept of corporate identity.

The key question behind analysis of metaphors, including the one of identity, is, therefore, whether it brings in any special semantic features of the analyzed constituents and, as such, reorganizes them, or whether it can be reduced to literal propositions based on the assumption that it involves only the process of mapping the pre-existent features of analyzed constituents which may have implications as to whether the criterion of similarity applies. The sense-making perspective attributing a meaning-creation capacity to metaphors and, thus, treating them as a cognitive tool (Cornelissen, 2003) clearly stands in opposition to the simplistic linear view of metaphor being only a way to picture the similarity and isomorphism of given constituents.

Using the image-schema approach, Cornelissen specified various meanings associated with the metaphor of organizational identity, depending on the research tradition in organizational sciences. A summary is presented in Table 2.1.

Table 2.1 Meanings of the 'organizational identity' metaphor

Organizational communication	Language constructs organization in the process of duality; i.e., communicating and organizing are both reciprocal. Communication tools such as language construct organizations and, therefore, identity can only reside in messages* where it is created in the sense-giving process. SENSE-GIVING, one way.
Organizational behavior	Organizational identity is 'material' in the sense that it resides outside of a cognitive area and expresses itself in detectable features in corporate strategies or practices, such as distinguishing a given organization from others. PRACTICES leading to CULTURE. One way or diffusion.

(continued)

Table 2.1   Continued

Cognitive framing	Organization is constructed in the cognitive process of its individual members – it happens through a collective consensus answering the question 'Who we are?' and relates to a collective awareness created in the sense-making process. Organization identity in this context serves as the perceptual lens allowing people to identify themselves with their organization. SENSE-MAKING, one way.
Discursive psychology	Organizations happen in social interactions, specifically in the dialogical situation where the nexus of discourses is created, which consistency serves to maintain the view of the surrounding reality. Organizational identity therefore has a collective meaning but is constantly reconstructed. TWO WAY.
Institutional theory	Organizations are actors by themselves and shall be treated as unitary entities rather than nexuses of relations or cognitions. Organizational identity is, thus, artificially constructed to position organizations against stakeholders – the process uses various levels of symbolic actions, including language (storytelling, narratives) and corporate culture constructs (artifacts, rituals, etc.).
Social identity	Individual cognitions and perceptions answer the question of 'what is shared' in organizations and, from such constructed social identity, organizational behavior patterns arise. 'Organizational identity is both ... mental and material fact' (Haslam *et al.*, 2003), combining the results of sense-making processes at the individual level with its results at the collective level.

Note: In this context a message relates to all types and forms of communication, including formal and informal, internal addressed to employees and external addressed to other stakeholders, expressed in various forms – e.g., press releases, corporate vision and mission statements and even marketing campaigns, with their individual features such as promotional adverts.
Source: Adapted from Cornelissen, 2006.

The analysis presented in Table 2.1 follows the logic of organizational ontology, from where the identity concept derives. Organization can be a predefined structure which gets filled by people performing the predefined tasks and roles (mechanistic view of organization) or it could be said that organization does not exist without people and therefore can not be treated as a separate ontological structure existing independently of its members – hence, envisaging a second approach treating organization as a virtual concept, which gets physical existence only through the creation process in people's minds.

Those two views – mechanistic and humanistic – bring to mind the now-classical metaphors of a machine and an organism applied to organizations by Morgan in his *Images of Organizations* (1997) – metaphors which seem to constitute the toolkit of analysis a researcher may adopt.

Organization and its message

Conflicting discourses

Corporate social responsibility, alongside increasing ties between business and politics, as well as corruption incidents, is one of the fundamental platforms for analysis of contemporary enterprises. A general consensus about defining corporate social responsibility is that it is a concept according to which organizations, mainly companies, voluntarily integrate social and ecological issues in their commercial strategies and their relations with the relevant market actors. The key aspect of such an approach to CSR is the postulate that corporations go beyond legal compliance in recognizing the needs of a broad spectrum of stakeholders and, thus, undertake actions which on top of generating the commercial benefits would also pursue a common good.[6]

Conflicting views in organizational theory provide a good illustrative ground for the discourse on corporate social responsibility or perhaps more, in particular, on the role of business in contemporary society. The way this role is perceived determines how one perceives the surrounding environment. The private sector, when looked at from the perspective of the social role it has (according to which it should be held accountable to a broad spectrum of stakeholders and be responsible for much more than just income generating), by definition acts in the environment in which its position is that of a partner and one of the actors, rather than the dominant one. This seems to be in disagreement with postulates of a mechanistic discourse, where organization dominates its environment and exploits its resources.

Mechanistic discourse in management, based heavily on the paradigm of productivity and the dominance of man over nature and its resources, competes with the ecological discourse, which promotes the vision of sustainable development founded over a balanced cooperation between equal elements: nature, organization, man and other stakeholder groups. This type of discourse is well reflected in the language of metaphors used in organizational science – for example, mechanistic or biological metaphors (Morgan, 1997).

Starkey and Cane (2003) proposed to move from the mechanistic discourse to the 'green' one (green narrative), contemplating the fact that ecological issues are not at the center of attention among managers or organization and management academics. Now, when this situation has changed profoundly and ecological aspects have dominated the management strategic discourse to a great extent, some started to voice discontent regarding what colloquially has been named 'ecology terrorism'.

One of the consequences of accepting the biological metaphor of organization is that this situates it within the context of its ecosystem. Such a naturological view of business operations interprets the socially responsible activities companies undertake as investment in long-term survival strategy (Hill and Cassill, 2004). In an environment where companies depend for survival on their stakeholders, they would share their resources, not for ethical reasons and philosophical beliefs that they owe something to the others, but for the sake of sustaining the market they live on. Furthermore, sustaining stakeholders would also be a strategy to build up the protection system related to the position of the entity in the social network of its constituencies. As animals enjoy safety in numbers as a member of the herd, equally corporate entities build their 'herd' through the policies of socially responsible behaviors and resource sharing, but also through competition, as they strive to secure a position in the network that is as central as possible. A further implication of adopting the ecological system point of view in organization studies would be to concentrate on the accurate identification of one's own social network and the position held in it, which is precisely what dialogue-based communication strategies aim at, thus facilitating not only good image creation, but also the identification of surrounding hierarchies and the competition to be central in the network at the same time.

Thus, depending on the paradigm adopted, organizational deeds, both in the context of socially responsible activities and of overall ethics, might be assessed differently. What might be perceived, under the mechanistic paradigm, as an unreasonable, socially underpinned postulate which interferes with the corporate ability to generate profit, under the terms of ecological discourse becomes an effective, justifiable and socially approvable behavior.

Reasons for right- and wrong-doing

It seems the recent decade has seen an unprecedented escalation of unethical behavior in management, inviting investigation into why individual managers ignore ethics in their decision-making (Armstrong *et al.*, 2004). To an extent, this can be attributed to the escalation of risk in decision-making and trivialization of evil.

What motivates organizations to get involved in socially responsible activities? Some authors claim that, under conditions of imperfect competition, it is possible to increase the value of the company through socially responsible activities (Amalric and Hauser, 2004). Potential benefits of such activities can originate from two sources: expectation from direct stakeholders that a given company will engage in such actions and envisaging new, obligatory regulations to be introduced by the state (law). Both of these sources are related to individuals' capacity to analyze the consequences of actions undertaken. For example, if an organization implements standards higher than those currently legally binding and later uses its power to promote those standards to introduce new and obligatory, state-imposed rules, not only is this beneficial for society but it also imposes the new duties on the whole sector; the initializing company can achieve a significant competitive advantage this way. Additionally, all rules and regulations are subject to cost implications. Therefore, if self-implementation of the new standards proves to be less costly than adjusting itself to comply with regulations imposed by the state, the company is motivated to act accordingly. Furthermore, if organizations attempt to block any new regulations it may cause the overall attractiveness of the sector to plummet.

However, companies also act in order to sustain the social acceptance of their own business, including the business of the competitors. For example, if one producer significantly decreases the quality of its products (for which there are lots of potential substitutes), this may jeopardize consumer opinion about the whole sector (*ibid.*). Thus, motivation behind engaging in socially responsible activities may be varied, but, irrespective of whether they are the results of strategic planning in organizations or the individual morality of its leaders, they do constitute an important aspect of identity, both internally and as the projected construct, and, as such, need to be communicated.

Communication process

Relations between organization and community are portrayed in the context of the ecological system, where organization is treated as the entity that transforms energy and attracts various resources from the environment. Such symbiotic co-existence of organizations can be viewed from two distinctive operational objectives: 'economizing', if the urge to preserve one's energy prevails, or 'ecologizing', if the paradigm to sustain all actors in the environment, including those who are weaker, prevails (Hill and Cassill, 2004). Hill and Cassill, in their bioeconomic skew selection model, postulate that philanthropy can be one of the tools stabilizing organizations against destructive change agents in organizations, presumably in the environment as well.

Given that, according to skew selection theory, sharing and, specifically, philanthropy should be viewed as investment and not cost, it is not surprising that getting involved in various forms of donations is indeed positively related to the dynamics of corporate income.[7] A skew selection model,[8] which translates organizational behavior using the notions of benign and malign greed, treats corporate sharing (in either form envisaged by corporate social responsibility policies) as a long-term survival strategy as opposed to altruistic giving. From that perspective, community relations should be designed with a view to building a corporate position as dominant (large) and central (within the social network of external actors). Having such a strategy in mind, corporations will aim at enhancing their visibility in the local environment (perhaps extending the local one as well), which can be achieved through various forms of donations and reputation-building exercises, like cause-related marketing. Furthermore, corporations will aim to moving onto central positions in the social networks they form with other market players (inclusive of all the stakeholder groups) through the structure of social dialogue, for example, or through other mechanisms allowing the company to maximize its power – for example, control of strategic resources or control of information flow. Using the framework proposed by O'Riordan and Fairbrass (2008), the whole CSR process is analyzed in this study of corporate identity construction, which may overlap with the CSR strategy development phase, namely values (vision, mission, objective, scope) and implementation, where actual stakeholder dialogue takes place. The diagram below (Figure 2.1)

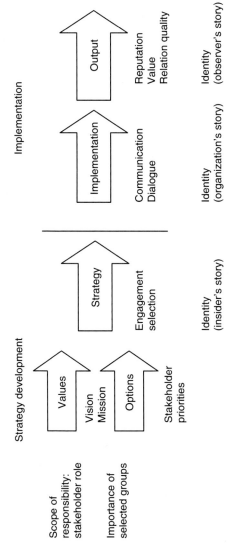

Figure 2.1 The CSR sense-making process
Source: Adapted from O'Riordan and Fairbrass, 2008.

overlaps with the sense-making process, because CSR is a special example of sense-making activity.

The CSR sense-making process (Figure 2.1) develops from the strategy development phase, when values-based perceptions of the scope of business responsibility interlink with the perceived role of stakeholders and, in effect, with the identity adopted by the organization. In parallel, the stakeholder prioritization exercise takes place, as the adaptation of certain role perceptions and the position towards corporate responsibility influences the importance attributed to local communities. Identity building unfolds in three distinct stories: those of the corporate participants (multiple identities), those of the organization and those of the observers – that is, the perception of the company by the market actors. Paradoxically, the process is composed both of linear relations (like the ones relating to the strategy development phase) and non-linear ones (distinct identity stories whose largely non-linear character is confirmed by the case studies presented in the course of the book).

The postulate of the symmetry of the communication process is parallel to the ethicality – in other words the more symmetry introduced in the communication, the more ethical the whole process is supposed to be (Huang, 2004). Ideally it should be designed to build a common way of perceiving things, both by the organization and by society, as opposed to asymmetric communication, where the key assumption is based on unitary-influence views, perceptions, behavior and changing behavior within society.[9] The ethical integrity of actions, on the other hand, is assessed on the basis of three teleological assumptions: open communication, information sharing aiming at leveraging the asymmetry of knowledge[10] and responsibility towards society for organizational activities and their consequences.

Morsing and Schultz (2006), building on public relations theory, propose three types of strategies depicting the way companies build their stakeholder relations. The strategies are defined by the interplay of the various proxy measures, which include the way stakeholders are viewed by the company and, in consequence, the role they are believed to have, the identification of CSR focus, the strategic task of the communication process, the key objective of the corporate communication department and, last but not least, the involvement of third parties in the design of the CSR initiatives. The relation strategies Morsing and Schultz define using those proxies originally assumed that information strategy – an exemplification of one-way communication – can be characterized through the perception of stakeholders as influential and thus requiring in-depth and accurate, objective information. Following from there, the strategic task of communication will be to inform stakeholders about positive actions taken by the company in the form of an appealing and well-designed message. The CSR focus will be defined strictly by the top management, while any involvement of stakeholders in the process of designing CSR policies would be perceived as unnecessary, if not completely unwelcome.

The asymmetric communication strategy would also see stakeholders as influential, but reacting to corporate initiatives. As they therefore require an assurance that their expectations will be thoroughly met, decisions on CSR engagements would be made within the organization on the basis of various market polls and surveys, as a means to enhance understanding of the expectations stakeholders have, while those responsible for the communication would focus on proper and accurate identification of key stakeholder groups.

The third generic strategy – a symmetric communication or a dialogue strategy – assumes partner relations between organizations and their constituencies. It sees the stakeholders as the co-designers of CSR involvements and defines the goal of the communication process as the relation-building exercise, with sustainability criteria applied. In such a setting, the organization would involve the stakeholders in various forms of 'conversations', such as regular focus groups.

3
Enterprises and Relations with Stakeholders

The Framework

Research method

The subject of the research draws from three parallel perspectives. Researching stakeholder relations strategies inevitably relates to the social aspect of the company operations, given that the company is just one of many actors in the social playground – embedded in the nexus of societal relations with other actors and generating micro-society internal relations on its own, at the same time. Thus, building relations with stakeholders is part of corporate societal activity and, as such, is subject to analysis of the scale of responsibility related to such actions. Naturally, the assumption here would be that relations examined are not those conducted on a daily basis, but instead are part of the long-term strategy to locate corporate operations strongly in the context of what is expected of the company and whether operations can be legitimized as a valid and socially needed expression of human activities. In this context stakeholder relations might be treated as something which exceeds legal obligations and, as such, is part of a wider corporate social responsibility program. Second, given that stakeholder relations are based on meaning creation, they become a sense-making exercise, which, depending on the communication strategy used, might evolve from quantitative, data-based fact-giving (information strategy) to narrative, epic construction, when, through engaging in two-way dialogue with stakeholders, a company co-constructs a certain reality and story. Third, given that stakeholder strategies are communication-based activities of enterprises, operationally they are translated into certain systemic aspects, like the system of decision-making (who has the ultimate say on what issue to focus on), the key performance indicator (KPI) structure of the communication department (what the ultimate goal of the communication process is and how the main responsibility of the person realizing this communication is seen) and how the role of stakeholders in this overall process is seen. The latter aspect seems to be a core value and the axiological foundation of the whole stakeholder relations approach, as it seems to predict how much stakeholders are instrumentally treated and how much they are involved in two-way communication.

Thus, a first assumption in the research process would be that there exists a kind of dichotomy in how the stakeholder relations process is designed in organizations, situating the latter between an instrumental approach (where stakeholders are a nuisance which regrettably, and thanks to pressures from environment, need to be incorporated in company statements and care for them demonstrated) and a socially responsible approach (where stakeholders are partners in the market, key to business sustainability, and with whom a dialogue is maintained to build mutual understanding and operational consensus).

The second assumption relates to the operational co-existence of stakeholder relations and communication strategies and takes a standpoint that both are synonyms. Definition-wise, however, while stakeholder relations might be treated as the strategic concept based on long-term planning and a certain ideological background, communication would need to be defined as the tool, which executes operationally the goals defined in the relations strategy. In this context, certain stakeholder strategies would require certain communication approaches – for example, using a pure information strategy, from which the company generates regular reports and makes them available to public without being interested in feedback, probably will not result in building a trust-based and ongoing relationship with stakeholders, although it might result in lowering the risk of the company being accused of withholding the information.

The third assumption relates to the definition of stakeholders as such and the mode of researching it. It seems quite obvious that stakeholder strategies and related communication modes may differ, depending on the stakeholder group targeted. Therefore, ability to generalize and draw standardized conclusions, when assessing the type of strategies companies use, becomes a trade-off for accuracy in describing in general something that might be case specific – that is, related to a certain, explicit stakeholder group. One of the possibilities to overcome this problem without the necessity of building an excessively detailed questionnaire treating all stakeholders groups individually, or a reduced questionnaire focusing on just one type of stakeholder, would be to use the commonly accepted definition of primary and secondary stakeholders. To test whether such an approach is justified, the research sample was tested for importance attributed to individual stakeholder groups[1] and for the intensity of communicating with those groups. The respondents were asked to assess the importance of selected stakeholder groups, as well as the frequency of their organizational relations with them on a five-point scale (1 – not important, no contacts, to 5 – very important, often contacts). Cluster analysis on both these aspects showed that organizations do not differ significantly in the importance attributed to certain stakeholders groups (Figure 3.1), although on average they tend to assign a higher importance to what is understood to be the primary stakeholder group and thus the concept of primary and secondary stakeholders presents an illustrative value.[2]

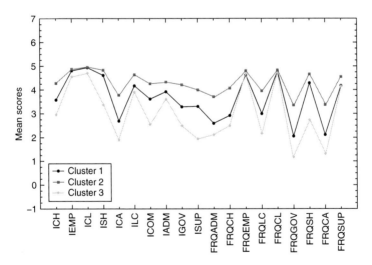

Figure 3.1 Major Polish enterprises: importance and the frequency of contacts with stakeholders

The fourth assumption states that, as organizations do not differ significantly in their attitudes towards primary and secondary stakeholders, the stakeholder relation strategies they use are based on the core systemic aspects related to how communication processes are organized, which are general and can be broadly defined in the quantitative research. Thus, questions related to the communication process aim to understand the processes, irrespective of which stakeholder groups they relate to.

Given the above, the subject matter of the research ranges between fact-giving and storytelling (as far as organizational communication strategies are concerned) and between an instrumental, risk management approach to stakeholders and an engaging, dialogue-building approach (as far as stakeholder relation strategy is concerned). The methodological implication of the above is the combination of quantitative and qualitative tools in the research process to capture both the systemic, structural aspect of communication strategies' taxonomy and the descriptive, interpretative, sense-making aspect of dialogue-based stakeholder relations, understood as part of corporate socially responsible operations.

The research builds upon two theoretical models. First, Morsing and Schultz's (2006) model of CSR communication strategies proposes to define three types of strategies: information, asymmetric communication and symmetric communication (dialogue) – the strategies being defined on the basis of supposed correlation between certain operational variables like decision-making hierarchy or KPI structure of communication department. Second, Basu and Palazzo (2008) designed a model which looks at CSR activities from the perspective of organizational sense-making processes, defining its cognitive, linguistic and conative part. Both models define corporate social responsibility from two distinct yet complementary standpoints: from the standpoint of how stakeholder relations are executed in daily operations (communication strategies) and what the axiological, internal background for it is (meanings used and created in sense-making processes). It might be considered then, that, while the sense-making processes model presents an internal, deeply cultural aspect of organizational positioning in the social environment, the communication strategies model presents its external manifestations in the shape of a given explicit strategy. The common denominator of both models seems to be 'relationship' with stakeholders and a perception of organizational relations and thus its role in the broader context of society and common good.

The first stage of the research was done using a CATI survey addressed to the heads of corporate communication units of 150 major enterprises operating in Poland.[3] After testing whether the organizations analyzed differ significantly in the way they attribute importance to the selected stakeholder groups, the communication strategies model was redefined on the basis of a pilot study, which resulted in formulating four main systemic variables – their potential correlations to define the exact communication strategy (Table 3.1).

In order to make the model more explicit and clear to the respondents, original aspects of stakeholders, stakeholders' role and third-party endorsement in CSR initiatives was translated into the variable 'perceived

Table 3.1 Revised communication strategies

	Information	**Asymmetric communication**	**Dialogue**
Perceived role of stakeholders	Influential, potential opposition to neutralize as they can support or show opposition	Influential responders to corporate initiatives	Co-constructors of corporate CSR strategy
Decision-making locus	Only top management and/or directors	Top management and/or directors on the basis of polls, surveys and research	Top management and/or directors with the representatives of key stakeholders
Goal of the communication process	Provide information	Prove that expectations are met	Create dialogue
KPI of communication manager*	Creating clear and convincing message	Identifying key stakeholder groups to communicate with	Creating and maintaining stable relations with key stakeholders

Note: *Communication manager stands for any person which, in a given company, is responsible for performing the stakeholder communication process – that is, the head of the communication department, which might semantically be stakeholder relations department, PR department or communication department.
Source: Based on Morsing and Schultz (2006).

role of stakeholders', which involves all the three aspects mentioned, as duly explained to the respondents by the researchers. The locus of the decision-making process (LOKUSDEC) reflects the identification of CSR focus, while the goal of the communication process (COMGOAL) and KPIs of the communication manager (MNGOBJ) reflect the strategic communication task and corporate communication department's task respectively. These are naturally variables of a qualitative nature, which were analyzed in the CATI questionnaire, where the respondents were ranking possible responses from the most to the least important.

As a result, it became possible to see to what extent the theoretical models of communication strategies from the Morsing and Schultz model are represented in their clear form in the tested sample. In due course, testing for the inter-correlations between variables also allowed verification of the legitimacy of the model as a tool for assessing operational strategies of companies.

The cognitive aspect of CSR-related sense-making processes was also tested at this stage. Since Basu and Palazzo (2008) defined it as a way in which organizations think of their relations with stakeholders and, to an extent, their views about the world and business at large, respondents were asked to express their perceptions on the scale of business responsibility. They could indicate a narrow scope (suggesting that organizations should be responsible only for profit generation for their shareholders), a moderate view (by which they accepted business responsibility for profits and fulfilling the expectations of clients and employees) and the broad view (by which the responsibility towards other players and groups on the market is added to the list). Since the cognitive aspect of a sense-making process includes also the concept of organizational identity, respondents were asked to identify themselves with three types of mission statements which were used as proxies for organizational identity orientation. Mission statements, being the verbalization of what organizations 'think of themselves', indicate quite clearly how they also position themselves in a broader microcosm of the market; thus, depending on whether the mission is formulated around notions of leadership, market fight, winning market share or notions related to trust and understanding of clients and/or employees or notions related to broader problems of society, people, life or planet, conclusions could be drawn about the dominant identity of organizations which could be individualistic, relational or collectivistic respectively. A certain degree of simplification is necessary at this stage of the research, given that CATI surveys are limited to a five- to ten-minute telephone conversation with respondents – for this reason the question about mission was limited to only three example statements. Any potential over-generalization of results arising from such an approach is well balanced in the second stage of the research, where mission statements were also analyzed using different methodology.

This stage is completed by a set of questions testing what types of CSR activities the sample organizations practice. Integrated categories of activities included social advertising, cause-related marketing, sponsorship, cooperation with NGOs, donations for local communities initiatives, support programs for employees (training, medical care, flexible working time), community volunteering and supplier selection. The categories are defined on the basis of extensive research in CSR practices done by Perrini *et al.*, (2007) and Russo and Tencati (2008);[4] however, activities related to formal CSR reporting and ecological engagements (i.e., ecological norms and standards) were excluded from the list for two reasons. First, the aspect of formal reporting was assessed in the second stage of the research using different methodology. Second, the research relates explicitly to stakeholders relations strategy; thus, non-person stakeholders – such as the environment – are not at the core of the interests. However, energy and water use reduction programs, as well as waste reduction programs, were left in the questionnaire as they also point to the important aspect of how an organization positions itself in the local community, building carefully its image as a non-polluting organization, for example.

In summary, the first stage of the research gives a picture of organizational perceptions on the role of business in the context of society at large and of the character of relations with stakeholders – this being expressed in identity orientation. It provides also information on how those attitudes and perceptions are transferred to the stakeholders in certain communication processes. Given that the respondents here fulfill the criteria of expert informants, it may be assumed that information collected is as accurate as it comes from persons leading the communication process and being directly responsible for it. Possible limitations of such an analytical approach can reside in a potential divergence between perceptions of top management and its strategic direction and of operational staff (communication managers), who execute the strategy. However, this is a discussion about where the strategic direction gets crafted and executed. Is it defined by top executives, who could be visionaries but not necessarily operation-oriented executors; is it well communicated to operational staff, well understood by them and executed accordingly; or perhaps it is orchestrated by operational staff (only because communication inaccuracies in the organization force middle managers to make sense of corporate strategic direction, internalize it and then give sense to stakeholders or because decentralization processes assume the empowerment of middle management to design a proper and flexible strategy of communication based on their educated sense-making of what the organization stands for)? Whatever the explanation, it seems reasonable to assume that the real strategy of relations is crafted where it is being executed – that is, in the communication department – and most probably derives from the perceptions of people who are responsible for it, rather than from the perceptions of top managers, which would need to be internalized and assimilated in the culture of organization. Giving priority to communication managers in the adopted research approach allows avoidance of systemic errors in the research which might occur as a result of not controlling for the quality of inter-organizational communication.

The second stage of the research builds upon the taxonomy of communication strategies examined in the first stage. From those organizations which represented clear strategy models, four were selected for further assessment of the effectiveness of the strategy used in local communities. The proxy used to assess the effectiveness was defined as the convergence of corporate identity perceptions between organizations and local community representatives. In order to examine local community perceptions, four random samples of 140 respondents each were selected and interviewed using the CATI method. Respondents were asked to identify themselves with three example mission statements, being proxies for corporate identities – they indicated which of the statements they believed best described the company in question.[5] They were also asked whether they were aware of the company's involvement in CSR activities, what corporate members declared they do, and asked about their general perception of the scope of business responsibility.

As a result, conclusions could be drawn on the effectiveness of corporate communication about CSR activities. Although the net results at this stage are presented as the outcome of the quantitative research, conclusions drawn might be of a qualitative nature only due to the fact that just four specific cases or organization–community relation nexuses were selected. In a sense, this part becomes more of a case study with an embedded quantitative component. Corporate identity assessment follows the interpretative paradigm of identity and treats it with self-reflective questions (Gioia, 1998; Corley and Gioia, 2004) followed by theory-building case study (Corley and Gioia, 2004). Last but not least, and perhaps more importantly, this part of the research gives interesting data upon local communities themselves and allows for conclusions about the influence of some independent variables like gender, age or education upon attitudes to business responsibilities.

The third stage of the research is a content analysis designed to test the linguistic part of CSR sense-making processes – that is, to analyze what companies say about themselves and what type of argumentation they use to justify the actions and deeds. The same sample of 150 enterprises was tested for the existence of web pages, or interactive web pages, treated as the instruments engaging stakeholders in a kind of a dialogue with organization. At this stage of the research, two sets of documents were analyzed. First, official corporate web pages and other formal documentation (i.e., reports and press releases), were tested for the existence of certain key words, as explained below. Corporate mission statements were looked for, either in the web page or, if no such page existed, a Google search was performed to determine whether the selected company has a mission statement. Mission statements were analyzed as well for the use of certain key words. Second, a database of press articles related to selected 150 companies was built to serve as a proxy for 'market' opinion about the firm. The archives of two nationwide newspapers were used for this purpose. Selected articles were then tested for the use of the same key words. The archives used belong to *Rzeczpospolita* (*Res Publica*) – a well-respected nationwide daily with a strong focus on economy and legal matters – and *Dziennik Polski* (*Polish Daily*) – selected for its strong representation of local editions covering smaller towns and thus providing a good coverage for the market and local communities specific for those companies in the sample that have registered offices in smaller towns, which, as such, might not be a direct interest of *Rzeczpospolita*.

Three sets of key words are used in this part of the research.[6] The majority of the verbal categories used in this stage (except for the ones relating to the type of argumentation companies use to justify the activities – the linguistic part of identity) is sourced from existing research, well described by Bart *et al.* (2001), who argue that the constant tendency of researchers to define new analytic categories rather than to use the ones already established as useful hampers the collection of solid mission statement research (after Williams, 2008).

The first set follows the categories established by Cunningham *et al.* (2009) in research exploring the link between corporate identity and sponsorship policies. By analyzing recurring themes in mission statements the authors tested the hypothesis about prediction of sponsorship by mission statements. Since sponsorship is one of the categories in social responsibility practices referred to by the companies in the *Rzeczpospolita* 2000 sample, and the link explored coincides partly with the hypothesis of this research, it seemed recommendable to include the same verbal categories in mission statements[7] to define identity. Moreover, sponsorship, being part of a wider marketing-oriented category of corporate communication with stakeholders, also presents the potential to be interpreted, together with other CSR-related activities, as the proxy for stakeholder relation strategies. We thus have the set A, which includes: company success, product superiority, focus on competitors, innovation, being the best, a focus on customers, diversity, value, ethics, an employee focus, being helpful, responsibility and improving quality of life (*ibid.*). These categories are used to portray the individualistic, relational and collectivistic identities.

Second, a linguistic dimension of identity requires to test what type of argumentation companies use in seeking legitimization. Categories proposed by Basu and Palazzo (2008) are legal, scientific, economic and ethical, depending what arguments are used. It could be related to law requirements and various regulations or there might be statements, citations or opinions from scientific experts and examples of the latest scientific advancements or discoveries or facts and data on economy and growth or arguments related to higher moral values and common good, respectively. These categories coincide, to an extent, with the principles of CSR activities, defined in the study mission statements and CSR reports of retailers by Lee *et al.* (2009). The type of statements used by the companies in that research (i.e., economic, legal, ethical and philanthropic) are not far from the Basu and Palazzo's legal, scientific, economic and ethical. Lee *et al.* defined these categories, following earlier work by Carroll (1991) who used them to describe dimensions of CSR, while Basu and Palazzo looked at them from the standpoint of getting a justification for corporate activities. While the first approach seeks to build a taxonomy of CSR engagements based on reporting and statements, the second looks for a deeper rationale behind the argumentation the company adopts, to obtain a social consensus in what they do. It thus makes sense to assume that the most relevant categories would be legal and economic, combined with ethical (including philanthropic motivations, as they seem to belong to the same value pool) and scientific. Based on this, set B of verbal constructs was developed, which includes: obligations, laws, sanctions, compliance, confidentiality, penalty, code of practice, science, experts, research, analysis, report, jobs, economic growth, unemployment, income per capita, economic development, economy[8] and GDP.

The third set of key words includes ten values determined as the most frequently occurring in the mission statements. The strong rhetorical value of the mission statement (Williams, 2008) locates it in the centre of the sense-giving activities of the company and makes it a central point in the communication toolset. On the other hand, value statements seem a focal point in corporate social responsibility strategies; thus, it seems reasonable to follow Williams' argument, that inclusion of positive values in mission statements can also be considered a strong identification strategy aimed at building an ethos of the company addressed to stakeholders – it thus can be also seen as a stakeholder relation-building strategy. However, given that CSR reports, communicated widely and aimed at the broad range of stakeholders, also aim to build certain relations, this research proposes to include CSR reports in the textual analysis of values. Set C of key words includes: excellence, integrity, innovation, respect, leadership, diversity, responsibility, citizenship, teamwork and safety (*ibid.*).

On top of dependent variables used in this model,[9] independent corporate variables, such as employment numbers, income and dynamics of income (year on year) were used, as well as independent stakeholder variables referring to community sample, such as age, gender and education. The scheme presenting the flow of analysis is shown in the Appendix (see Figure A.1).[10]

Identities generated and community relations

Looking at the companies from the perspective of the relations they built, one sees them not only as elements in the wider social network organizations create, but also as vehicles and platforms of the multidimensional communication flows of which they are both receivers and senders. Such circumstances embed the analysis in the concept of organizational sense-making and sense-giving (Weick, 1995) and in the stakeholder theory perspective (Freeman, 1994). Organizations constantly create and give sense to the process of leadership and motivation, but also to the process of creating a corporate image projected to the outside environment. In parallel, a sense-making process occurs, based on the interpretation of surrounding phenomena, actions and events – this is a process performed both by employees and outside stakeholders, enabling them to identify themselves with the organization and to adopt their individual attitude towards surrounding reality. Sense-making theory has its foundations in the paradigm of anti-realism, which means that reality does not exist independently from our cognitive structures, but rather is created by us (Nijhoff and Jeurissen, 2006). Given that we perform various interactions in organizations on a daily basis and the quality of these interactions is getting more important to the success of the organization, it might sound acceptable that, through interpersonal deeds, we precede the creation of hard structures which, in effect, proceduralize and standardize our behaviors. The more unclear the situation, the more sense-making processes are needed.

The research also deals with questions about relations between the role of business in a society as perceived by the managers and attitude to stakeholder relations. It seems to depend on the model of business role the company adopts – generating profits for the owners (i.e., private responsibility [Baron, 2001]) or generating common good and service to society (i.e., social responsibility [*ibid.*]). In the first scenario, if the goal of the company is perceived only in the category of profits, which, under certain circumstances, are positively correlated with financial results[11] (Hillman and Keim, 2001), and relations are looked upon solely from the perspective of an area to be managed, the temptation is to regard the surrounding environment – including stakeholders – as a threat. In the second scenario, if the goal is perceived as generation of common good (altruistic CSR, which does not generate positive financial results [*ibid.*]) – the stakeholders' goals become more internalized and a more profound process of consulting stakeholders takes place (sense-making).

The sense-making perspective of corporate social responsibility is created through stakeholders' engagement in a dialogue with organization. This aspect of relating to environment is covered by the model proposed by Morsing and Schultz (2006), suggesting that organizations use three generic strategies when they communicate various social activities to the outside world: information, asymmetric communication and symmetric communication or dialogue. As could be expected, the scale of stakeholder involvement escalates in each, respectively. Depending on how intense it is, organizations can choose the information strategy (where stakeholders are hardly involved *per se*), asymmetric communication strategy (where corporate messages are designed in a way to convince the stakeholders that the organization is aware of their needs and includes them in its operations) and a dialogue strategy (where social consultations are being performed to enhance legitimacy of certain corporate decisions).

At the same time, CSR, seen as a sense-making process as presented in the Basu and Palazzo (2008) model, determines corporate identity – that is, it aims to differentiate itself from the surrounding environment, positioning itself as the aggressive competitor fighting for the market share, as the partner in social relations or as an actor belonging to the wider systemic macrocosm, where it has a mission to extend effective money-making – for example, by generating wealth for the community, enhancing quality of life or creating some kind of common good.

The cognitive dimension of this sense-making process facilitates the assessment of corporate identity (how organizations think of themselves), while the linguistic dimension helps define what type of argumentation companies use to justify their operations and whether the information they convey is transparent and clear (what firms say about themselves).

The research presented attempts to explore the hypothesis that there is a relation between corporate identity, as declared in generic types of mission statements, and the stakeholder relation strategies and this relation is intermediated by sense-making activities expressed by perceptions of the role of business in the surrounding environment. Supposedly, organizations where the sense-making process aims to define a wide role for business in society build their relations on a dialogue and on social consultations, while those with an individualistic identity use the strategies of information or asymmetric information.

Perceptions of the role of business are measured by the proxy defining the scale of business responsibility towards the shareholders only (private responsibility concept) versus the responsibility towards the wider range of stakeholders (primary and secondary stakeholders). Supporting questions suggest that companies building dialogical relations are more often perceived by their stakeholders in accordance with their projected image, while those using information strategy and asymmetric communication experience divergence between projected and perceived image, ergo, dialogue strategy seems more efficient. Convergence between projected and perceived corporate identity is used as a measure of the effectiveness of a given strategy. Detailed research questions include:

- Are corporations getting involved in dialogue with stakeholders?
- What are the differences between the companies in the scale of stakeholders involvement and what does it depend on?
- What is the mechanism of consensus building in the company; who makes the decision on what is important and what should be the focus of CSR policies?

Furthermore, the research explores some supporting hypotheses. One supporting hypothesis assumes that sense-making practices, intermediated by perceptions of the role of business in society adopted by companies, determine the stakeholder relation strategy companies use. The hypotheses to be verified are complemented by a set of detailed tests aimed at verifying the following:

0.1.0 Companies dominated by the narrow view on business responsibility (private responsibility) build relations based on the information strategy.

0.1.1 They believe that stakeholders are influential and, as they may oppose or support corporate actions, they should be treated as potential opposition to be neutralized.

0.1.2 They are companies where the strategy of social responsibility is mainly defined by management.

0.1.3 They are companies which limit their communication to recording those of their actions which they perceive as attractive.

0.1.4 They are companies where the main task of a person responsible for stakeholder communication is to design an effective message.

0.2.0 Companies dominated by the narrow view on business responsibility (private responsibility concept) also build relations based on the strategy of response (asymmetric communication).

0.2.1 They believe that stakeholders are influential, but only react to corporate actions.

0.2.2 They are companies where strategy on CSR is defined by management, but is often based on previous research, market polls or analysis.

0.2.3 They are companies which aim at proving to stakeholders that their expectations are met.

0.2.4 They are companies where the main task of the person responsible for stakeholder communication is to define the key stakeholder group.

0.3.0 Companies dominated by the wide view on the role of business in the society (social responsibility), mainly use the relation strategy based on dialogue and stakeholders involvement.

0.3.1 They believe that the stakeholders' role is to actively co-construct corporate social responsibility strategy.

0.3.2 They are companies where CSR strategy and focus is defined by a process of social consultation.

0.3.3 They are companies which enter into regular dialogue and interaction with stakeholders.

0.3.4 They are companies where the main task of the person responsible for communication is to build proper and sustainable relations with stakeholders.

The second supporting hypothesis assumes that sense-making and sense-giving practices (expressed by the proxy of social consultations) influence corporate perceptions of the role of business at large measured by the perception of the scale of business responsibility towards various stakeholder groups (shareholders only, primary or secondary stakeholders). The more the company is engaged in social consultations the more it strengthens its view on business responsibility being towards primary and secondary stakeholders as well.

Organizations: the portrait

The sample of enterprises consists of 150 companies randomly selected from the database of 2,000 major companies in Poland.[12]

The selection covers the whole country and all business sectors and includes companies from the locations of various sizes (see Figure 3.2).

Companies also differ according to the number of employees (Figure 3.3) and, to an extent, according to the dynamics of their revenue, although they all show significant positive revenues, in the majority of cases exceeding 100 per cent year on year (see Figure 3.4).

As seen in Figure 3.2 and 3.3, respectively, the vast majority of the sample consists of enterprises either from small towns of up to 50,000 inhabitants (39 per cent) or from big cities with more than 500,000 inhabitants (25 per cent). Large enterprises employing over 250 people dominate the sample (58 per cent).

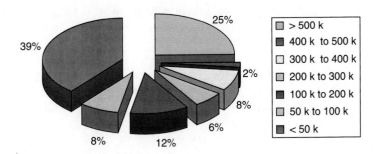

Figure 3.2 Enterprises by size of city of origin

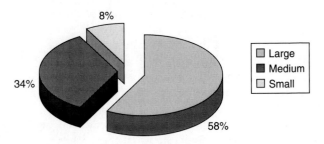

Figure 3.3 Sample by size of company

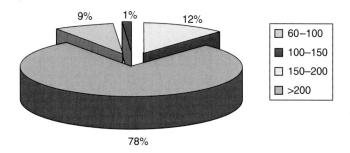

Figure 3.4   Enterprises by dynamics of revenue

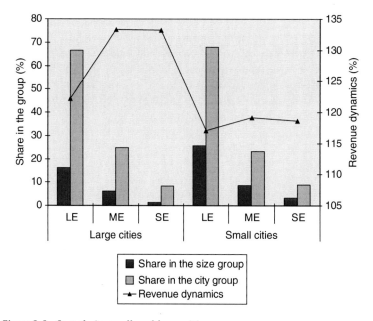

Figure 3.5   Sample in small and large cities

A closer look at the sample (Figure 3.5) reveals that, while all enterprises (large, medium and small) represent a similar share in both large city and small city sub-samples, small enterprises choose to operate in small cities rather than in large ones. Interestingly enough, substantially more large enterprises choose to operate in the small cities as well (25.7 per cent as opposed to 16.2 per cent), although the dynamics of their revenue seems slightly higher in large cities than in small ones (122 per cent as opposed to 117 per cent). Nevertheless, the difference between their revenue dynamics depending on the location seems much more modest, in comparison to numbers shown by SMEs, where the difference in revenue dynamics exceeds 13 per cent, showing higher numbers in companies operating in large cities.

This may indicate that, while medium and small enterprises may be able to generate substantial economies of scale deriving from operating in large environment, large enterprises seem to show less elasticity of revenue dynamics. One of the possible interpretations of those numbers may be that large companies consider small cities more beneficial as the main operating point, as they give them the possibility to become a key employer and benefit from all the advantages of local labour markets,[13] which usually show higher unemployment figures. At the same time, being a key employer in town enables the companies to build different, deeper stakeholder relations, based on the strong local embeddedness of local communities, as opposed to cosmopolitan orientation, usually shown in case of large cities where the migration trends are much stronger.[14]

Identities perceived and the effectiveness of relation-building strategies

This part of the research covers the supporting questions about envisaged effectiveness of strategies used by the companies, measured by the convergence between the identity projected and that perceived by local communities. It is presented primarily as a case story and narrative because, although the data relating to local communities is quantitative (about 140 respondents in each community), it covers only four pre-selected communities. It is possible, therefore, to draw statistical conclusions about certain features of the communities, but it is not possible to generalize statistically regarding the reasons for convergence or divergence of corporate identities.

Randomly selected respondents gave their opinion on the perceived mission of the company in question (ranked proxy for identity orientation), on the scale of business responsibility at large and on their observations of CSR-related activities undertaken by the company in question (perform, does not perform, do not know).

Research questions analyzed included:

- Do companies differ from local communities in the way they perceive the responsibility of business at large? This question is designed to facilitate the definition of the operational nature of community that surrounds the company and thus give some information on whether the company operates in the scenario of poorly adjusted expectations.
- Does this perception depend on independent variables such as education, age or gender and, therefore, can the expectations of local communities regarding business be predicted either geographically or demographically? This might support the hypothesis that, in some locations, which are virtually stable demographically and where the idea of locally embedded community holds, a company may be able to foresee certain sociological features which may impact their future operations – that is, a community with exuberant expectations regarding business may carry more risk of hostility if the company presents a modest and shareholder-oriented profile of CSR involvement.
- Is the identity projected by the selected companies perceived accurately by their local communities? Potential convergence of those identities may indicate further that the relation strategy a company uses is based on effective communication strategy with stakeholders.
- Are there any features of the local communities, independent from the company, that may intervene in the way the community perceives corporate image – that is, can demographical structure, education or age influence perceptions of corporate missions, irrespective of the relation strategy the company adopts for its environment?

Local communities: the portrait

Local communities, analyzed here in the form of four sub-samples, can be viewed from the perspective of features of the environment in which corporations work. A closer look at the structure of various variables, such as gender, age and education, as well as at the perceptions of business responsibility across locations, gives a good

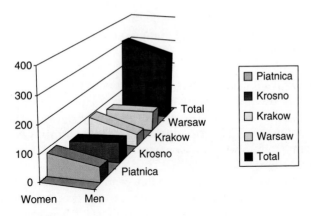

Figure 3.6   Gender comparison of the samples

overview of the aspects which might be important from the perspective of a relation-building exercise.

The overall sample (over 500 respondents) is well balanced in terms of the variables mentioned above. It represents men and women (45 per cent and 55 per cent, respectively) and covers a range of age cohorts (people below the age of 25 [12 per cent], between 25 and 39 years of age [31 per cent], between 40 and 54 [29 per cent] and 55+ years of age [28 per cent]). As far as level of education is concerned, the sample represents people with basic education (10 per cent), technical education (37 per cent), secondary education (16 per cent) and higher education (37 per cent).[15]

Individual sub-samples differ in two cases (Krakow and Krosno) from the structure of the overall population analyzed, as seen in Figures 3.6–3.8.

In the cases of Piatnica and Krakow, women are over-represented in the sample (61 per cent and 67 per cent, respectively), which is consistent with the general trend observed in the overall sample (55 per cent). This is reversed in cases of Krosno and Warsaw, where women represent 44 per cent and 48 per cent, respectively.

The general sample represents mainly people of production age (87 per cent); however, the category 55+ (27 per cent of the sample) may also include those already retired. This is ignored for the sake of the analysis, based on the assumption that people in the cohort 55+ are considered slightly disadvantaged from the labour market

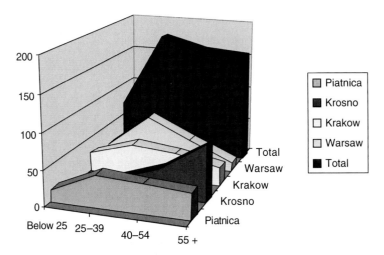

Figure 3.7 Age comparison of the samples

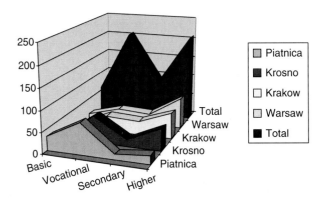

Figure 3.8 Educational comparison of the samples

perspective and there seems to be a consensus that it is more difficult for them to find a new job as employers show a strong preference for younger people, even though they might not have equally substantial experience. This trend is confirmed by various governmental activities and NGO campaigns to promote employment of this group.[16]

The strongest category in the sample includes young working people of age 25 to 39 – this is also reflected in the structures of sub-samples Piatnica and Krakow. A digression comes to mind, however, when observing Krosno and Warsaw, where two distinct trends can be noticed. In the first case, there is a strong over-representation of people in the 55+ cohort (56 per cent of the sample), while, in the second case, this category is the smallest (9 per cent of the sample). A possible explanation might relate to migration trends and labor market specifics – that is, young people from smaller cities, such as Krosno, migrate to bigger ones looking for good jobs, while, in big cities, which are the main concentration of labor market opportunities, the influx of job seekers creates certain imbalance in the population age structure.[17]

The vast majority of the sample is distributed between two main categories – vocational education and higher education –together forming over 70 per cent of the population examined, which seems natural given that majority of the overall sample consists of people of working age, and both primary and secondary education, as defined here, are only intermediating stages in the process of completing education. It might be assumed, therefore, that people with primary or secondary education only are, to an extent, those in the youngest group of the respondents (below 25 years) who are still in the process of obtaining a higher diploma. Nevertheless, there seems to be a clear division line visible in the age structures of sub-samples, with vocational education dominating smaller cities (Piatnica and Krosno) and big cities clearly showing the biggest share of people with higher education in their samples (Krakow and Warsaw).

In conclusion, the environment within which the enterprises in question operate consists of populations dominated by women, mainly of working age, with an emphasis on people in the first years of their careers (25–39 years), either highly educated (with the university qualifications) or, alternatively, with professional, vocational training. This is also a population expressing strong migration trends related to job seeking, which leaves smaller towns with a relatively strong over-representation of older people, influencing the balance in age structure of big cities by providing a strong influx of young and educated new entrants to the labor market. The latter seem to have the academic qualifications and aspire to posts in highly specialized sectors of complex business processes, such as professional consulting, banking and finance, etc. At the same time, people with vocational training choose more often to stay in smaller towns, where a great deal become entrepreneurs, setting up businesses of their own.[18]

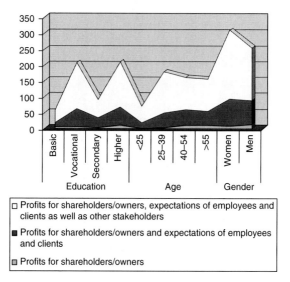

Figure 3.9 What should the business be responsible for (by education and gender)?

Surely, in diverse communities, there will be many diverse perceptions of what role in society business should play. As the notion of business responsibility developed substantially over recent decades, evolving in meaning and significance, together with the evolving nature of business and changing societal trends, as described in detail in the introduction to this book, local communities and other stakeholders, previously not involved in the subject, felt rightly that they should build their own opinions about the issue.[19]

Local communities were tested regarding their views on the desired scale of business responsibility (Figures 3.9 and 3.10), being asked to choose one of three possible options offering different ranges of stakeholders having a potentially justified claim towards a business *sensu largo*.

The vast majority of the overall sample supports the view of a wide business responsibility as opposed to a narrow one, where only capital owners would be entitled to expect anything from organizations. Not surprisingly, the view that business is responsible to various stakeholders, including indirect ones, is voiced more often by women than by men, by people over 25 years of age through to those of 55+ and

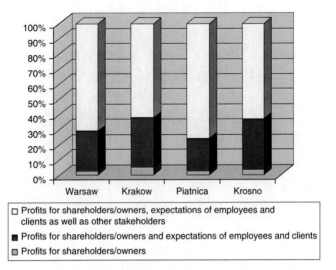

Figure 3.10   What should the business be responsible for (by city)?

mostly by people with higher or technical (vocational) educational qualifications. Except for the fact that the demographical structure of the sample might be responsible, to an extent, for such a result, it seems fairly obvious, given the psychological and emotional features attributed to their gender, that women show more sensibility towards interests of others, while men remain more task-focused. The fact that the mercantile approach to the idea of responsibility starts to show with increase in age might indicate that, as people progress in their careers, a certain percentage of them gives up their altruistic approach, which they may perceive as 'idealistic', and adopts a narrow view, which helps them stay focused on business and concentrate on profit maximization. This might also be the group of people who, from the corporate governance perspective, might be those showing more inclination to short-term profit maximization as opposed to long-term sustainability building. Also the fact, that people show a greater tendency to focus on consumption than on savings as they progress in age, seems not insignificant here.[20]

There is a large proportion of people with higher education in the group supporting a wide view on responsibility, as well as those with vocational training. A possible explanation might be that this group

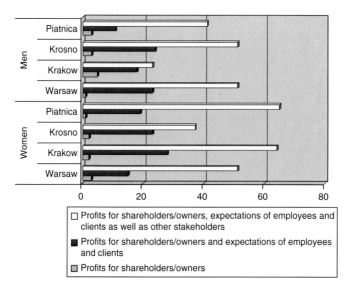

Figure 3.11   Gender and responsibility

consists of entrepreneurs and/or people involved in SME sector; thus, their support for the wide concept of business responsibility might derive from direct contacts with clients and, therefore, higher working awareness of the importance of trust-based relations; this contrasts with the awareness of those academically educated, whose experience is often theory and philosophy based.[21] A purely mercantile view, attributing corporate duty for responsible actions only to the group of shareholders and owners, seems to show only in the age cohort below 25, but as they progress in age it seems to decrease, then returning as they enter the group of 55+.[22] The same sample of 150 enterprises was tested for the existence of web pages, or interactive web pages, treated as the instruments engaging stakeholders in a kind of a dialogue with organization. At this stage of the research, two sets of documents were analyzed.

Looking at the comparison of the sub-samples (Figure 3.10), a fairly high consistency across individual cities may be seen, with only Krakow and Krosno showing, perhaps, a noticeable similarity in the pattern of responses.

There is little surprise in response patterns between men and women across sub-samples (Figure 3.11), except for the fact that most

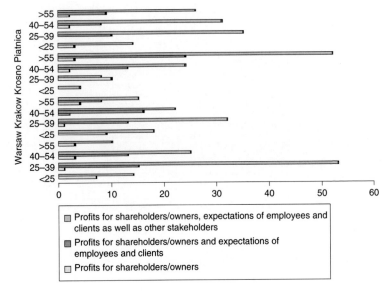

Figure 3.12   Age and responsibility

mercantile-oriented women seem to reside in Warsaw, while the majority of mercantile-oriented men are in Krakow. A possible explanation, though anecdotal only, could be that, to make their way through to higher business posts, women need to show much higher levels of determination, skill and focus, which often turns into certain forms of business aggression. Also, in smaller cities, a narrow view of business responsibility is more often represented by men than by women.

The question arises as to whether there are any differences between cities in the way the perception of business responsibility evolves together with age, which may present an interesting story (Figure 3.12). First, it seems that a mercantile attitude to corporate responsibility (i.e., one which approves of the fact that business is responsible solely to its shareholders) does not occur until people start their professional careers. Once it does occur, it seems to increase as people progress in age. This trend is most visible in the Krakow sample. Local exceptions from this rule are visible in smaller cities (Piatnica and Krosno), where people start to sympathize with this narrow view of responsibility relatively later (after they are 40 as opposed to earlier age group of 25–39 in big cities), while in Warsaw this trend disappears in the cohort 55+.

Why do more mature employees in Warsaw seem to be philanthropic and altruistic than in smaller cities? Perhaps the explanation can be found in the differentials in income patterns and asset status of respondents in those cities. More wealthy people in Warsaw exceed a certain psychological barrier beyond which they do not have such a strong motivation to further benefit from their accumulated wealth and are prepared to share more.[23]

A wider attitude towards corporate responsibility that accepts that other stakeholders, including indirect ones, also have legitimate claims and expectations towards companies, follows more or less the same pattern. It increases, reaching its apogee in the age group 25–39 – that is, among people in the relatively early phase in their careers – and then decreases with age. Krosno is an exception to this pattern, showing a clear growing trend for a wide perception of business responsibility, with the apogee in the cohort 55+.

In summary, local communities examined experience various demographical shifts, such as a general domination of women in the population and strong migration shifts from smaller cities to bigger ones, the results of which could be observed in the age structure of smaller cities (more mature people) as compared to big cities (saturated by the younger generation). The big–small city shift is also visible in education structure, where vocational training characterizes more the smaller cities and higher education clearly dominates in big ones. In such demographical settings a view promoting corporate responsibility towards a wide range of stakeholders seems dominant as opposed to a mercantile view, which would prefer to restrict responsibilities to shareholders only. Except for Krosno, where the awareness of wide corporate responsibility increases significantly with age, people tend to attach more importance to the broad responsibilities of businesses when they are building their careers progressively – that is, when they are between 25 and 39 – shifting their focus more towards narrowing the legitimate group of stakeholders when they get older.

Potential relations between demographic specifics and public perceptions of the scale of business responsibility show that local communities can differ significantly in their attitudes towards business. The perception of business responsibility depends on the gender of the respondent – for example, women favor the concept of wide responsibility (towards all stakeholders) much more than men – while in case of narrowly defined responsibility, focusing on primary stakeholders only, men sympathize with the concept more than women. Also age and education influence perceptions of the role of business; those people who adopt the view that business should be responsible towards its owners and shareholders only tend to be older than those opting for a wider scale of responsibility. Also more educated people believe that business should be responsible to the broad range of stakeholders (see Appendix, Tables A.2a and A.2b). However, this result holds only in Krakow.

Socially sensitive organizations

Mission and vision: corporate identity and business responsibility

Inter-correlations between mission statements reveal that the mission defined in terms of leadership and domination (strong competitive fight underpinning individualistic identity) is strongly and negatively correlated with the mission defined as gaining trust or contribution to solving social problems (–0.77 and –0.62, respectively, significant at p<0.001).[24] Given the above, it might be expected that corporate identities – seen through the lens of the mission statement and reports and defined on the basis of key words, as described in the framework – will indeed be mutually exclusive.

A first look at the corporate sample from the perspective of two key questions posed in this research – those are, what is their identity and what are their perceptions on the role of business? – reveals that, contrary to what might be expected, the fact that a given company uses aggressive and competitive language to identify its mission, thus expressing individualistic identity, does not immediately imply that it focuses on shareholders only, excluding non-direct and secondary stakeholders from its area of business responsibility. In other words, companies expressing a deep belief in their responsibility towards a wide spectrum of stakeholders do not see any contradiction between such philosophy and a competitive market fight (Figure 3.13). Given that Basu and Palazzo (2008) are right about the background of identities being deeply rooted perceptions of the nature of relations between the firm and the environment – that is, atomized relations of firms pursuing self-interest (individualistic identity) through to a profound bond with the world in organizations pursuing the vision

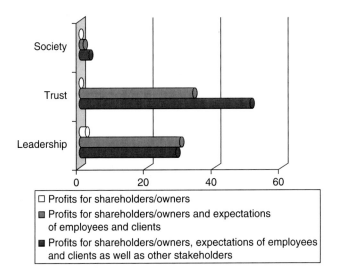

Figure 3.13 Mission and vision

of extending its direct obligations (collectivistic identity) – the only explanation of this divergence between identity defined through mission and perceptions of the role of the business is that either organizations do not integrate their internal values related to the perception of their role into their operational strategies (i.e., they experience a hidden organizational conflict as the execution of the strategy is not adjusted to its core assumptions) or they verbalize and communicate a false message, which aims to enhance their image. In the first case, they might not be doing what they are thinking, in the other case, they might not be saying what they are thinking – both being an example of a conflict of identities. Further examination of corporate formal communication (text analysis) presented below sheds more light on the issue.

The first signs of this potential discrepancy in the assumptions behind the definition of what corporate identity is show themselves in the structure of identities, where individualistic and partner (relational) identities can be attributed to 41 per cent and 56 per cent of the sample, respectively, while the collectivistic identity only to 3 per cent (Figure 3.13 presents these categories using key words from the mission statements for better clarity – leadership, trust and

society – presenting individualistic, partner and collectivistic identity, respectively). At the same time, the vast majority of companies
in the sample define their responsibility in broad terms – that is,
respecting all stakeholders and all primary stakeholders (56 per cent
and 43 per cent, respectively) – while only 1 per cent admits limiting
its responsibility to shareholders only. Not surprisingly this 'narrow
responsibility' minority is shown to have, almost exclusively, an individualistic identity (leadership and competitive fight). Nevertheless,
a significant number of companies declaring a responsibility to all
stakeholders express also partner or individualistic identities. While
the first is understandable and the category of trust, being a key
value for these companies, inevitably situates them in the context
of strong relations with their environment (over 70 per cent of
this category confirms engaging in social consultations), the latter
is surprising and might point to the existence of identity conflicts
described previously (this relates to 19.3 per cent of the companies
in the examined sample).

In terms of the hypothesis about relations between corporate
identities and the perception of the scale of business responsibility,
the above conclusions seem to open the door to further analysis.
Although those companies which identify themselves as affiliated to
wide social problems (collectivistic identity) indeed express views in
keeping with the broad scale of responsibility (to all stakeholders),
the narrow view of responsibility (shareholders only) is more preva-
lent in the case of those who show competitive orientation (individualistic identity), which seems to advance the original hypothesis; it
is difficult to deny that the concept of wide responsibility dominates
also other categories of identities. Irrespective of the corporate identities declared (Figure 3.14), the majority of companies claim to engage
stakeholders in active dialogue with the organization.

Equally, companies seem to perform various forms of social consultation
irrespectively of perceptions on the scale of business responsibility they
show. However, when asked to provide details about such consultations, many of them mention various forms of sponsorship, charity or
cause-related marketing. Only in a few cases did companies undertake
some actions on the basis of suggestions from representations of local
communities – for example, participation in social actions organized
by local media or NGOs, organizing a budget bar for local youth,
cooperation with the local council in organizing social events and

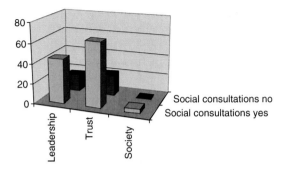

Figure 3.14 Mission and dialogue

providing mentoring for business classes in local schools or donating funds for activities specified by the local community. Nevertheless, these can be considered part of a responsive CSR policy rather than proactive dialogue, which would engage stakeholders in more complex, policy-setting exercises. The latter still seems a rarity – only a few companies gave examples of their cooperation with local councils and with employment offices, where they discuss aspects of the regional labour market and undertake to shape it actively through a previously agreed employment policy. Some also mention maintaining active dialogue with representatives of tax offices and customs, stating the aim to 'achieve mutual benefits'. These contacts are maintained through the network of intermediaries (defined by the respondent as 'advisors'); however, no further details were disclosed. In summary, the only category of consultations mentioned, which fulfill the criteria of active dialogue and involvement of stakeholders in the corporate decision-making process and its strategy to an extent, is that with a wide range of representatives of local or central public administration. This is further confirmed by the fact that companies which declare that decisions related to social aspects of operational activity are made in consultation with stakeholders also happen to be those who attribute more importance to public administration (local and central government) than those where decisions are made in a more centralized and authoritarian process (see Appendix, Table A.3a).

The direct implication might be that a dialogue approach occurs where the process is underpinned by corporate motivation to mitigate operational risks or maximize benefits related to exploring the legal and political environment – a correlation between the revenue and the frequency of contacts with central administration and government (0.28, p<0.01) seems to be shedding some light on the latter. In other cases, it is clearly a response approach, in which case organizations either agree to fulfill previously openly voiced petitions or engage voluntarily in charity actions.[25] In summary, as much as a clear form of dialogical relations between companies and stakeholders is rare, a dialogue is also confused in terms of relations between a firm and its environment, which is part of standard operational exchange between entities in the market, be it the client and the company, the provider and the receiver, the company and its subcontractors, etc. This raises the question of whether examples of social involvement were given to illustrate dialogue because of confusion regarding the term or corporate policies, or are the described situations genuinely and purposefully interpreted as dialogue. In the first case, the reasons might be attributed simply to faults on the side of the respondent, be it personal lack of knowledge or organizational inadequacy of actions in comparison to strategic assumptions. In the second case, however, an interpretation is needed on the extent to which a day-to-day exchange with market players can be justifiably considered a dialogue. Given that one of the fundamental assumptions behind a notion of dialogue, as used in this work, is that it should be based on a partner-type relation whereby parties involved are inter-related but independent decision-wise and operation-wise, any relations between parties inter-connected through various contractual or institutional arrangements (e.g., the mother company and the entity it controls through ownership structure, or the key corporate client and its suppliers and subcontractors) should be naturally excluded from the definition of a dialogue.

In the sense-making context, corporate identity is a cognitive part of the process of creating meanings in organizations, which is complemented by the linguistic aspect. The latter, however, when analyzed from the perspective of key words reflecting generic types of identities (partner, relational and collectivistic) used in formal corporate communication, does not show any significant relation with the verbalized mission statement declared by respondents. Nevertheless, significant relation exists with certain individual key words. For example, companies focusing on the mission verbalized in terms of leadership and competitive fight (individualistic identity) would tend to use the rhetoric related to the quality of life in their written mission statements and scientific arguments to justify the operations. It is almost as if they are trying to appeal dema-gogically to high expectations of second-tier stakeholders, maintaining at the same time an undisputable justification for their operational deci-sions (backed up by scientific arguments). The more important the mis-sion related to gaining trust (relational identity) the less frequent the use of argumentation related to quality of life in formal mission statements, almost as if the organization were trying to avoid incorporating notions over which they do not have much influence in their strategies, so as not to create the impression in the market that they diverge from the core business and concentrate on third-tier aspects, which they cannot directly influence. This is not surprising, given that, from the managerial perspective, the best way to create trust-based relations is to demonstrate high professionalism and a razor-sharp focus on business matters. Those companies strongly demonstrating individualistic identity and verbaliz-ing the mission related to leadership and competitive fight also tend to use rhetoric related to unemployment in formal mission statements, as if they were transmitting a hidden threat to the environment, reminding it that strong and empowered corporations are the only remedy against poor economy and should be valued as job creators. The more important the verbalized mission of solving social problems, the more frequent the use of rhetoric such as 'meeting expectations' or 'excellence'.[26]

One of the key questions which comes to mind when observing how companies internally verbalize their identities and how they later project them formally in reports or mission statements is how they relate to the perceptions the market expresses about those organizations. Indeed, companies verbalizing strongly competitive and leadership-based individualistic identities tend to be portrayed with significantly less use of the rhetoric such as 'relations' or 'meet-ing the expectations'. At the same time, relation rhetoric is used more often to describe companies where the trust-building is the strategic priority. The collectivistic identities – focused on solving social problems – tend to be described with rhetoric structured around words like 'community' or 'meeting expectations'. They also often appear in the context of economic arguments, like 'GDP', almost as if the market perceived them as vital elements of the overall wealth of society.

All formal corporate communication, specifically mission statements and reports, should consistently express identity, which logically should be the same both in its verbalized and internal version, as well as in the projected version. In ideal circumstances, a consistent identity picture should also find its reflection in the coherent identity perceived by the market and expressed in professional texts of market analysts and also by journalists assessing a given company.

This clearly does not mean that all these texts need to be based on the same sets of key words. On the contrary, since the words might carry different meanings depending on context, it could be expected that key words will form certain patterns in terms of how they are used – that is, they would probably be grouped in some natural way around major paradigms or conceptual ideas they define. Second, at least some of them, those more particular and sensitive to potentially different meaning, would also show variations between mission statements, reports and press texts. Indeed, analysis of the texts of mission statements, reports and professional texts by market commentators reveals certain groups of factors which indicate the types of projected identities companies create, on the one hand, and market perceptions, on the other (please see Appendix, Tables A.4–A.6).[27]

All the above categories are constituted by three elements: identity aspect (which locates them in relation to the surrounding environment), justification aspect (which defines the area of legitimization of corporate actions) and axiological aspect (which indicates the core values around which the culture is formed).

The factor analysis of mission statements (see Appendix, Table and Figure A.4a) reveals that, on top of unified identities (e.g., purely collective), mixed-type identities can be found as well – for example, collective individualists. The dichotomy in this case can be illusionary if reference to the key word 'best' or the phrase 'being the best', which according to Cunningham *et al.* (2009) points to an individualistic and competitive nature for the given identity, is treated as complementary to 'society' and 'social problems'. In such cases, the interpretation could be that the organization aspires to be the best in fulfilling the mission wrapped around societal aspect of the business environment and a paradigm of contributing towards solving social problems. Following that logic, the main types of identities found in the text analysis of mission statements are as follows.

Collectivists mainly use economic and scientific argumentation in order to build the legitimacy for their deeds and differ in the definition of their core values. One group uses the argumentation of leadership and citizenship, which may imply that, although they see their role in the context of contributing to a better world through

Table 3.2 Corporate identities and communication channels

Mission statements	Reports	Articles
Collectivists; economic and scientific legitimization; values: leadership and citizenship	Individualists/relational; economic legitimization	Collectivists – economic justification
Individualists; legal legitimization	Collectivists/individualists; value: integrity	All IDs, value of responsibility and scientific rationale
Collectivists/individualists; values: respect and teamwork	Collectivists/individualists; value: diversity	Collectivists, legal legitimization, value of diversity
Individualists; scientific legitimization; value: integrity	Collectivists; economic, scientific and legal legitimization, value: responsibility	Individualists, scientific justification and the value of innovations
Individualists/relational; legal legitimization, value: security and excellence	Relationists; legal and scientific legitimization, value: teamwork	Relational ID, ethical justification and the value of respect
Collectivists; economic legitimization; value: responsibility	Collectivists/individualists; value: leadership	

their business, operationally they see themselves dominating the environment and adopting a leadership role (leading collectivists).

The values of citizenship and leadership support collectivistic identity expressed by 'diversity' and 'help', coupled with economical and scientific argumentation to get legitimization backed by 'economic development' and 'science' – this situates the company as a compelling partner in the surrounding environment, which accepts its role as a leading citizen in the diverse market microcosm and sees its role largely as a contributor to growth and development, operating on the basis of scientific analysis and rationale.

The second group emphasizes the value of responsibility and, as such, may be perceived as more cooperative and less aggressive in terms of propaganda used. Individualists mainly use scientific or legal arguments to support their conduct and operational decisions and do not define any specific core value as their business guidance (pragmatic individualists); they adopt 'integrity' as their key value, understood as internal coherence with what is acceptable and legally justifiable and external coherence in market decisions, mostly backed up by various research and analysis, currently deemed accurate (coherent individualists).

Individualistic collectivists practice values of respect and teamwork; however, they see their role as fulfilled through actions aspiring to make them the best on the market – this element of the individualist identity is seen here as an operational tool rather than a feature of individual identity conflicting with a collectivist one.

Last, but not least, are relational individualists. These are individualists; however, the elements of relational identity they exhibit are addressed only towards the internal labor environment, which operates under the key values of security and excellence and relies on the law and formal obligations to justify its deeds. Judging by further analysis of reports and web pages, this group also uses economic justification as a linguistic part of its sense-making process.

Textual analysis of formal communication of companies (websites and various reports) confirms, to a great extent, the above typology as far as collectivist identity is concerned. However, it spreads the catalogue of the key values as far as individualistic collectivists are concerned, adding 'leadership', 'diversity' and 'integrity' to it. Clearly, this group can also operate under the axiological umbrella of 'leadership'. The other two values relate to collectivist and individualistic aspects of their identities. Reports and other formal communication papers allow the group to be defined as having relational identity, supporting their legitimization with legal and scientific arguments and focusing on the value of teamwork.

In conclusion, mission statements as well as other types of formal corporate messages (i.e., web pages, reports, press releases) coincide with the typology of sense-making processes organizations perform, of which corporate identity is a part.[28]

Key words, when considered as the semantic carriers of meanings, always carry some kind of sense-giving potential, some stronger, some weaker.

The process of building stakeholder relations, if considered from the perspective of creating meanings and understandings, based on a certain structure of the communication process, requires the authors of the communication, be they companies or market-side analysts and commentators, to utilize the language to differentiate emotional load and perceptions it might be creating.

The overall formal communication between companies and their constituencies can be described by the clearly visible factors which differentiate the population of texts analyzed. Moreover, the factors are different across the type of communication (mission statements, reports, articles), although the analysis was run against the same set of key words, thus implying that there might be some kind of qualitative difference between the emotional load of the words used. A further look at the semantics of formal communication, both on the company side and on the market side, showed that the use of certain types of words is related to the particular type of the communication. These are:

- those inherently related to generic identities, including: success, quality, competition, dominance, leader, information (individualistic identity), employees, fulfilling the expectations, ethics (relational identity), help, community (collective identity);
- those related to argumentation used to justify corporate conduct (or to describe it) including: obligations, penalty, code of conduct (legal), experts, research, analysis, report (scientific), job places, economy, economics, GDP, GDP per capita, economic growth, economic development (economic);
- those related to the values of the company, 'excellence' (please see Appendix, Table A.7).

In these categories, there are significant differences in the use of words between the types of the communication, while, in the case of other key words, the differences are not explicit. The conclusion is that certain words have emotional load particularly suited to a given type of communication (see Appendix, Tables A.8–A.10) (Figure 3.15).

There are some phrase areas which show significant differences in their use patterns across the mission statements, reports and articles. Their position in the centre of a given area illustrates their embeddedness in this area in preference over the other two. For example, a nexus of meanings related to the argumentation companies use (competition, obligation, etc.) is used much more often in articles than in either mission statements or reports, whereas while 'analysis' is used also more in articles than in reports, there is no significant difference between its use in articles and in mission statements. In

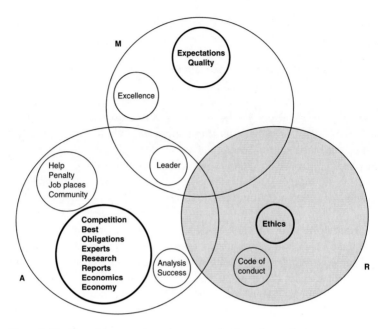

Figure 3.15 Use of key words and communication channels

a similar way, 'expectations' and 'quality' dominate mission statements much more than articles or reports, while 'excellence' is
significantly more often used in mission statements than in articles,
without explicit differences in its use in reports.

'Quality' is attributable to mission statements much more than
reports and articles. 'Competition' and 'dominance' are attributable
to articles much more than missions and reports. 'Leader' is more
often utilized in mission statements and articles than in reports.
'Expectations' are cited more often in mission statements than in
either reports or articles. 'Help' appears more often in articles than
in mission statements. 'Obligations' are cited more often in articles
than either mission statements or reports. The same applies to the use
of 'experts', 'research', 'report', 'economics' and 'economy'. 'Penalty'
dominates discourse in articles rather than in mission statements. The
same applies to 'job places' and 'community'. 'Analysis' and 'success'
are used more often in articles than in reporting. 'Excellence' is attributable to mission statements rather than articles. 'Ethics' is more often

utilized in reports than it is in mission statements or articles, while 'code of conduct' more often appears in reports than in articles.

Apart from potential metaphysical divagations on the possible meanings of the fact that these words happen to be grouped in a certain way, two immediate thoughts come to mind. The fact that phrases related to the justification of corporate conduct locate themselves within market-originated communication indicates that it is the external environment which interprets corporate conduct, qualifying it as legally or economically justified or not justified; therefore the whole process of legitimization is dominated by the sense-making activities of corporate communication recipients rather than by explicit sense-giving by the message sender.

Second, reporting seems to be dominated by only two notions, which appear to be used in this forum more often than in mission statements or articles. 'Ethics' seems a central notion, thus implying that companies tend to overuse ethical aspects of their activity to 'sell their image' to stakeholders, irrespective of whether this is aligned with the mission and true values they represent. 'Code of conduct' appears an often-cited instrument in this context.

Sense-making and sense-giving processes seem to be polarized between explicit identity, constituting a message embedded in mission statements, and contextual interpretations in market-side communication. Furthermore, analysis of reports and formal corporate communication serves only as a check of the internal corporate consistency in meaning setting; however, it cannot be treated as the ultimate and effective platform of communicating with the external environment. Identity is set predominantly in mission statements, however symbolic they may be and formulated in the iconic manner.

Reports are dominated by an ethical perspective and, in fact, they do not mediate the sense-giving and the sense-making process, as it seems that reception of corporate identity happens only through the sense-making process and is based on the contextual interpretation of the latter embedded in the current circumstances (e.g., those of the economic crisis at large or those of the economic success or failure of the company).

Looking into the ontology of corporate sense-making and sense-giving, one might be tempted to conclude that there are two flows defining the meanings. One is generic and constituted of the phrases and notions freely interchanged between communication channels – that is, with the equal possibility of being used in mission statements or formal reports or press articles; for example, 'value', 'responsibility', 'trust', 'respect'. Another is based on the core notions specific for a given communication channel, where notions carrying certain value, like, for example, 'excellence' or 'quality', are strong mission setters, while those carrying an explanatory role serve as the context for assessments (e.g., when analysts formulate opinions about corporate conduct or results achieved in the context of economy, law, obligations, etc.).

The fact that values are not represented explicitly in corporate communication is less surprising in the case of reports, since they should be rather an objective, fact-finding and emotion-free information flow. In this context it is surprising that an emotionally loaded notion such as 'ethics' finds a central place in reporting systems. Mission statements, however, are expected to be emotionally loaded declarations of what the company stands for. Their value emptiness remains a subject for further research, as well as the question of how to interpret the fact that the market takes over interpretation functions, utilizing phraseology one could rather expect in reports.

Business responsibility and the role of stakeholders

Perhaps not surprisingly, companies almost unanimously sympathize with two dominant views of the scale of business responsibility. Over 55 per cent admit that business should be responsible towards all stakeholders, direct and non-direct, while over 43 per cent would limit this responsibility to primary stakeholders only. The orthodox view that business should care for business only, limiting its responsibility to shareholders as much as possible, can be considered negligible as it is represented only by 1 per cent of the population analyzed.

Although, social consultations are encountered in companies with all types of identity, there is a clear and noticeable trend – that companies which declare business responsibility towards all stakeholders are more inclined to perform social consultations than those declaring responsibility towards primary stakeholders only (chi^2(2) = 9.19; p = 0.010, see Appendix, Table A.11). At the same time, companies with a narrow perception of business responsibility, limited to the primary stakeholders, tend to attribute more importance to certain stakeholders (i.e., consumer associations and public administration at central and local level); they also communicate with those groups more often (see Appendix, Tables A.12 and A.13). Although being responsible towards all stakeholders intensifies the process of social consultation as such, without suggesting which stakeholder groups would be specifically addressed in this process and recommending any prioritization of stakeholders, it is a limited responsibility concept, which allows such conclusions, however paradoxical. This might indicate that declaring an all-stakeholder responsibility approach occurs in companies without a clear vision on prioritization of stakeholders and representing a kind of 'big picture' approach. The fact that companies declaring responsibility limited to primary stakeholders attribute, at the same time, more priority to secondary stakeholders becomes an interesting paradox, as one would expect that a company attributing its duties as towards primary stakeholders only would automatically assign more importance to these groups than to others. However, this is not the case. The answer may be hidden in the way those companies perceive the role of the stakeholders, specifically local communities and public administration. Indeed, the way the companies perceive their scale of responsibility (i.e., the role of business at large, in a sense) is significantly correlated with the way they perceive the role stakeholders might have. The more the company admits a wide concept of responsibility, inclusive of secondary stakeholders, the more it sees stakeholders as the co-designers of the strategy. Limitation of the responsibility to primary stakeholders implies a perception of the role of stakeholders as neutral, yet influential and receivers of corporate communication which need to be carefully managed ($chi^2(2) = 12.62$; $p = 0.002$ (see Appendix, Table A.14). When seen from the perspective of management rationale, this becomes more logical. Since all groups not within the circle of direct stakeholders seem to be denied a justified claim to any corporate responsibility by companies, they are perceived as part of the totally external environment, which poses a potential threat to the company in its quest to fulfill duties towards its 'legitimate stakeholders'. This is confirmed by the fact that stakeholders are viewed not as partners but as playing at management. Accordingly, such a perception of stakeholders relates also to corporate identities, as it shows significant focus on mission statements defining partner-like relations between the company and the environment, where gaining trust is paramount (partner identity) (see Appendix, Tables A.15 and A.16). In such cases, trust might be viewed as the instrumentally used tool to manage and control those groups, which the company perceives as critical, yet requiring attention.

In conclusion, attributing importance to a given group and admitting responsibility to it are two different things. The companies expressing wide concepts of responsibility seem to lack strategic impetus in terms of how to execute this concept in practice; on the other hand, companies who, from the start, adopt a focused approach (primary stakeholders only) immediately translate it into operational terms regarding who is important and how they should be treated.[29]

This brings us to the debate about operational features, which, as a consequence of the above, might be determined by philosophical aspects of CSR policy – that is, scale of responsibility or perhaps corporate identity. In their model, Morsing and Schultz (2006) mention a few key aspects, described previously (see Table 3.1).

Perception of the role of stakeholders not only implies the importance attributed to them by companies, but also influences the way key objectives are defined for the communication manager. Perception of stakeholders as 'opposition' which needs to be neutralized weakens the importance attributed to relation-building, presumably for the sake of objectives defined as accurate stakeholder identification or for the sake of designing a convincing message.

While the personal attributes of stakeholder relation strategies, such as the way the communication job is defined or stakeholder prioritization done, are influenced by the perception of the stakeholder role, resultant from the adopted scale of business responsibility and from corporate identity (whereby the perception of the stakeholder role would act as the intervening variable), organizational attributes of the strategy – that is, the way the goal of the communication process is defined – and the social consultation process seem to be determined by the size of the company, as well as by its identity. Such is the case with individualistic and collectivistic identities, which relate, respectively, to the lesser and greater importance attributed to the communication goal defined in terms of dialogue building (–0.24** and 0.25**, respectively, see Appendix, Table A.17). The social consultation process intensifies with the growth of the company (chi^2(2) = 7.41; p = 0.025, see Appendix, Table A.18). The bigger the company, the less important it is to prove that stakeholders' expectations are being met (0.26**, see Appendix, Table A.17), which contributes to the view that big corporations are sometimes characterized by a certain degree of arrogance as far as individual stakeholder group management is concerned. Instead, they prefer to adopt generalizations, with a unified approach to all stakeholders, often through implementation of generic CSR strategy.

Operational features, as defined by Morsing and Schultz (2006), do not show internal relations and cannot be perceived as a stable nexus of predictors indicating a specific strategy, as described in the model. The fact that only a very limited number of companies (25 out of 150 companies) show strategy patterns as described in the model (information strategy, asymmetric communication and symmetric communication – dialogue) seems to confirm that the model serves illustrative purposes only and the individual features it includes (perceived role of stakeholders, decision-making locus, goal of the communication process and KPI of communication manager) form a matrix of specific managerial processes which, when combined, result in many more than just three basic strategies. What is certain, though, is that, within these strategic figures,[30] the only one with predictive power is the perception of the role of stakeholders as analyzed previously. It relates directly to the scale of business responsibility the company adopts, as well as to the corporate identity expressed in a mission statement and intermediates the way in which the company sees the role of its communication manager (KPI of the communication manager) as well as the results of the stakeholder prioritization exercise (importance attributed to certain stakeholder groups).

In summary, given that the Morsing and Schulz model may be treated as the descriptive and illustrative tool for discussion about CSR-related communication strategies, it might be said that the strategy of asymmetric communication based on the perception of stakeholders as responding end receivers of communication who need to be managed, results in defining the mission in terms of trust-building, which, in a sense, is synonymous with creating partner corporate identity too.[31]

How organizations engage in social activities

Companies perform various forms of socially sensitive activities, ranging from sponsorship and donations through to energy saving and CSR-embedded selection of suppliers to various forms of cause-related marketing. If certain strategic figures of stakeholder relation strategies, such as the objective of the communication manager, the perception of stakeholders' role, social consultation or the goals of the communication process depend on corporate identity and the size of the company, would the latter impact also on the type of CSR activities the companies engage in? Or do some of the strategic figures determine the exact activities as well? A first glimpse at the types of actions companies undertake reveals three generic groups determined in the factor analysis (Table 3.3).

The first group, including CSR-based selection of suppliers, donations, cooperation with NGOs and addressing various social aspects in their own advertisements, can be regarded as image-related activities addressed to the surrounding environment at large (generic stakeholders and widely understood public) in order to create certain, favorable perceptions of company activities. As these seem to relate to corporate policies at the central level (international and national scale, as well as general company policy, as opposed to initiatives and programs of local or regional offices), they will be treated as external, generic CSR.

The second group includes employee volunteers, energy-saving and emission-reduction programs and local community sponsorship,[32]

Table 3.3 Generic types of CSR

	Generic	Local embeddedness	Internal engineering
CSR-based supply chain management	.713		
Donations	.592		
Cooperation with NGOs	.530		
Socially sensitive advertisements	.496		
Employee volunteers		.462	
Energy-saving and emission-reduction programs		.819	
Sponsorship		.544	
Social packages for employees			.824
Cause-related marketing			.647

and can be seen as activities addressed to local society specifically in order to embed the firm in the local environment and create its sustainable perception as a responsible local citizen. This is local CSR.

The third group, including social packages for employees and cause-related marketing, can be interpreted as internal engineering CSR. In this case an organization uses effectively the strategic capacity of CSR and, by integrating it with core business, aims to gain concrete, tangible results. For example, cause-related marketing (such as assigning part of the income from sales of products to charity, or other socially sensitive goals) thrives on the existence of the niche market segment, composed of middle-class people who make purchase decisions not on the basis of price but on that of ethics. Such a trend, known as ethical consumerism, in a sense can be compared to the rise of other relatively new market segments, such as organic food or the fair trade movement, which portray the evolution of markets from those satisfying the basic needs to those addressing more sophisticated ones, although it still remains a basic product market. On the other hand, social packages for employees are a proven tool for ensuring employee loyalty and effectiveness. Specifically, the existence of formal codes of conduct or other formal CSR programs do not improve the ethical position of employees (i.e., they are not effective in reducing corruption and fraud activities), while benefits such as training, medical care, various social benefits and a motivational remuneration system significantly decrease the risk of fraud (Turek, 2010).

The majority of organizations in the sample seem to be spread between local CSR and internal engineering CSR (37 per cent and 34 per cent, respectively; see Figure 3.16), which does not mean that they do not engage in other forms of CSR at the same time. Surprisingly, only 10 per cent admits to aspects of generic CSR – surprisingly, as one

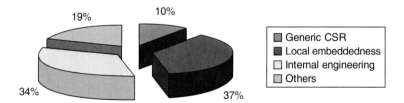

Figure 3.16 CSR activities of companies

might get the impression that, since most of the firms have standard ethical codes and codes of conduct and they heavily publicize their social responsibility, they will concentrate mostly on those aspects which appeal to a wide public and thus may be marketed easily.

Since all three groups of activities seem distinct from the perspective of their scope and ultimate goal, they relate differently to the relation strategy used and, in some cases, are even predicted by the size of the company.

In the first case – generic CSR – neither the size of the company, nor the specific elements of communication used predict whether the firm engages in certain types of activities. In case of local embeddedness CSR, the bigger the firm the less engagement in the activities building strong relations with local communities ($p = .002$, $R^2 = 0.06$; see Appendix, Table A.19). This type of activity is also related to communication strategy (i.e., the goal of the communication process and KPI of communication manager) ($p = 0.016$, $R^2 = 0.11$); however, it is not possible to determine which of those predictors are statistically significant. This type of CSR engagement also differentiates the perception of the role of stakeholders – that is, the enterprises which show a preference for perceiving stakeholders as potentially active opposition get involved in activities of local embeddedness CSR much more than those who perceive stakeholders as neutral end receivers reacting to the corporate communication only. Not much can be said about companies declaring the role of stakeholders to be co-designers of CSR strategy, as, statistically, these groups are not significantly different from the other two (see Appendix, Table and Figure A.20).

The companies engage in the internal engineering irrespective of their size; however, there is a relation between some communication strategy aspects and these types of activity ($p = 0.061$, $R^2 = 0.09$), specifically the companies engaging in internal engineering are those which attribute much importance to the goal of the communication process being defined in terms of proving that stakeholder expectations are met (see Appendix, Table A.21).

Understanding local communities

How communities see business operations

Four cases were chosen for further analysis of their strategies of relation-building from the perspective of effectiveness of these strategies measured by the convergence or divergence between companies and their local environments in three respects:

• views on the scale of business responsibility as a whole;
• perceived identity of companies interpreted through the perception of their mission statements by local communities;
• local awareness of the CSR initiatives companies engage in.

The general trend seems to be that, while representatives of local communities more often sympathize either with the view that business should be responsible to shareholders only or, quite the opposite, that it should be responsible towards all stakeholders, companies more often present the view that business should accept responsibility towards primary stakeholders only. In conclusion, local communities tend to be more polarized, while companies usually present a coherent and strategically focused view (chi^2 = 12.94; p = 0.002; see Appendix, Table 22).

However, in Krosno, Piatnica and Warsaw, both companies and communities unanimously indicated the same scale of expected responsibility towards all stakeholders. The difference occurs in Krakow, in case of 'B', where local society expects wide responsibility of business, while the firm presents the view that it should be limited to owners, employees, clients and customers.

In terms of perception of mission statements, serving as proxies for corporate identities, in three cases (Krakow, Krosno, Piatnica) local communities perceived the companies in question more as emphasizing leadership and presenting an individualistic identity as opposed to the companies, who identified themselves as having partner-type identity. In the case of 'O', a big nationwide firm located in Warsaw, local communities saw the firm more as partner- and relation-oriented, while the firm identified itself with aggressive, individualistic identity.

Table 3.4 presents a schematic overview of the awareness of corporate CSR actions in companies' local communities. While 'O', with headquarters in Warsaw but operating on the national scale, seems to be the leader in terms of types of engagements, showing generic and local embeddedness as well as internal engineering activities, it also seems least effective at the same time, as, paradoxically, the perception of its activities among representatives of local communities is virtually zero. The other three cases, to a large extent,

Table 3.4 Coherence of CSR activities and their perception by the local community

	'O', Warsaw	'B', Krakow	'KHS', Krosno	'OSM', Piatnica
CSR-based supply chain management	⚐			
Donations	⚐			
Co-operation with NGOs	⚐	⚐	⚐	⚭
Socially sensitive advertisements			⚐	
Employee volunteers	⚐			
Energy-saving and emission-reduction programs	⚐	⚐	⚭	⚭
Sponsorship	⚐	⚭	⚭	⚭
Social packages for employees	⚐	⚐		
Cause-related marketing	⚐			⚐

Notes: ⚭ the actions undertaken by the company are confirmed by the local community
⚐ the actions undertaken by the company are not confirmed by the local community

adopt local embeddedness initiatives which seem to create some level of local community awareness, specifically in the case of companies operating in smaller towns. In the case of Krosno, both energy- and emission-saving programs and sponsorship are noticed in the community. In the case of Piatnica, the community also acknowledges the cooperation of the company with various NGOs. Interestingly, all four case study companies belong to the group of big firms employing more than 250 people, therefore increased awareness of their activities in communities could be attributed to the fact that, in smaller towns, they become a kind of 'category killer' as dominant employers, thus having a chance of their activities being recognized more readily. Qualitative observations indicate not only that the generic type of CSR seems less effective in winning public attention effectively; it also is negatively related to the bottom line, as active involvement in donations means lower revenue dynamics (see Appendix, Table A.23).

Analysis of press texts related to the four selected case studies was undertaken twice using different approaches. A search of the texts for key words relating to types of identities returned very ambiguous results. First, key words are usually used in different contexts; for example, 'value' more often relates to the value of the firm than, as expected by the model, to some generic value set indicating that the market sees the company as operating with clear observance of a value code. Second, in some cases the finding is not relevant, as it does not relate to the analyzed company at all.

The second approach was based on the careful reading of source documents, coding them using QSR NVivo software against the same key words – this time not to calculate frequencies but for the sake of checking the contexts in which given words were used. This specific triangulation exercise largely confirmed the coherence of the organizational portrait presented in the texts. Given the assumption that the press articles related, in their general context, to the selected case companies, offering a picture of what types of identities the companies present, it is possible to conclude:

(a) whether the key words used for the initial analysis are interpreted in a similar way by journalists and by companies;
(b) whether they return the same or a different type of identity in terms of what the companies define;
(c) whether there is any new structure emerging from the new contexts which relate to key words and from links between them.[33]

In summary, the same set of key words might be interpreted differently by different groups of respondents – that is, they may indicate different things to companies and to analysts. Alternatively, the same concept may manifest itself differently in various groups that is, it may be verbalized differently.

Why some local communities are more special than others

One of the interesting outcomes of this research is that the relation between perceptions of scale of business responsibility and corporate missions are demographically sensitive – that is, they occur only in certain cases.[34] It seems as if this result fulfills all the necessary conditions to be treated as a 'surprise', as defined by Robert Merton (1982). This result was unexpected, and was not targeted for testing in this research; it occurred as a side effect of testing the main hypotheses and seems counter-intuitive to common knowledge. This finding should have a significant capacity to extend existing theories describing what we know about the social environment of organizations; it might also be important in the methodology of stakeholder relations-building. The theoretical background allowing explanation of this phenomenon is provided by the concept of the cosmopolitan versus locally embedded influential people, coined by Robert Merton (*ibid.*). Merton researched the behavioral patterns of influential people in the context of mass communication media. During the course of his research, he defined two types of people who had the capacity to influence others: those locally embedded and cosmopolitans. They differ in the patterns of their career development, in the way they construct and use their social networks, in the backgrounds of exercising their influence over others and in their attitudes towards media, specifically the press.[35]

The structure of local communities defined by the proportion of locally embedded and cosmopolitan people might be one of the possible means to explain why perceptions of the role of business is different in some locations than in others. One potential extension of this research might, therefore, aim at verifying whether the cosmopolitan or local orientation of the local communities relates to the way they perceive organizations.

It might be also interesting to analyze whether the concept of local and cosmopolitan orientation can be extrapolated to organizations, as corporate citizens. Given the positive answer to this question, further research might verify how locally embedded and cosmopolitan organizations build their influence patterns and social (stakeholder) networks. The latter seems particularly tempting, since the organizations analyzed differed significantly in the roles they play in their communities – that is, there is a difference between a company operating among many others in a large city and a company that is the dominant market player and key employer in a small town. The scale of operations also seems significant, considering that companies operating globally, for natural reasons, will aim for a more or less standardized and global approach to business strategy; even if they adopt a multi-local approach, with a reasonable scale of local adjustments, they are more likely to look for economies of scale and standardization, if not globally, at least on the regional level. Additionally, this research showed that not only do companies differ in the types of CSR activities they engage in (one of them being locally embedded CSR), but they also do it according to various criteria – size, for example. If companies give up locally embedded CSR, together with growth, it is also possible that they might lose local orientation as they increase their operations.[36]

Last, but not least, since cosmopolitans and locally embedded people differ in their attitudes to mass communication, another area for exploration might be how the structure of local communities relates to attitudes towards formal communication of the company and market communication about the company (identity communicated and reinterpreted by the market commentators). As people with different orientations read communications differently,[37] a hypothesis worth debating might be whether their orientation influences the meanings which they attribute to the same messages – that is, whether it influences their sense-making process.

Perhaps, then, the key to successful stakeholder relations and communication strategy is a thorough knowledge of the structure of the local community, as far as the cosmopolitan versus local orientation is concerned.

The communities and local environment the companies operate in may, obviously, fall into one of those categories and, depending on whether the community is dominated by cosmopolitans or by locally oriented citizens, it may provide a fertile ground for demographically bounded expectations towards business. The two orientations mentioned differ significantly in what might be called the 'ways of gaining the influence over others'.

Among locally bounded aspects are the polarizations of importance attributed to corporate missions defined through trust-building among men and women and the above-mentioned demographically determined perceptions of the business responsibility. One possible reason why gender does not show as an explanatory determinant in all locations is the possibility that it loses its illustrative power due to the process of uniformization of views between men and women. In other words, men and women are not that different from each other in the way they see various aspects of today's life.[38] On the other hand, in those locations where gender plays an explanatory role, women tend to widen the scale of business responsibility while men seem to lack flexibility in this respect.

In terms of the relation between role and perception of the identity (through mission statements), a direct conclusion is that 'trust' becomes an instrumental variable. Those entities where the stakeholders are perceived as the end receivers, reacting only to corporate deeds, also define the mission in the context of trust-building; however, it might also be possible that entities which pay attention to trust-building prefer to see stakeholders simply as end receivers of corporate actions. Indeed, once you have the trust of your constituencies, what else is needed? There does not seem to be any necessity to engage stakeholders profoundly. In other words, this is a good illustration of the optimization exercise managers perform as far as stakeholder relations are concerned.

The geographic specificity of the perceptions of corporate identity expressed by careful positioning of the enterprise in the nexus of social network, as individualist, partner or collectivist, may be related to perceived quality of life, as it is not completely impossible that social problems might be transferred to expectations towards enterprises. In the case of those locations where trust seems to be more appreciated than elsewhere (e.g., in Krakow), it might be related to the fact that Warsaw represents a typically cosmopolitan city with no embeddedness.

Last, but not least, age and education determining the perception of business responsibility might also be correlated with the wealth respondents enjoy. It is, therefore, not impossible that older people, putting more weight on the private business responsibility (towards the shareholders only), do so because they become the beneficiaries of corporate dividends. Perhaps those more educated express a tendency to enlarge the scale of business responsibility because they are satisfied with their wealth status and their life and, as such, they can 'afford' to share corporate benefits with other constituencies.

The perception of mission statements also depends, in some of the communities, on the gender, age and education of the respondent. Such is the case with Piatnica, where women, as opposed to men, attribute less importance to 'being the leader' and more importance to 'trust-gaining' (see Appendix, Tables A.24 and A.25). The latter holds also for Warsaw.[39]

Local communities also differ in the way people of various age and education levels perceive the mission statement. In the case of 'B' (Krakow), the more educated the people, the more gravity was attributed to leadership missions (i.e., individualistic identities). The same applies to Warsaw. Additionally, the more educated the people, the less importance they put on trust-building (Krosno) and on the solving of social problems (Warsaw) (see Appendix, Table 26).[40] In krosno, the higher the education, the lower the importance of leadership missions.

The four pictures

The value added of the qualitative approach

The four case studies[41] mentioned should be examined from the perspective of their identity declared through verbalized mission statements, identity projected in formal communication, stakeholder communication strategies examined against the basic Morsing and Schultz model and the coherence of the overall perceptions of corporate identity analyzed through the effectiveness of the communication process, measured by perceptions of corporate actions by the local community. The overall context of the local community follows.

Since this part of analysis combines quantitative and qualitative methodology, some theoretical explanation is needed. The main differences between qualitative and quantitative research are the following:

- distinction between explanation and understanding;
- personal or impersonal role of the researcher;
- difference between knowledge discovered and knowledge constructed.

Quantifying researchers are pressing for explanation and control, while the focus of qualitative research remains with understanding the complex relations between everything that exists. It could be argued, as von Wright says, that every explanation furthers the understanding; but understanding has a psychological feature, which is lacking in explanation. Understanding is a form of empathy or re-creation in the mind of a scholar; it is also connected with intentionality (we understand the purposes, meanings of the symbols and significance of everything which surrounds us) (von Wright, 1971). Qualitative research facilitates reader understanding. For a quantifying researcher, uniqueness will always be a case of error outside the system; for a qualitative researcher it will be a particularization and important point in understanding of a specific case within its context. To focus on understanding, qualitative researchers will always assess what is happening in key episodes or testimonies and present happenings with their own direct interpretation of the story (Stake, 1995). Qualitative inquiry is, therefore, oriented away from causal explanations and towards personal interpretation and holistic treatment of phenomena – qualitative epistemology is non-determinist and constructivist. Because phenomena may be related to various coincidental actions, understanding them requires looking into a wide range of contexts (historical, personal, political, cultural, economical). Patterns in qualitative studies are equivalent to correlations and co-variations in quantitative research.

Qualitative research is bound to be subjective, as subjectivity is considered a crucial element of understanding. This is the main reason why the role of a researcher in qualitative studies cannot be objective. The role evolves towards being a participant observer – a teacher, reader, storyteller, advocate, evaluator or consultant. The decision on what role to employ and to what extent is made intuitively. In this particular case, I adopt the storytelling perspective.

The researcher liberates the reader from simplistic viewpoints and narrow interpretations. Being constructivist, at the same time the researcher provides the reader with good raw material to enable a readers' own interpretation (*ibid.*). Stake defines the main types of triangulation as follows:

- data source triangulation: is the case or meaning of conclusions the same under different circumstances?[42]
- investigator triangulation: is researcher interpretation accurate, would different researchers come up with similar interpretations of the same raw material?[43]
- theory triangulation: is there an effort to adopt co-observers, panelists or reviewers from alternative theoretical viewpoints?[44]
- methodological triangulation: to enhance the confidence in accuracy of our observations and conclusions, we may follow them with additional reviews of old records.

I treat the four cases presented as idiographic (interpretative and individualizing) and heuristic. Heuristic case studies are constructed to seek out theory. This gives a study which is used deliberately to stimulate imagination and discern important general problems, also seeking their solutions. This is done because ad hoc additions to the theoretical framework are isolated from the rest of the sequence and used as a theory-seeking medium. Heuristic case studies are often aimed at formulating testable hypotheses. After they are formulated one does not necessarily proceed with testing them.

Case study is a study of the particularity and complexity of a single case, coming to understand its activity within important circumstances (*ibid.*). The qualitative researcher emphasizes episodes of nuance, the sequentiallity of happenings in context and the wholeness of individual. The real business of a case study is particularization, as Stake explains. This research combines the quantitative and qualitative approach. I choose, then, to accept that initial meanings can be redirected and, thus, research questions can be modified in the middle of the research process, although an initial variable set was included in the cases under the shape of key words.

In social sciences, common conceptual organization centers around hypotheses. Specifically, in qualitative research, what counts is the uniqueness and complexity of a case and its embeddedness within a certain context. As hypotheses and goal statements sharpen the focus, thus minimizing interest in the situation itself and its circumstances, issue questions, used in the standard case study approach, force attention to the complexity and contextuality of a case. Issues are problems about which people disagree, complicated problems within certain contexts and situations (*ibid.*).

So we now have two main notions to be used as a basis for the conceptual structure of research: the case itself, which is dominant in intrinsic case studies, and issues, which are the main focus of instrumental cases. Issue statements can sometimes appear as cause and effect relationships; however, they should not be confused with information or evaluative questions, neither should they be too broad and enduring (*ibid.*).

Etic issues are brought in by the researcher from the outside; they may derive from the larger research community, colleagues or writers – they evolve over the course of work. Emic issues are those from inside the case – they are likely to emerge or to be brought up by the actors belonging to the case (*ibid.*).

Qualitative researchers come to conclusions either through direct interpretation of an individual instance or through aggregation of instances, which can result in defining some conclusions as to their class. The search for meaning is a search for pattern and consistency within certain conditions – it is called correspondence (*ibid.*).

The report of each of the cases is prepared according to guidelines by Stake (1995) and it describes individually the major components of the case. The issue questions relating to these particular cases were:

- Is there a correspondence between declared corporate identity and the expressed one? Does the verbal one imply that promoted in the formal communication?
- What is the nature of relations between corporate identity and the stakeholder relation strategy declared? What are the circumstances in which dialogue-building is possible?

Topical questions, portraying the need for information and data or the main topics of the case study otherwise, are:

- a structure of CSR communication strategy, as declared by the corporate informant;
- corporate identity declared compared to that expressed in formal communication;
- perception of corporate identity by the local community and visibility of the CSR engagements (perceptions of those engagements by the local community).

The described cases should serve as instrumental and comparative case studies for two reasons.

First, they seek to understand in what circumstances and how dialogue-based stakeholder relation strategies develop. CSR communication strategies, based on the Morsing and Schultz model, served as the criteria for picking up the cases; in particular the cases were selected on the basis of fulfilling the criteria for a stakeholder symmetric communication strategy.

Second, the cases differ as far as corporate identity is concerned and declared sense-giving processes (social consultations); therefore, comparison of their formal communication patterns, as well as CSR engagements, and the actual quality of relations in their local communities (analyzed from the perspective of visibility of CSR activities for the community and in the context of the news the company attracts) may shed some light on possible emerging patterns of causality between the identities companies adopt and later express to the external environment and the stakeholder relations companies build.

Identities, arguments and values: consistency of communication as the foundation for relation-building

Judging by quantitative analysis of mission statements, press releases and reporting documents, where key words for identities are calculated, 'O' is a company predominantly individualistic in its projected identity and it is equally perceived as such by the market, where journalists tend to use most words specific to individualistic identity – especially in the cognitive part of the sense-making process. In terms of linguistic aspect, 'O' is described predominantly with economic and legal argumentation justifying their deeds, while the company itself restricts argumentation mostly to the economic one. What does the company mean, exactly, when it situates itself within the 'individualistic identity' setting?

The communicated meanings relate mostly to the notion of the success (22.2 per cent) the company managed to achieve in a very competitive environment, which is mainly cited in the context of growing competition characterized by changing structure and new players, to which the company has a strategic answer. Although the semantics of being the most dominant in the market are used rather in the historical context, where the company describes its long tradition, the claim of indisputable market leadership is often made in formal communications. Another aspect of individualistic identity is related to the way the company manages its information flows. Indeed, in case of 'O', there are often citations of the information policy of the company; however, the main focus relates to an explanation of why some of the codified ethical provisions for public companies implemented by the Polish Stock Exchange (GPW) will not be implemented. Such positioning of the company as a good law observer, compliant with all legal requirements but neither prepared nor willing to extend its communications activities beyond the necessary minimum, not only indicates the identity distancing itself from surrounding stakeholders but also serves as a clear example of stakeholder communication strategy based on pure information provision, rather than on building a more sophisticated network of relations.

The semantics related to collectivistic identity, based on invocations towards socially sensitive issues, is expressed only on a general level, either through general invocations such as 'the world of business today must respond to social expectations' or on an instrumental level, where the company admits participating in social action 'Discover Our Own Anew', aiming to promote Poland as a tourist destination, which in fact is a type of customer loyalty and marketing program. Notions of 'responsibility' and 'values' – which could constitute the very core of corporate identity if used in an axiological context – do not appear otherwise, in the purely economic or operational sense – that is, as the value of the company for its shareholders and as the scope of responsibilities of the top management, respectively.

Traces of a relativistic identity – which could be attributed to invocations about the reporting system the company has, allowing conclusions to be drawn regarding the extent to which it includes a wide range of stakeholders – point to a strong asymmetry towards the of employees. Again, on a general level the company voices its policy of treating its employees as the capital of the firm ('We would like to thank our employees, who are our most important capital, for their hard work' – a formal statement in a speech made by the president), but it sees its obligations towards them only in the context of the legal requirement (agreements with trade unions or necessary budget reserves for redundancy payments, legal obligations related to the processes of restructurization) or in the context of investment in the productivity of this capital (training); in some formal communications the company also voices explicitly the limited responsibility it has towards its employees (required minimum, covering the cost of social benefits).

A deeper look at the context of the semantics specifying identities clearly shows that, although, nominally, 'O' uses key words pointing to elements of relational and collectivistic identity, as well as to the predominant individualistic one, contextual interpretation proves that it is a deeply individualistic organization, concentrated predominantly on its shareholders and stock value creation as its predominant responsibility. While shareholders are seen as the key stakeholders in this context, employees are situated on the opposite end of the continuum of relation strategy, where the company seems to concentrate on careful management of minimum necessary legal requirements related to labor law. Although, occasionally, employees are cited as important, the message is unconvincing, superficial and almost trivial and obviously does not carry the quality of a genuine aim to build partner relations. In fact, there is much effort to satisfy shareholders and assure them that any employee-related costs are minimized wherever possible, although such careful management of employee-related risks did not manage to safeguard the company from a court case started by a group of employees questioning the legality of lay-off procedures related to the liquidation of one of the group hotels in Warsaw in 2005.

Interestingly enough, there is a clear contextual polarization around the notions related to success and market leadership, in the sense that, while in formal communications addressed to shareholders market competition is always mentioned as the natural trend to which, even if it is getting more fierce, the company has a good strategic response, in communication to outside stakeholders (in press interviews; for example, in *Rzeczpospolita* in 2008, an interview with the president of 'O' at the time and, later, interviews with the vice president of 'O' in 2009, reacting to plans for a VAT increase) it is described as a threat and danger to the competitiveness of the company. The same applies to the notion of 'being the best' – while, in communication with shareholders, the company claims to be constantly striving to maintain its dominant position, in press interviews it is not mentioned, other than in the context of being a serious barrier for company development. The conclusion might be that the company optimizes the message for its shareholders through the enhancement and enforcement of positive communication in reports, which could mean it becomes difficult to make an objective assessment of market risks and the actual situation. The way these verbalizations are structured serves almost to prepare the path to a 'market exit' strategy, indicating that there are objective and strong reasons within the market which might justify corporate failure, should it happen. While company representatives point towards objective reasons shaping the bad results of the company, experts and analysts concentrated on poor-quality strategic management decisions.

In summary, while the company expresses a strong individualistic orientation, verbalized in competitive semantics and corporate propaganda, it also confirms its alienation from the widely understood market by acknowledging only the priority of shareholders' interest and by showing a skew towards perceiving the internal environment (employees) as a potential threat (trade unions) and the source of costs. Such an underlying message is not, in any case, mitigated by occasionally mentioning the overall responsibilities of business and courteous speeches acknowledging employee value, which in this context sound superficial and almost trivial.

Furthermore, there is a strange divergence between the meanings created for shareholders (to whom an 'assurance message' is communicated) and other recipients of formal communication such as press interviews (wherein the message conveyed sounds almost like an exercise in excuses justifying possible future failure. In normal circumstances, one would expect market analysts, commentators and experts to receive a razor-sharp message about the strategic capacity of the company to compete, rather than an exhibition of early signals of internal weakness.

'KHS' presents itself as an individualistic company, while it is perceived by the market as of a relational and collectivistic type of identity.[45] In terms of argumentation, press discourse about the company is dominated by economic justification, while, in formal communication, the company freely navigates between scientific, economic and legal arguments. Strong invocations regarding competitiveness in reports is mostly related to structural ways of maintaining competitiveness (technological investments) and analysis of international competition on the key segments of glass production. There are invocations also to quality as the key aspect of building competitiveness. The company clearly perceives itself as a market leader. Detailed descriptions of the corporate governance follow, where the company describes its understanding of and structure for providing information to its constituencies and, in a similar way to the case of 'O', strong effort is made to explain where the company does not comply with the code of conduct of the Polish Stock Exchange.

The case of 'KHS', analyzed from the perspective of the formal communication of the company (sense-giving), presents itself as being purely individualistic in identity much more explicitly than 'O', since there are hardly any aspects of relational or collectivistic identity mentioned (with the minor exception of a section about wartime employees, whose loyalty to the company allowed its quick renovation after it was bombarded and set on fire by the withdrawing Nazis in 1944).

While there is no trace of stakeholder relation-building efforts on the side of corporate formal communication, a significant discourse about the economic problems of the region related to the bad condition of the company surfaces in the press. The significant article, titled 'Problems of the glass factory: a drama of the region' (*Rzeczpospolita*, 16 December 2008), clearly emphasizes how strong relations are between a key employer and other stakeholders, specifically the local community. Interestingly enough, among the voiced opinions of local council representatives and those of the trade union, partly blaming management for the bad situation, the voice of a representative of the company is lacking. Not only, then, is it a negative communication, but it is also a skewed and asymmetric one, with its roots, perhaps, in the skewed stakeholder relation strategy of the company, which ignored the voice of stakeholders previously. The big picture, arising from analysis of various contexts around formal communication, one of an individualistic organization, self-concentrated, detached from the local stakeholder environment, although, paradoxically, it remained a key employer with a significant tradition and long-term history in the region and, as such, was embedded at the core of local communities.[46] This criticism, that in times of problems the company leaves its employees without any help whatsoever, sheds even more light on the nature of relations between the company and its workforce. Not only do we have a case of opportunity lost, where dialogical relations built in the time of prosperity might have eased problems which surfaced during the crisis, we also have a case of moral negligence as a consequence, confirmed by the fact that over 200 employees who were made redundant took the company to the court, claiming the overdue salaries (*Rzeczpospolita*, 28 March 2009). The press reports surrounding the crisis were full of emotional descriptions of people who had worked for the company for generations and now did not have any means to prepare and pay for Christmas. This way of constructing the discourse, perhaps typical for the smaller town in which almost half of the population was related somehow to the company, puts even more pressure on the company in question to incorporate the issue of stakeholder dialogue in its core strategy of relation-building. The employees mentioned by the press are always portrayed in the context of fighting for their rights or being disadvantaged in the conflict with the company. Interestingly, this is also an example of the contextual importance of text analysis, where, although key words used in press texts relate to the area of relations between the company and the stakeholders, the context in which they are used does not constitute a relational identity of the company; it rather points to the void of what, in other circumstances, should have been proof of corporate relational identity but is not.

In summary, this is a case of individualistic identity, ignoring the stakeholder environment.

'OSM' sees itself as an individualistic company, using mainly legal argumentation to justify its deeds. At the same time, its perceived identity remains individualistic, as well as the argumentation used to describe it (legal). The company presents itself as a pioneer of innovations, with the most ground-breaking and best technological investments in the country. It claims that their success is due not only to technological advancement but also to the highest product quality and an implemented quality management system (ISO 9001). At the same time, the company admits its respect and feeling of responsibility for the local environment, which is fulfilled by the implementation of the standard ISO 14001; it does feel responsible for the quality of the product and, in a sense, for the employees – their health and safety and work standards. The quality of the product is seen as a way of fulfilling expectations (surely only at the client side of stakeholder relationships). Interestingly enough, it is the 'responsible goal' which is cited by the representative of the company as the key success factor – not profit in itself but long-term quality and best price for its members – this is the key objective of the company.[47] The relational side of identity is restricted to the employees only, while the collectivistic element of identity can be seen, in part, in the claim to be responsible and to care for ecology and the surrounding environment.

In summary, this is a case of individualistic identity with restricted relational awareness and a generic positioning of the company as part of the surrounding environment; however, it is far from a collectivistic identity, where the entity does not position itself as superior to other 'beings' in the world – instead, it identifies itself with the standpoint of being one of many participants in the market and its environment. The company has been ranked as the best in its field, with 20 per cent growth dynamics in the report prepared in 2008 by Dan and Bradstreet; it is no surprise that this fact is used as a key message in corporate communication. Also, even competing producers voice the view that some of the products of this company are exceptional.

'B' is presented as a company with relational identity dominated by a legal and scientific interpretation of its operation and professional conduct. Much attention in formal communication is paid towards employees and methods of motivation and professional training. The workforce is seen as an integral part of the company, whereby the development of people and of the firm should happen in parallel as they are strongly correlated. However, it is worth pointing out that the statement should be seen rather as an internal political declaration than a reflection of economic fact ('our strong motivation to improve the quality and the engagement of all the employees allows us to reach the planned results enabling a further and visible development of the firm and all the workforce') ('Quality Policy', 'B' webpage). At the other end of the continuum are customers, with respect to whom, the company has an ambition to fulfill 'the highest' expectations, admitting, at the same time, that they cannot afford to minimize those expectations.

The projected identity also focuses around quality and the quality assurance system the company implements, whereby a lot is said about customer satisfaction and exceeding customers' expectations through profound engagement of employees. Furthermore, the notion of a systemic achievement of quality is interpreted as the foundation for building trust in the client relationship.

In summary, this is relational identity polarized between customers and employees as key stakeholders, with instrumental orientation towards stakeholders – which is a skewed one, since it is only primary stakeholders who are mentioned in corporate communication. There is very little about the company in press communications, except for purely informative announcements relating mostly to public works tenders for which the company applies.

The companies in dialogue with the communities

The second aspect of these cases relates, following the sense-making process taxonomy of Basu and Palazzo (2008), to the actual engagements companies undertake and whether these are perceived, and how, by local communities. Local perceptions are established by formal market assessments of companies, such as by journalists and analysts.

'O', although it identifies itself as being in an individualistic position in the market, using competitive language, verbally declares an almost pure dialogue communication strategy, with the only exception that decision-making related to CSR strategy is made by management on the basis of polls and surveys. At the same time, it declares a wide concept of responsibility, acknowledging primary and secondary stakeholders. While the company is coherent with its identity claim, both on a cognitive and on a linguistic level (the company thinks and says the same), its declared perception of the strategic stakeholder role and a broad responsibility of the company does not find any confirmation at the linguistic level. The semantics used by the company confirms its strong individualistic identity, which, in a sense, results in a 'withdrawn' communication process mainly targeted at shareholders. As a result of such divergence between declared approach and actual operations, there is virtually no awareness of corporate activities among local community members. The company gets involved in the total spectrum of CSR activities, including: generic (which, indeed, do not depend on the size of the company); local embeddedness strategy (surprisingly), which seems more specific for smaller entities; and, logically, in internal engineering, which is coherent with the fact that the company attributes much importance to proving to stakeholders that their expectations are met. In other words, the company does not execute any strong sense-giving activities either to external or even to internal stakeholders, except for shareholders.

The conclusions from this case can be twofold. First, although the company is coherent in its identity claim, declared and verbalized, there seems to be a strong divergence between declared perceptions of stakeholders (as co-constructors of CSR strategy). Therefore, irrespective of the coherent identity communication pattern, there are no traces of execution of a declared dialogical relations with stakeholders, which might be related either to wishful thinking of the communication manager or to inefficiency of operations.

Second, a chaotic approach to the relation strategy can be seen in the inconsistent engagement in the wide span of CSR activities. In terms of explicit CSR communication, 'O' is the only one out of the four cases present in the country-wide annual report 'Responsible Business in Poland', published by the Responsible Business Forum (www.fob.org), credited, in 2004, with having one of the best corporate governance systems (Corporate Governance Ranking 2003, *Rzeczpospolita*, 26 January 2004), followed by a report in 2006 describing the eco-responsible program 'The Earth Guests', implemented in all the hotels belonging to the group and based on the New Scorecard for Environment Protection, and on its partnership with the UNICEF program supporting children.

The company functions in a specific environment where trust-building is perceived as more important, in comparison to other cities, where it is preferred by women more than by men. Moreover, the local community is characterized by its sympathy towards the wide sense of responsibility (primary and secondary stakeholders) and perceives the company through the lens of its demographic characteristic, as a trust-building and relational company; even though the company considers itself an individualistic entity, the local community expresses the same attitude towards scale of business responsibility as company informants – that is, they agree that it should include a wide array of stakeholders.

In this environment, the importance of trust depends on sex, being promoted mostly by women. The ultimate managerial outcome of this for operations dictates that, if you locate your business in Warsaw, you should take into consideration that the environment values trust highly (as compared to Krakow, for example), which is an important issue, particularly if your constituency is dominated by women who attribute more importance to this value than men.

'KHS' is a case of declared relational identity, together with elements of asymmetric communication/information stakeholder relation strategy. However, in formal communication the identity communicated appears purely individualistic, similar to 'O', as far as perceived identity is concerned. The domination of relational and collectivistic discourse in market-side communication not only fails to confirm corporate identity, but also, rather, voices all the relational aspects neglected by corporate communication strategy. It might be assumed that market-side communication serves as a mirror, showing the discrepancies in corporate communications by exposing what is expected of a company but is not executed. If, in the case of 'O', market-side communication shows a relational void because of skewed corporate communications favoring shareholders only, in the case of 'KHS' it shows a relational void because of the lack of acknowledgment of any significant outside environment of the company. First, there is a divergence between declared and communicated identity, although a declared asymmetric communication and information-based relation strategy seems more plausible if the company restricts dramatically its surrounding environment. As a locally embedded company, 'KHS' engages in local embeddedness CSR activities and, not surprisingly, as this company perceives its stakeholders as potential opposition. The awareness of these activities among the local community is fairly high, which might be interpreted either as proof of the effectiveness of the information strategy or as a sociological fact related to the strong embeddedness of the company and high interdependence of the local community upon their key employer.

This is the environment which attributes more importance to the corporate mission of solving social problems – that is, it would expect collectivistic identities much more than people in Warsaw; other than that, there are no further location-specific expectations towards the business.

'OSM' sees itself in the context of trust-building being the main mission of the enterprise, thus positioning itself as a relational identity and, although it declares a dialogical stakeholder relation strategy, the fact that it perceives stakeholders as being only passive end receivers of corporate communication implies that, indeed, trust-building will be much more important for them than for those entities convinced that stakeholders are their partners in a strategy setting.

Interestingly, the linguistic side of the identity shows a strong individualistic affiliation and is equally perceived by the market, mainly due to the real economic success the company managed to achieve – a success also confirmed by the company's competitors, who, although fiercely competitive, admit objectively to the high quality of their key competitor. For example, the boss of the biggest Polish milk conglomerate Mlekovita, when asked about 'OSM', said impulsively: 'The scale of the production is not the same; we are the power – they just a small factory.' But he immediately restrains himself: 'We have very correct relations with them. It is a good producer with success. But it sells mostly in the country, while the market is being regulated by those who sell a lot for export' (*Rzeczpospolita*, 27 June 2008). Or, elsewhere, the vice president of another competing enterprise, Mlekpol, said: 'they do have a few good products there which sell very well, but one of them is exceptional. It is so good, that it does not need any promotion. One can only congratulate' (*Rzeczpospolita*, 27 June 2008).

The declared relational orientation is partly confirmed in the linguistic sphere of the identity, with a marked importance assigned to educating employees and exceeding the expectations of clients, although, again, this is a polarized approach to stakeholders where only primary ones are included.

The clear declarations of a deep responsibility felt for the undamaged and precious local environment (ISO 14001 implemented) situates a discourse also very close to a collectivistic identity. The individualistic perception of the company by the market (using competitive language, which creates distance between a given company and other market players) is related to the fact that the significant economic success of 'OSM' is widely commented on in the context of their competitiveness, the quality of the product considered to be one of their fundamental strengths.

Since this is also a locally embedded enterprise, in a similar way to 'KHS', it engages in local embeddedness CSR and achieves an accurate awareness of its activities in the local community. This is a community which shows a similar pattern of allocation of the importance of trust as Warsaw – that is, women believe that trust is more important than men do and, equally, that leadership is less important in corporate identity. The comment about the gender balance of corporate constituencies, therefore, applies. Given that Piatnica is dominated by a female population, the conclusions for stakeholder relation-building seem obvious.

Finally, 'B' perceives itself through the relational lens and consistently builds this message in its formal communication. The company believes in the role of stakeholders as co-designers of CSR strategy and declares a strategy of dialogue-building with stakeholders. This is confirmed by clear messages about various investments the company makes in the quality and education of its employees; most importantly, this is seen as the way towards developing the company together with its people. Clients are mentioned in the context of not only meeting but also surpassing the expectations of 'dear clients' (Quality Policy, corporate website of 'B' 5) in an attempt to meet necessary standards to earn the trust of clients. Interestingly, the company builds its formal communication by appealing to the pride of the local community through emotional statements like: ' "B" is situated in the beautiful city of Krakow by the Vistula river – a historic city with rich traditions, and a capacity for surprising'; or, elsewhere, 'The city of Krakow obliges. One cannot, living and working here, allow oneself to minimize the expectations of potential customers.

A client has a right to expect perfectionism' (description of the firm on the corporate website).

Although, due to the specific structural setting of the company (it belongs to a group), the exact entity which was analyzed is not perceived clearly as a separate entity on the market, the brand itself is well recognized as occupying a decent position on the Krakow consumer map, according to 27 per cent of spontaneous answers from respondents (SMG/KRC research published in 2007, 'Developers brands. Which firms we know'). Whether this is a desirable situation is difficult to assess, since the perception of the whole group, although related to relational aspects and thus consistent, raises the issue of possible negative repercussions of exposure in the case of wrong-doing and dubious treatment of clients attributed to other group members.[48] 'B', a member of the group, is mentioned by the market only in the context of its professional conduct, various operations it gets involved in and tenders for and significant works in the region that it applies for.

It might be, then, that the company enjoys a purely professional perception, with no emotional connotations. Such a standpoint requires the assumption that identity is always emotionally defined and, as a construct built out of the deepest sentiments towards certain values or ideas, expresses itself through emotionally loaded notions, such as 'responsibility', 'help', expectations', 'competition', 'leadership' and other key words in mission statements. Information about the involvement of the company in consecutive tenders and other purely professional engagements is deprived of any qualifying dimension other than just being an informative text. Another possibility is that, due to the complex group structure to which the entity belongs (which operates under one brand name, but gets involved in a wide span of diverse activities), the individual identity is embedded in a group one.

The company constructs its CSR strategy partly around generic CSR, achieving a very poor communication result, as those activities do not seem to be visible for the local community at all. However, it is locally embedded CSR which forms the core of corporate strategy, not surprisingly given the strong emotional affection for the city in the formal communication; regrettably, however, local awareness of these activities is also very unsatisfactory. The reason for the latter might be lack of perceptional clarity due to confusion between the group and its members, whereby the perceived corporate identity might be diluted across the members of the complex relational nexus.

In terms of local community, this is the most peculiar case out of the four. On the general level, it is agreed that much more attention is paid to the idea of corporate identity wrapped around the mission of solving social problems than in Warsaw. Also, the social expectations towards the wide spectrum of business responsibility, including all stakeholder groups, is polarized between men and women, the latter of whom are much more enthusiastic about the idea. Given that the city has an over-representation of females in the population, the corporate entity operating there might expect a strong asymmetry in the scale of social involvement expected of it by society.

It is not only that the more educated the people get here the more they broaden the spectrum of the stakeholders they accept as having legitimate expectations towards the companies, which clearly shows the importance of educating constituencies to promote such a standpoint, but also, more surprisingly, older people develop significantly narrower views on business responsibility, ultimately promoting the shareholder model of private responsibility. Given that the local community sample in this case is dominated by highly educated people, as well as those within the age range promoting the social responsibility concept, a business operating here can expect another asymmetry, which, together with the dominance of the female population, enforces the trend to scrutinize the business and locate social expectations in the private sector, especially that social problems are more appreciated here than elsewhere.

Synthesis

The synthesis of the above case studies draws out a few lines of thoughts requiring further research. Big enterprises operating in cosmopolitan environments, which manage to align their declared identity with their linguistic dimension and remain consistent in the message they convey, are perceived by the market through the same identity emotional lens, irrespective of their actual economic success. Big companies operating in the smaller markets, usually locally embedded, where the message conveyed differs from the declared identity, will be perceived according to the identity verbalized if their performance is successful. Such is the case of 'OSM', which, in spite of declaring itself as relationist, focused on dialogue-building, constructs a strongly individualistic discourse around its competitive and market-winning abilities; but, since this indeed is the case, the market accepts this message. One may speculate about the reasons: perhaps, for example, it is a deep identification with its key employer, whose success is a source of pride for the local community – a hypothesis which could be in line with Merton's concept of locally embedded communities.

Should the company, however, be unsuccessful and thus fail to satisfy the hopes and expectations of the surrounding environment, the market is likely to expose the void between the identity declared and that communicated, pointing to what is lacking in the overall identity picture of the entity. Such was the case of 'KHS', where the company, in spite of declaring itself a relationist, built a strong individualistic identity and, since it failed economically, its market perceptions became overshadowed by relations-focused discourse, exposing, in a sense, a scale of disappointment with company's operations.

The above observations might serve as an illustration to the saying 'The winners do not get asked'. Above all, the social perceptions of the enterprises by other market players, including local communities, are born through the economic lens, it seems. From this perspective, a further hypothesis that market perceptions of businesses depend upon the long-term economic calculation of probability with which a given entity has a capacity to enrich its environment in purely commercial terms and on the underlined systemic wisdom of natural systems thriving to survive, does not seem unjustified.

However, the second part of the case study, deriving from analysis of local communities, sheds a bit more light on the dynamics of the enterprise and local community, showing that some local environments express strong phenomena which might have the power to affect stakeholder relation strategy. These phenomena, the demographic perceptional specifics, which I named *location enforcers*, include demographically bounded value systems, where, for example, the perception of mission statements (and thus corporate identities) will depend on the gender of the respondents and demographically bounded tendency to locate the businesses in the social network – that is, when the perception of the wide responsibility of the business (that towards all stakeholder groups as opposed to primary stakeholders only) would depend on the age, gender and education of respondents.

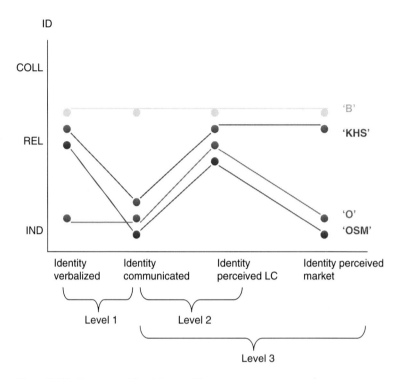

Figure 3.17 Corporate identities profiles

Such is the case of Krakow, which is the only one out of the four case studies, where the above-mentioned relations exist.[49] It might be possible therefore, that certain locations facilitate certain stakeholder relation strategies.

Looking into the cases presented from the perspective of consistency of corporate identity (Figure 3.17), three spheres of consistency become apparent.

Level 1 consistency is between identity verbalized and expressed linguistically by the company. Level 2 consistency is between the identity expressed formally and the one perceived by the local community. Level 3 consistency is between identity expressed formally and the one perceived by the market in general, represented by the press.

How the identity verbalized by corporate managers responsible for designing communication and building relations with stakeholders fits with the formally communicated identity statement raises the issue of internal processes in organizations. The distortions between those two messages may be the result of a faulty design of the formal communication, as well as a poor sense-making process or internal strategy communication, resulting in managers not understanding or not knowing what the company stands for culturally and in terms of value. Level 2 and Level 3 spheres will depict how well the message was understood within the direct external environment of the company (local communities) and within the market in general.

Let's start with broad market perception of the identities transmitted. The analysis of the four case studies shows that three of them are perceived according to the identity conveyed and only one not. Two of them ('O' and 'B') happen to have a consistently built identity at Level 1, hence we might conclude that this is the source of correct perception by the market. Two other cases show distorted identity (they define themselves differently than the message they later construct). They are both big companies and they both operate in relatively smaller cities; however, one of them is very successful economically ('OSM'), while the other is not ('KHS').

Thus, the first emic issue occurring is whether the correspondence of identity transmitted by the company and perceived by the market depends only on consistency of corporate identity built (Level 1) or on economical success of the entity as well? Furthermore, it will be interesting to know whether this process may be conditioned by the local environment, in the sense that it is different in bigger cities as compared to smaller towns.

Consistency of perceptions by the local community with the corporate identity constructed by the company shows only in one case ('B'), which is, incidentally, an example of perfect consistency across all levels. In other cases the local community perceives the identities of companies differently to that communicated, irrespective of whether companies are coherent internally in this matter. The only case where these perceptions are aligned is 'B', which is the company operating in a unique environment with location enforcers.

Thus, the second emic issue deriving from the study is whether the identity perceived by the local community depends on the consistency of corporate linguistic identity or derives from specific features of the local community – that is, location-specific determinants.

Given the above conclusions, thinking strategically about the relations companies built with their stakeholders encourages adoption of

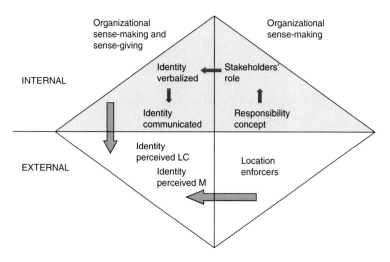

Figure 3.18 Strategic relation-building model

a synthetic model of relation strategy-building (Figure 3.18), which combines the key areas of sense-making practices between the constituencies engaged in the process and the competencies needed.

It is important to understand whether we are talking about the tactical or operational model of building relations or about strategy. Clearly, operational execution of strategies might be as varied as the business models of the companies; however, certain uniformity of the stakeholder environment across businesses, differentiated by contextual issues much more than by typology of stakeholders and their potential interests, allow us to think about stakeholder relations in the strategic context, answering the question of whether there are any underlying phenomena at the foundations of the relations-building, which is clearly the sense-giving process.

All the significant elements included in the strategic aspect of relation-building constitute the organizational perception of the stakeholders' role, which is conditioned by corporate attitudes towards the scale of responsibility (private responsibility as opposed to corporate social responsibility). The role perceptions determine identity constructs, which, in consequence, relate to the definition of communication goals. Thus, there exists a three-dimensional strategic construct which includes perceptional variables (ROLE and

RESPONS[50]), which are purely cultural, and the identity construction process (sense-making and sense-giving), which intermediates the goal of the communication process, thus positioning the organization as seeking dialogue or using asymmetrical communication based on manipulating the message to convince stakeholders about certain aspects of organizational reality. In this case, the asymmetric communication patterns might be regarded as enforcers of sense-giving practices. On top of inter-organizational aspects – value-based attitudes towards the scale of responsibility and the role of stakeholders, and the culturally embedded process of creating the meanings – there might be the external enforcers related to certain locations. While we do know the relations between the intra-organizational aspects of relation strategies, the causality of successful relation strategy (based on a coherent identity communication process) is a surprise, specifically in the context of location specifics.

The above interpretation serves as an example of the narrative seeking a coherent story to clearly explain the causality and relations between certain facts and messages conveyed. In that sense, it is chronological in as much as it attempts to understand the causality between various identities voiced. On the other hand, however, what we observe here is, in a sense, a fragmented and polyphonic (multi-voiced) story[51] recording various identities as seen by various actors involved in the organizational identity. Additionally, the explanation offered is speculative, statistically unverifiable, and, as such, qualifies as a sense-making and storytelling exercise rather than a pure narrative.

Other managerial conclusions include:

- the split of the Morsing and Schultz model between the operational and perceptual aspects;
- a new dimension of local environment, while there are homogeneous groups of stakeholders and we tend to believe that it is only the business model of the company which might determine somehow the prioritization of stakeholders' claims, there is now a completely new dimension –which is inherent to a given local community;
- the focus should be on the integrity of the sense-giving procedures which are visible in the process of corporate identity forming.

Stakeholder relations insights

Contemporary markets, dominated economically by transnational corporations, where classical economy is contested for obvious reasons, such as information asymmetry and growing interdependence of enterprises interlinked via capital relations, exposed the notion of corporate power and its abuse at the cost of those less advantaged, mainly societies. The sources of this power are numerous, but, on top of capital accumulation, extensive relational network, often obscured in lack of transparency, seems to be playing a critical role. Relations, used by entities to execute power, at the same time become a subject of scrutiny for regulators, who intend to tame the business through various governance mechanisms in order to ensure a balance between market actors.

Social activism, in its various forms, and a discourse about corporate social responsibility are both an answer to what is perceived as the oppressive corporate state, on the one hand, and a market generated risk for corporate freedom, on the other. Potential answers on how to manage relations with stakeholders to ensure long-term sustainability of business need to be embedded in a discussion on what the business entity is, what its nature and relations with the surrounding environment is and whether the new and still-changing status of big business imposes any new, additional responsibilities on it.

My answer is this: corporations and business are, basically, the way we create them. However, to know exactly what they are is not easy. The apparently untamed nature of their evolution does not allow analysis as a given object, but rather imposes a necessity to observe something which is a living organism in the making. For that reason, organization science looks for new methods of research and analysis, where mechanisms rather than solid organizational structures will be the subject of observation. From the perspective of stakeholder relations, a sense-making approach, based on acknowledging that markets are formed with multiple and parallel stories generated by different interpretations of reality by stakeholders, seems more accurate than a linear approach, which inevitably must end with the goal alignment problem.

Relations formed and executed in the communication process are not only the channel for a power exercise on the individual level. When targeted at a specialized audience they also carry certain senses and meanings, thus allowing the construction of stories – interpretations of the surrounding world. It is the communication process where the meanings are negotiated, and notions such as responsibility executed and interpreted into actions.

The quality of the stakeholder relations the company executes depends largely on how it perceives the scope of its own responsibility, whether it wishes to include secondary and indirect stakeholders as legitimate claimants and whether stakeholders are seen as potentially active opposition and a threat. The relation, defined in the sense-making terms as a consensus about the meanings the company communicates and the stakeholder interprets, is largely constructed on the foundation of the identity the company adopts and communicates. Relational identity, based on trust, indeed occurs when the stakeholders are seen as partners and involved in organizational processes, but, on the operational level, it is fear of opposition which makes companies focus on relation-building. When stakeholders are fairly passive, the company does not have any motivation to concentrate on dialogue-building activities.

Companies tell us stories. When they communicate their culturally embedded identities as a sign of what they stand for and who they are, they offer a certain story which gets reinterpreted by various market constituencies – differently and depending on the context. The latter, among other things, is constituted by their particular interests. This transfer of meanings is done in the standardized condition of the same language, notions and phrases. The number of notions which have the potential to carry a special meaning, reserved for certain context in which they are being used, is surprisingly low. The recipient of the corporate communication is forced to navigate between thousands of phrases, which can carry various meanings depending on the circumstances in which they are used. When one looks into the range of material of corporate communication, a first impression is that companies tend merely to hint at what they stand for by using language in a very free and uncoordinated manner. One might even get the impression that a certain abuse of words such as 'excellence' is taking place, especially in mission statements, with other forms of formal communication, specifically reports, treated as deposits for tailor-made information. The latter also gives a disturbing impression of a certain devaluation of the notion of 'ethics', which seems heavily overused in reports; rather, it should be objective and avoid emotionally loaded phrases. At the same time, while companies often leave a void in information they provide, market observers, specifically the press, take on the burden of interpreting the reality for other market participants. Given that the goals of companies and market analysts (press) can be different, the meaning generated by the organization is likely to get distorted. The answer is a direct dialogue with stakeholders – something the Polish organizations hardly do.

Organizations also 'talk' through certain socially responsible actions they undertake. The more they want to prove that they do what stakeholders expect them to do, the more they engage in internal engineering activities, such as systems of benefits for employees or assigning a certain sales margin on their products for a good cause. However, companies tend to lose interest in providing evidence of stakeholder orientation and responsibility in line with the company's growth – although the bigger the company, the more it declares performing social consultations.

Growth in the company also distances it from its local communities, which is visible in diminishing involvement in local CSR, such as cooperation with local communities or supporting local initiatives.

Given, that the perception of the company does not depend only on the endogenous factors such as corporate strategy and operational professionalism, but also on the exogenous ones, deriving from the specifics of the stakeholder environment, the almost academic postulate of getting to know stakeholders better is not unreasonable. And there are surprises hidden in local communities.

Community perception of the scope of business responsibility might depend on the gender, age and education of a person. Also, perception of corporate mission might depend on the demographical structure of the environment; however, these relations are geographically determined – that is, they occur only in certain locations. For example, men tend to think about corporations as being responsible more for generating income for shareholders and fulfilling the expectations of primary stakeholder groups (i.e., employees and clients), while women perceive the responsibility in the context of a much broader scope of stakeholder groups (including primary and secondary); however, such gender-generated phenomena are not visible in the overall sample of local communities, but only in one specific location (Krakow, in this case). What people expect of the company, and how they perceive it, depends on very locally embedded phenomena.

Older people more often choose income-creating for shareholders as the key responsibility of the business, as opposed to fulfilling the expectations of broadly understood stakeholders. However, those who are more educated prefer a broad definition of corporate responsibility (primary and secondary stakeholders) as opposed to primary stakeholders only – that is, shareholders, employees, clients. Again this relation is locally specific, implying that while, in some locations – free from such dependencies – the company might be able to ensure its proper image and perception successfully via a standardized approach to stakeholder relations, in other locations, the approach would need to incorporate very unique, local aspects.

The fact, that the views of managers and those of the local community upon the scope of business responsibility differed from each other only in Krakow, where there is a demographic determination for perceiving the role of business, while in the other three cases, where there is no such relation, managers agreed with the local community in the views, seems to confirm that such local specifics can successfully distort corporate understanding of its stakeholder environment.

One of the obvious conclusions which comes to mind is that, while the Morsing and Schultz model of CSR communication strategies serves as a good illustration for possible operational solutions when building a relation strategy – that is, defining the task of the communication process or the key responsibility of the communication department – it does not differentiate between different ontological and axiological backgrounds of the construction elements used in strategies. Specifically, the perception of the role of stakeholders, which is by nature a cognitive and deeply emotionally grounded aspect of strategy, seems to carry a much stronger determining force than defining the communication goal or the key task of the communication department, or finally deciding about the decision-making process structure, which are all technocratic aspects of organization, driven by the paradigm of efficiency and productivity.

Indeed, it is the perception of the role of stakeholders which predicts the task of the communication department, pointing to the relation between seeing stakeholders as potentially active opposition and concentrating communication department efforts around building strong relations. It is also the perception of the stakeholders' role which structures corporate identity, as, paradoxically, those companies where stakeholders are considered as end receivers of corporate communication tend to focus efforts around trust-building much more than those where stakeholders are considered co-designers of the strategy. It is fear that drives the organizations to create dialogue-based strategies and it is emotional distance to stakeholders which helps them construct relational, partner-oriented identities. From the identities constructed, operational aspects of relation-building strategies are born, as the identity constructed facilitates the definition of the goal of the communication process.

It is, however, not the relational identity which defines options for strategy-building, but extreme identities, such as individualism, which negatively influence dialogue-building, and collectivism, which facilitates it, while discouraging instrumentally defined communication aimed at proving that stakeholders' expectations are met.

The *spiritus movens* of the whole process – the perception of the role of the stakeholders – derives from strong sense-making processes, such as a perceived role of business and scale of responsibility towards stakeholders, on the individual level, and social consultations procedures, on the organizational level. Managers arrive at certain organizational settings (inevitably embedded in the cultural context) where certain processes are already in place. They see these facts and, based on them, they build certain perceptions – the perceptions which help them construct their identities, which later become subject to strong sense-giving actions expressed, for example, in the linguistic dimension of corporate CSR process, through reporting or other forms of formal communication. The failure of sense-making procedures results in possible inaccuracy of corporate communication at the level of mission statement and formal reporting.

The key message is, therefore, that, on the managerial level, it is the sense-making process which resides at the foundations of relation-building strategies and it is the way we educate and condition our managers which can become the root of the operational problem. On the operational level, firms become complacent about good dialogue, allowing their focus on relation-building to lapse until they perceive stakeholders as a threat.

Given the above, the relation strategy model should be seen as a managerial approach, which is based on multi-level flows of meanings: social consultations serving as social facts, on the one hand, and a strong sense-giving procedure for managers, on the other. Such sense-giving or educational procedures for managers would need to include crafting perceptions of the role of stakeholders and those of business responsibility, from which corporate identity is constructed. The operational outcome of such an approach would be expressed in the goal of the communication process.

The question remains as to why perceptions of the role of business by constituencies depend on the demographic structure of the local community in some locations, but not in others.

The portrait of stakeholder relations executed by companies consists of a specific stakeholder map, where some stakeholders are more important than others and some have the power to initiate a social network. Companies tend to attribute more importance to primary stakeholders with which they are linked via direct exchange – for example, work for pay in the case of employees, capital for the dividend in the case of shareholders or price for product in the case of clients. The importance attributed to secondary stakeholders tends to be, on average, lower; there seem to be no fundamental differences between the companies in the way they perceive the stakeholder environment.

In conclusion, there are no significant differences between companies in the way they appreciate the importance of stakeholders – they concentrate on the external environment, where the perception of importance of capital lenders and local administration predicts strongly the frequency of contact with central government and the perception of importance of local communities predicts the importance of contacts with consumer associations.[52] Intensified relations with central government, indicating greater appreciation by the organization of its primary stakeholders (specifically capital lenders) may be related to seeing the government as the main and important rule setter, whose decisions might be lobbied. Intensification of relations with consumer associations, wherever local communities are more appreciated, points to the role of institutionalizing the voice of stakeholders, as these are organized forms of voicing concerns, which are likely to capture the attention and become a noticeable player in the game.

The issue with the importance attributed towards stakeholder groups is that some stakeholders can influence the overall social network of the company more strongly than others. This means that it might be possible to predict the social networks of companies on the basis of their stakeholder maps constructed as a result of organizational processes, such as the way the decision-making process is organized or the way the communication manager's objective is defined, which sheds some light on the internal mechanisms of mapping stakeholders.Operationally, those social networks are constructed only around external stakeholders.

Importance attributed to stakeholder groups is linked to both internal systems of management – for example, how decisions are made and corporate identity defined. Individualistic companies, expressing themselves though mission statements praising leadership and market fight, treat local communities as less important, while those companies which define themselves through mission statements acknowledging social problems and corporate contribution to solving them tend to attribute more importance to local communities (see Appendix, Table A.3b).[53] Interestingly, the more communication management focuses on relation-building, the less they think about local public administration; however, paradoxically, secondary stakeholders gain importance, together with narrowing of the perceived scope of business responsibility (see Appendix, Table A.12). When managers function in a company which believes that business should be responsible towards its primary stakeholders only, they acknowledge the importance of associations and government (at central and local level) as important rule-setters; however, when they are requested to execute a razor-sharp relation-building strategy, they tend to deprive local administration of importance, almost as if they perceive the administration in an antagonistic context.

Once there is general consensus about stakeholder relations in management objectives, companies leave a lot of freedom and discretionary power to their staff as to how to execute their key objective.

Companies differ from local societies in the way they perceive the scope of business responsibility. Respondents drawn from the sample of local societies more often chose creating income for shareholders only or creating income and fulfilling the expectations of both primary and secondary stakeholder groups, while respondents from the corporate sample chose more often creating income for the shareholders and fulfilling expectations of other primary stakeholders. This might suggest that corporate representatives are very consistent in perceiving relations between companies and stakeholders, while local societies' respondents tend to be polarized when it comes to a somewhat epistemological discussion on what business should be responsible for.

What predicts the strategy of stakeholder relations the company uses? Given that the strategy of stakeholder relations is composed of a cognitive part, relating to the perceptions of business responsibility and the role of stakeholders resulting in stakeholder mapping, and a sense-giving part, related to identity construction and its communication, there is an interesting internal dynamic of this process, which includes the following. Those companies who define stakeholders as a potential threat to be dealt with (risk management category) will attribute lower importance to relation-building (understood as the key communication task) than companies which perceive the stakeholders either as neutral end receivers of corporate communication or as co-designers of CSR strategies who should be incorporated in the whole decision-making process – that is, relation building is facilitated by reduction of possible tensions between company and stakeholders. In other words, a risky and active stakeholder environment stimulates companies to undertake a more short-term objective-oriented approach to stakeholder relations – that is, focused around designing an exact message, for example, rather than on building long-term partner relations.

Companies dominated by the perception of stakeholders as potentially active end receivers of corporate communication attribute more weight to gaining trust, as their key mission, than those who perceive stakeholders as co-designers of their strategy. This, in a sense, is surprising, as one might expect that relations of trust would show significance wherever the stakeholders are more involved in strategy-building and engage more in the co-construction of corporate understanding of CSR and expectations of various actors – that is, with the intensification of the mutual sense-making process. The above result, although understandable – if the stakeholders are perceived somewhat in terms of being in opposition, the company needs to gain their trust in order to make such communication effective – shows, at the same time, the manipulative character of corporate attitudes towards stakeholders. Companies which perceive their responsibility in broad terms (responsible both for maximizing profit and for fulfilling the expectations of stakeholders; responsible both towards direct and non-direct stakeholders) more often perform social consultations than companies which limit their responsibility only to direct stakeholders.

A detailed assessment of CSR involvements can serve as a balance and check tool for stakeholder maps. In other words, careful observation of CSR activities may give an insight into the operational stakeholder map of a company. The following relations might be helpful:

- companies including social aspects in their advertisements and engaging in sponsorships tend to attribute more importance to local communities;
- those who work closely with NGOs attribute more importance to local administration; those who implement energy-saving programs pay attention to capital lenders, suppliers, local communities and government (this might be linked with a more or less subconscious response to current market expectations – i.e., capital lenders will assess the company more favorably and will assign more credibility to it if it has such program. This may influence the cost of capital. In a similar manner, local communities will be reassured that the company cares about surrounding environment, governmental actual or future legislatory expectations will be fulfilled and, last but not least, proper good practice will be delivered, thus sending a message to suppliers and subcontractors);
- donations imply a greater importance attributed to local communities and consumer associations, but also to local and central administration;
- companies with extensive social packages for employees observe closely their relations with local administration;
- engaging in employee volunteer schemes implies importance attributed to employees, local communities, suppliers and local administration.

The hypothesized relation between corporate identities and the CSR-related communication strategies can be confirmed by the fact that organizations which see stakeholders as end receivers of corporate communication, thus are intent to perform asymmetric communication strategy, also focus on gaining trust in their mission statements, showing tendencies towards relational identities. At the same time, individualistic identities (leader- and market fight-oriented) hardly create dialogical relations as opposed to collectivistic ones (see Appendix, Table A.27).

In the context of both supporting hypotheses, which linked generic communication strategies with the adopted model of responsibility, there is a confirmed relation that a narrow concept of responsibility, including only primary stakeholders, tends to stimulate companies to treat stakeholders as end receivers of corporate communication, which, in Morsing and Schultz's terms, would indicate a tendency for an asymmetric communication strategy, while including secondary stakeholders in the CSR concept indicates that they are seen as co-designers of corporate strategies. Dialogue activities in various forms of social consultation are intensified when an organization accepts the legitimacy of all stakeholder groups.

Notes

Introduction

1. Please see the discussion on the common good by Rafael Alvira in 'B. Fryzel and P. H. Dembinski (eds), *The Role of Large Enterprises in Democracy and Society*, Basingstoke: Palgrave Macmillan 2010.
2. What does a 'proper' environment for business operations mean? Should the government be obliged to exercise stakeholder prioritization analysis to decide whether it is society or business that has a more legitimate claim? Who should the government be representing in the first place: its citizens who elected it in a democratic process and cover the financial burden of its maintenance through the tax system or the businesses who make the economy run and pay taxes as well? Given the above, the stakeholder concept seems an astonishingly confusing one, not contributing significantly to solving main axiological questions seeking the balance between often-conflicting interests. Moreover, the stakeholder concept seems a technocratic term which, when treated as a substitute for managerial morality, covertly dilutes the responsibility for one's own actions, replacing it with the dubious analysis of stakeholder priorities, often against the criteria of urgency of the issue or power of the stakeholder.
3. Balmer and Soenen proposed the Acid Test Process of assessing CI, where communicated identity is one of the four parts, together with actual identity (values, performance, competitive position, history structure, management style and corporate behavior), ideal identity (optimum dimension of the before-mentioned constructs) and desired identity (visions of stakeholders, senior executives and shareholders). The test was developed as the consultancy tool to facilitate and manage the change programs. For more details see Balmer and Soenen, 1999.
4. The discussion about the 'organization' in its ontological context – whether it is an object and 'being' in itself or whether it remains only an adjectival quality portraying various forms of humans' activity – exceeds the scope of this book, although the view taken in this analysis derives from the 'sense-making' concept of organizations, treating it rather as the nexus of relations focused around axiologically bounded goals and embedded in meanings.
5. The first aspect is researched on the sample of the 150 best Polish enterprises using statistical methods of data analysis; the second one follows partly the case study method proposed by R. Stake, but is, however, heavily influenced by the storytelling approach proposed by D. Boje (2001); and the third concludes with the statistical analysis of the sample of 564 respondents selected randomly from the four local communities related to the four case studies.

1 Corporate Social Responsibility: A Response to Growing Corporate Power

1. The World Investment Report (2007) gave figures on the long-running trend of increasing corporate profits, while a recent report on corporate taxes by KPMG (2009) confirms that a long-running trend to reduce direct corporate taxes has slowed down only recently. The report also confirms the observation that, as the governments are pressured by the recession scenario to secure their national budgets, a slow-down in corporate tax reductions is coupled with the moderation of the economic incentives programmes. These, however, are only recent and crisis induced changes, which seem to mark an end to the decades-long prosperity during which enterprises increased their earnings while benefiting from the favorable tax legislation in countries competing for foreign direct investments (FDIs). See also P. H. Dembinski (2010).

   Although the financial crisis, which generated massive public aid to rescue corporations, undermined the long-term trend of profitability for a while, it is surprising how quickly the companies managed to generate profits again. The fact that rising profits are not translated into jobs and employment growth at the same time undermines public trust in the private sector. See Rampell (2010) and Hathaway (2010).

2. According to the World Bank, poverty in the world has decreased – that is, a number of people living below the poverty line of US$1.25 per day has decreased globally – however, most of this decrease is explained by the trends in the East Asia and Pacific region, while in other regions the numbers have, in fact, increased. Please see the World Bank, Poverty Reduction and Equity, Poverty and Inequality Analysis at www.web.worldbank.org/WBSITE/EXTERNAL/TOPICS/EXTPOVERTY/0,,content M DK:22569498~pagePK:148956~piPK:216618~theSitePK:336992,00.html (accessed 29 October 2010). Other sources shed some light on subtleties such as that the original estimates for poverty rates were revised upwards. Also the good message from the falling rate masks regional situations, where, in most countries (including European ones), poverty has not reduced, indeed has actually increased; the fall in global figures can be almost completely explained by trends in China, which is unique as a country meeting Millennium Development Goals well in advance, see Shah (2010). More importantly, however, income distribution inequalities are rising, portraying the trend for growing social stratification. The vast majority of OECD database countries show an increase in the Gini coefficient from the mid-1980s to the mid-2000s (www.stats.oecd.org, accessed 29 October 2010); see also OECD (2008) and World Income Inequality Database (2008).

3. Empirical evidence from the USA showed that this was not unimportant – nearly all major US companies were tied up in a single network with banks and insurance companies being at the center of the network – their position unrivaled over the course of the twentieth century, although

there were differences in the density of networks over time (Mizruchi, 2004). However, later evidence given by Mizruchi points to the declining centrality and importance of the banks in the network, partially due to their shift from lending to financial services and thanks to the bigger number of opportunities for capital supply (*ibid.*).

4. This would be an interesting hypothesis to test, especially in the view of the discussion as to whether the internationalization of management leads to the creation of a new class of managers – specialized in managing cross-border operations and with the significant capacity to understand and manage cross-cultural issues. Mizruchi polemized with the argument of financial globalization, claiming that 80 per cent of economic activity still takes place within national borders and that the level of economic cross-boundary activity in 1997 was comparable to that in 1914 (Mizruchi, 2004). However, globalization processes have shown significant dynamics from that time and, given the simple measures such as the share of profits generated abroad or percentage of foreign assets in the asset structure of international companies, those statements would certainly require another look and verification.

5. More insight into the process and its cultural and economic significance can be found in *The Selling of British Telecom* by K. Newman (1986).

6. This type of research evolves around the question of how a CEO can affect board processes. Following from there, the key interest of the researchers is whether boards can be an effective tool for management control or whether they are just a 'rubber stamp' for managers. See Herman (1981), Fama and Jensen (1983), Pfeffer (1972) and Zajac (1990).

7. The critical contingencies theory says that, since the departments or individuals do not share the same definitions of what is a critical contingency, they cannot be expected to agree on who has the power to control them; therefore, to define who has power one must answer the question of who defines the critical uncertainties (Pfeffer and Salancik, 1977; Enz, 1988). Enz suggests that to be able to define the critical contingencies one must express the value similarity with top management, because it involves it in a decision-making process (the author proves that top managers ascribe more power to those who independently perceive their values to be similar to top management; the greater the perceived similarity of values with top management and between departments the greater the power) (*ibid.*).

8. Perceiving power as a tool to achieve society's goals encourages the legitimization of its asymmetry, even if it is treated as a voluntary obedience based on common interests or legal legitimization (Weber, 2002). Voluntary obedience paradoxically can enforce asymmetry through granting what Hobbes called a 'sovereign power'. The sovereign accepts the power given to him voluntarily by others; however, as he was not a part of the agreement between those who gave him the power, he does not hold any obligations towards anybody. Any attempt to govern a sovereign becomes unjustified unless the Lockean interpretation of

a legitimized power is adopted, which assumes that its ultimate aim is the wealth of others, therefore the power must ensure the continuation of efforts to achieve those goals. This is based on the assumption that goals are the expression of a desired wealth. However, as long as this assumption is valid at the individual level, at the group level it gets obscured by a decision-making process. How are the decisions being made to ensure that they reflect the common goal and how can we be certain that common goal reflects the individual goals of the group members? For these reasons, one of the proxies for a group power, in its corporate context, could be participation in a decision-making process.

The state–society platform is where the relationship between power and goals manifests itself in ruling. To rule is to design the communal activities through defining their goals. The question arises of how the power can rule. According to Marcuse (1991), the key ruling tool is the notion of 'freedom' used in democratic societies, where democratic election only helps to seal the existent structure of power and enforce the goals of those who already possess it. Such enforcement and the manipulation of the notion of freedom are undertaken through conditioning from early childhood through the systems of media and education. The manipulative character of power manifests itself also through the creation of habits through which people are led to false desires, preventing them from seeing what is really good for them (Lukes, 1974). Such habits are usually built through repeated experiments of pleasure and discomfort. An everyday example could include introducing a public transport system based on electronic access tied to personal data of the holder stored in a central computer, such a system being, on the one hand, questioned for its attributed breach of human rights to freedom and being accused for introducing a 'big brother' philosophy and a policy state, but, on the other, cheaper than standard cash-paid tickets. Similar discussion applies to attempts to introduce biometrics on 'ID' cards, or strengthening security policies at airports, or on imposing preferential rates on electronic payment versus cash. In all examples, argumentation spreads between a benefit (more comfortable and cheaper) and threat (security).

9. The discussion on the relation between corporate power and democracy is far from being US-centric. Please also see a Polish text by J. Osiatyński, 'Czy korporacje zniszczą demokrację?', at www.polityka.pl, 10 May 2009 (online version, accessed 29 October 2010).

10. Given the development in the sophistication of methods for image creation, reputation-building and public relations activities, what was a personality-based power in the writings of Galbraith, attributed to leaders, today might become associated with the corporate and organizational identity.

11. This is the case in post-modern society, though the role of property is clearly becoming crucial with those individuals and organizations who accumulated significant capital becoming trend-setters and often consulted opinion-givers at the same time; more importantly, through

the increased structuralization of the ways in which the influence can be exercised (i.e. lobbying), the property seems to be a determinant of the effectiveness and range of influence at stake. One of the aspects of property–power relations can include the analysis of growth dynamics of PR and advertising industries.

12. For detailed analysis of economic power, please see V. Smith Hilmann and A. Scott (2010).

13. Some of the measures proposed to assess the procedures of governance clearly show how the latter provides an effective interface of relations between the entity and its constituencies. Apart from the dominant research related to boards, their processes, structure and diversity (Wan and Ong, 2005; Filatotchev *et al.*, 1997, 2001, 2002; Morck *et al.*, 1988; Weisbach, 1988; Beatty and Zajac, 1994), governance research focuses also on the scale of external involvement in corporate processes such as ownership structure and concentration (Earle *et al.*, 2005; Beatty and Zajac 1994, Goodstein and Boeker, 1991; Halpin and Naresimha, 1999) and the non-executive interlocks. While the first group of research exposes mainly the structural aspect of relations concentrated internally, specifically through the diversity of the boards where employee representation is inherent to the governance system adopted (Germany, France), the second looks at the external stakeholders tied to the company with the relation of ownership, either concentrated and, in such an instance, usually institutional or fragmented and dispersed among the mass shareholder base. Both groups represent a specific type of relations the company has with its stakeholders –one intermediated by work contract, in the case of diverse representational boards, or one intermediated by the capital, in the case of shareholders.

14. European Transparency Initiative details and current status can be found in the thorough analysis by Melich (2010).

15. More details about a long battle for the software patents directive and alleged accusations about extensive and misleading lobbying practices, which are said to be associated with the procedure, can be found at www.archive.corporateeurope.org/lobbycracy/C4Cbackground2. html, www.theregister.co.uk/2005/07/06/eu_bins_swpat/and www.ciaran. compsoc.com/software-patents.html

16. Some documents touching on the issue of legal governance mechanisms and the aspect of independency of board members include: *European Governance, A White Paper* (2001), *The Tyson Report on the Recruitment and Development of Non-Executive Directors* (2003), a report by D. Higgs on the role and effectiveness of the non-executive directors (2002) and the *Combined Code of Corporate Governance* (2003).

17. The concept of organizational or industrial democracy seems to be complementary to social responsibility (although it is much older), in the sense that it attempts to structuralize the postulate to involve employees in the organizational processes, coming from the standpoint that their loyalty to the organization would exceed a standard relation of

work and pay. Interestingly, though, the concept does not focus on the internal environment only, whereby its structural concept simply means the equalization of power and behavioral involvement of the employees in the decision-making process via leadership, trust, negotiations or corporate culture. In its external dimension it relates to the stakeholder democracy and organizational influence on the environment in the structural and behavioral context, respectively.

18. Corporations negotiate with government or other market players directly or indirectly using governmental channels – for example, bilateral (China and France), multilateral (EU accession case) and global trade (WTO). This is a new corporate diplomacy and, as big business becomes a player in the international politics, its bargaining powers need to be planned for with other players, often in procedures reaching far behind standard business dealing. Please see Henisz and Story (2003) for more details.

19. This chapter builds on the first version of my 'Governance of Corporate Power Network', published in *Finance and Bien Commun*, 4 April 2005.

20. The alignment of goals such as common good, helping others and increasing own economic standing at the same time was proposed by M. Porter and M. Kramer in 'Strategy and Society: The Link Between Competitive Advantage and Corporate Social Responsibility', *Harvard Business Review*, December 2006, and in the global context by C. K. Prahalad and A. Hammond, in 'Serving the World's Poor Profitably', *Harvard Business Review*, September 2002. The book by J. Perkins, *Confessions of an Economic Hitman*, provides a slightly different perspective of the motivations behind the politics of introducing new markets into the liberal economy zone. Please see Perkins (2004).

21. An astonishing account of the degeneration of the pharmaceutical industry as far as its mission to save lives and help suffering people is concerned, is provided in Petersen (2008). The book provides real-life examples and cases portraying the scale of dubious standards and procedures manipulating clinical tests, R&D policies, results dissemination and promotion through a very deep reach in the academic community and, in extreme cases, the systemic cooperation of some of the researchers with PR agencies used to prepare the publications and speeches. The sector, where the key stakeholder was redefined from the patient to a lifelong consumer of drugs, would not be able to execute such fundamental changes in its modus operandi if not for underlying changes in the philosophy of medicine, which seems to anecdotally assume that there are no healthy people – only those who have not been diagnosed yet. Please also see S. Saul, 'Unease on Industry's Role in Hypertension Debate, *The New York Times*, 20 May 2006 and Moynihan and Cassels (2005).

22. Compare   www.igs.berkeley.edu/library/research/quickhelp/elections/ 2004general/htHealthCare.html and http://epionline.org/studies/yewwitz_ org.2004.pdf

23. First place is occupied by the product quality interpreted as the category of responsibility towards the client; second place is occupied by profit

generation. Social goals such as providing a job placement in line with the capabilities of an employee, decent and genuine advertising and equal opportunities for employees occupy 12th,14th and 15th place, respectively.

24. Donaldson proposed a model of corporate obligations based on three types of laws: laws people cannot be deprived off (e.g., ownership rights, a right of the honest court proceedings), laws which the company has the obligation to protect (e.g., a right to education, a right to freedom of speech) and laws which impose upon the company the obligation to help those disadvantaged.

25. De George (1993) proposes a set of rules that he claims as useful for enterprises in defining higher norms – for example, honest paying of taxes, observing the human rights, cooperation with host governments in defining the ethical institutions.

26. Research done in the Netherlands shows that the majority of entrepreneurs believes CSR measures should be designed specifically to reflect the circumstances of a given economy sector; however, this is very difficult in practice. The suggested model of a CSR-balanced scorecard is difficult to implement for some organizations, especially those from the SME sector.

27. Four approaches to the CSR concept include: CSR through the compliance of corporate activities with formal rules and regulations as well as with the law; CSR motivated by profit, where social and ecological initiatives should contribute to the financial results of the company; CSR motivated by the commonwealth, where the balance of the goals is reached through the engagement of all stakeholders; and CSR stimulated by a synergy, where the creation of economical, ecological and social value takes place in the situation of the aligned goals of all stakeholders (win–win).

28. For further discussion on 'common good' in the local context, please compare W. Gasparski, 'Ethical Infrastructure for Business with Special Emphasis on Poland: Designing for the Common Good', in H.-C. de Bettingnies and F. Lépineux (eds), *Business, Globalization and the Common Good* (Peter Lang, Bern 2009), pp. 227–50.

29. Given the five main aspects of CSR defined by the EC, including the office, environment, market, local communities and the values, it is characteristic of SMEs that, while they usually show high awareness of CSR-related issues in the areas of office (employee-related) and the market, their general level of awareness fluctuates, depending on the position occupied (owner, manager or a staff member), they reject the idea of having substantial obligations as far as the local communities or the environment is concerned. The owners and managers in those companies would naturally express a better awareness (measured by the percentage of 'do not know' answers). The rejection of the legitimacy of corporate obligations towards the environment and the local communities is expressed by the very high percentage of answers stating that the problem is either not relevant for their business or confirming that they haven't got any implemented CSR procedures in those areas (more than half of the respondents). More interestingly, only about 30 per cent of the

respondents acknowledge that they have implemented the procedures related to the codes of values in organizations, although all the entities the respondents represent belong to the professional association which has the ethical code of conduct implemented. The conclusions come from my discussions and interviews, as well as the survey research done, during the CSR training sessions for tax and accounting advisors organized by the Tax Advisors Forum in Poland. The sessions took place during the course of 2010 and earlier in 2008.

2 Creating Meanings: A Sense-Making Perspective of Corporate Social Responsibility

1. Clearly the uncertainty, being the inherent element of the operational environment, is dealt with both on the individual level and on the corporate level as part of the strategy setting. The process of defining meanings (sense-making) is therefore individual as well as organizational, the latter being obviously embedded in the cultural context of defining common and shared understanding of what the company is. On the strategic organizational level, areas of managing uncertainty include:

   - politics in the context of directing the will of people into certain tasks as the traditional powers of state get dispersed among other actors sharing the authority with them;
   - markets which became people centered and knowledge-focused information systems, with the driving force being the entrepreneur and not the state any more;
   - ideologies explaining human collective behaviours – e.g., free global economy against the nation-state-centered interests;
   - geopolitics – i.e., economic competition between the US and Western economies, Middle East and Africa with its huge potential for transition economies.

   For more details please see Henisz and Story (2003).
2. The method of metaphor use assumes that a metaphor, to have value, needs to transcend the illustrative level and be able to generate knowledge on the examined subject. To do this it needs to fulfill the criterion of isomorphism (structure similarity), as well as the hypothesis of comparison, meaning that if both subjects of the metaphor (primary and secondary) are fairly similar there might be implications that there is a basis for further theoretical relation between them (for details, see Cornelissen, 2003).
3. I reflect on culture here since I treat it as a basic medium for meaning sharing and communication. The fact that a person responsible for building relations with the corporate constituencies points to a different identity than the one which can be read from the formal communications either means that the organization is incapable of building internally a strong and uniting value system, which could ensure the coherence of all verbal expressions by its members, or that the respondent is not

integrated internally strongly enough to incorporate the organizational value system.

4. As to the relation between identity and culture, two options seem viable: one which treats culture as the derivative of identity and one which treats culture as the context of identity expression rather than its variable or determinant (Melewar and Jenkins, 2002).

5. Agency theory has it that managers employed by investors (shareholders) play a stewardship role with respect to the capital and other resources they manage and, as such, serve as agents accountable to the shareholders.

6. 'The *common good* is ... something objectively given that perfects the human being. In essence, directly or indirectly, all true good is common, as the perfection of each individual cannot be dissociated from social perfection. And what perfects human beings and what is damaging to them can be determined. It is what makes human beings truly grow or perfects them. Whatever takes something away from them, be it no more than time, is damaging' (Alvira, 2010). Rafael Alvira elaborates on the notion of common good in his paper 'The Dialectics of Democracy'.

7. The result was confirmed in a study of the largest Polish corporations; further details in Chapter 3.

8. A skew selection model, which looks at organizations and their behavior as if they were living organisms in the environment, fighting to survive, recognizes two currencies which can enhance their chance for survival: income and capital. Whether the company shows benign or malign greed depends on whether it accumulates resources when they are abundant and thus maximizes its chances, but not at the expense of others, or whether it accumulates them when they are scarce, thus depriving others of the possibility. of satisfying immediate survival needs. The extinction of suffering masses as well as their rebellion, may both lead to predation of those malignantly greedy, therefore to avoid it the latter decides to share some of the resources. Philanthropy is therefore an investment and not a cost. Furthermore, enlarging one's physical size, surrounding oneself with others (herd) and competing for a central position far away from the edge of the group, are also biological mechanisms for survival (Hill and Cassill, 2004). For further reading see Frederick (1998).

9. Huang's research was done in the context of public relations; it seems, however, that such a definition of the symmetric communication process can be treated as universal.

10. This is based on the assumption that the owner of the communication process should be acting as an advocate of the interests of her clients.

3 Enterprises and Relations with Stakeholders

1. Questions related to a standard set of stakeholders, including: capital holders and lenders, employees, clients, shareholders, consumer associations, suppliers, local communities, competitors, local public administration and central government representatives.

2. The adjustment of the analysis to include only two clusters does not show any significant differences between the companies. Please compare Appendix, Figure A.2.

3. The sample of 150 enterprises was selected randomly from the list of 2,000 major enterprises published annually by *Rzeczpospolita*. The list is prepared on the basis of financial information submitted by the companies together with their answers to survey questions. The companies invited to submit the data are preselected on the basis of the income threshold reached. For more details about the methodology, please consult www.rzeczpospolita.pl

4. The authors did not define such a category as NGOs explicitly in their original research, however, given that the subject matter of this project are stakeholder relations, it seems obvious that NGOs should be included as building relations with them seems the integral part of organizational dialogue building techniques. It also expresses a participatory character of corporate strategy, i.e. integrative with civil society interpreted as important sphere of expression of public thoughts and sentiments.

5. Local community samples relate to one of the four model strategy organizations each. Those organizations all represent well-recognized brands nationally; therefore, whether their local community is a big city or a small town, the brand awareness is high enough to justify the question about community perceptions of 'who' the company is. Additionally, in two cases, companies were selected that have their registered offices in small towns; due to the size of organization and its dominance on the surrounding market, they play the role of a major employer. In those cases, due to the different, closer bond between local community members and the company, deeper conclusions on company perceptions are enabled.

6. The first and third sets are based on existing research (Cunningham *et al.*, 2009, and Williams, 2008), whereby the categories of words are the result of textual analysis done in accordance with Insch *et al.*, (1997) methodology, which gives specific recommendations for coding and further data analysis.

7. Cunningham *et al.*'s (2009) research followed the same logic of defining corporate identity through identification of certain verbal expressions in mission statements. Interestingly enough, the authors treat sponsorship policies not only as the end result of identity but also as the intermediating construct between identity and corporate image, thus attributing strong sense-making features to sponsorship practices. In this context, sponsorship, and presumably other CSR-related activities, become both the reason and the result of certain projections companies use to 'give sense'. A mission statement is one such type of projection, expressing corporate identity.

8. As these words are translated from Polish, 'economy' includes two different Polish words; one indicates the meaning of 'economy' as the area of science and the other relates to the economy and the economic system of a given area (national, international, global, etc.).

9. The list of variables is presented in the Appendix, Table A.1.

10. To keep the clarity of the diagram, only those tests which returned positive results were included. Some of the variables were used in various contexts, both as dependent and independent variables; for example, perception of the role of stakeholders in the communication strategies (ROLE) explains some of the corporate identity declarations, but the specific perception depends, at the same time, on the perceptions of the role of business (RESPONS).

11. The potential relation of CSR activities to the ability of the company to enhance its financial results is subject to many studies and theories. The main lines of thought to be mentioned include the concept of responsive and strategic CSR, proposed by Porter and Kramer in their *Harvard Business Review* article (2006), and the concept of private and social responsibility (where corporate actions related to social goals do not relate at all to financial results, or at least do not generate positive effects on them (Baron, 2001). Separately, there exists a great deal of research returning positive, negative or neutral results in terms of the relation of CSR with financial results.

12. The database is put together on an annual basis by *Rzeczpospolita* (a high-quality, economics- and law-oriented Polish daily).

13. Labour is usually considered one of the strongest predictors for investment decisions of large companies. Key aspects analyzed are not only unemployment rates (the higher the better), but also issues like labour market sustainability. On top of this, investors also pay attention to the fact that in larger towns, more saturated with investments, their negotiation capacity to gain incentives from local government is much lower, as well as the general level of possible public aid, which is set by the EU and depends on the state of economic development in a given region. From such a perspective, it seems more attractive for investors to consider locations where the benefits related to poorer economic development are higher as opposed to developed cities where it is more difficult to compete for employees and inflation pressure on wages is much higher. Having said that, one should consider that second-tier cities usually become the point of interest for investors once first-tier cities become saturated. It looks like Poland is, at the moment, at the point where the overall foreign direct investment (FDI) figures are decreasing, preference being shown for countries further east and further south (as they offer better incentives and equally skilled but cheaper labour); thus, second-tier cities are becoming FDI targets across the whole CEE region. The process described was slowed down by the 2009 crisis.

14. This is based on the hypothesis of local versus cosmopolitan orientation in creating influence over others, proposed by R. Merton (1982). However, Merton defined his theory using people as the unit of analysis and defining various determinants of getting power of influence over others, one of them being local embeddedness. It remains open to question whether the theory may be fully applicable using enterprises as the unit of analysis, to describe the case of local embeddedness of large enterprises, which

definitely play a dominant role in creating jobs and generating economic growth in smaller cities. I elaborate on this issue more in the corporate case studies, presenting the results of research in local communities.

15. Original categories used in the research are consistent with those used by GUS (Polish Statistical Office) and include more detailed categories, however as some of them returned very small statistical significance in the research, they were cumulated to four main categories. These are: basic education (covering primary school and college below A-Levels), secondary education (covering general colleges with A-levels and the post A-levels), higher education (studies with bachelors or masters degree) and technical education (both primary and secondary specifically related to vocational training).

16. The Minister of Labor and Social Policy implemented the '55+' program, financed by European funds and aimed at activization and employment of the people above 55 years of age. The program is realized through the network of local labor offices.

17. Specifically, in case of Warsaw, the indigenous population is dramatically dominated by newcomers, who usually live in rented flats. As the research is based on CATI of the sample randomly selected from the telephone numbers database, it might be the case that a substantial number of respondents from this group were among those reached by interviewers.

18. However, a first glimpse at the entrepreneurial indexes of Polish towns and cities indicates that, on average, big cities have higher indexes than the small towns and also enjoy far bigger dynamics in the index (Regional Data Bank of Polish Statistical Office, number of entities registered in the national REGON database per 10,000 inhabitants, data for 2002–9). Thus, to evaluate fully whether the sample structure, as presented in this chapter, hides any long-term statistically significant trends, a longitudinal study would need to be performed. Nevertheless, in assessing the entrepreneurial capacities of the cities the index of innovativeness also proves to be helpful. In case of Poland, it seems to be geographically dispersed, pointing towards disadvantaged areas on the East. It also shows a tendency to gravitate towards the bigger cities and seems to be directly related to the accessibility of education. Please compare Salamon, 2004, and Guzik, 2004.

19. It remains the subject of discussion to what extent this growth in the interest 'ordinary' people show in economic and business-related matters is a result of education per se or a result of more direct relations between business and non-business members of society, in which people are simply more exposed to the consequences of various business activities.

20. This might depend on the individual level of income and material status of the person, as well as on their belonging to a certain social class.

21. This hypothesis would need to be tested in further research to determine to what extent it is the type of education which determines our perceptions in this context and to what extent it is the size of the sector a respondent operates in. A different logic in perceptions of business responsibility between people from SMEs and from large enterprises seems to be a fact,

often confirmed during training sessions in CSR. Often, representatives of SMEs perceive their duties towards others as natural and deriving from the fact that we all function together in the limited area and we are all dependent upon each other. They tend to react strongly and negatively to the ideology which links responsible business with the potential of enhancing returns, while people from large enterprises, are more often intent on considering responsibility in the context of a business case, which is understandable to an extent, given that owners of assets have different possibilities in terms of allocating them and are free in their actions, as compared to managers in big companies who act as stewards for assets which do not belong to them.

22. It can be easily imagined that a person who invested savings directly on the stock market (or indirectly through pension funds) does not support easily the reduction of current dividends for the sake of long-term business sustainability or future gains, especially given that people of advancing age focus more on consumption than on further saving. As shareholders expecting returns on their investment, they might perceive issues of business responsibility differently than they would if they were still in managerial posts and involved in current business operations.

23. The recent report, 'The World Giving Index 2010', confirms that giving is correlated more strongly with happiness than with wealth and that the older people get the more inclined they become to share and give. However, locally, Polish people express a higher score in terms of life happiness when they experience a better material situation as well and, indeed, this index seems to be increasing in big cities' populations. Please compare the 'Life Satisfaction' research report (BS/3/2010) done by CBOS (Public Opinion Research Centre).

24. Please see Table A.17 in the Appendix. In the same table, the correlation between the size of the company and the goal of proving that stakeholders' expectations are met is 0.26**; however, since the COMGOAL variable is ranked adversely, the result in this case should be interpreted as showing negative relation – the bigger the company, the less important it is to prove that stakeholders' expectations are met.

25. Examples of such openly voiced petitions include requests from various local stakeholders (e.g., sport clubs, schools, hospitals, foundations, associations) and usually are specific for smaller towns and the companies within the SME sector well embedded and recognized in their communities. Large enterprises would more probably engage voluntarily in various actions based on a well-crafted and predefined policy. Although, in both cases, such an approach can be attributed to a responsive CSR policy, there is an operational difference in the way this is performed. 'Politicization' of the forms of social involvement of the companies seems to be increasing, together with their size, while in the SME sector there is a much bigger probability of ad hoc reactions to immediate community claims, underpinned not so much by the strategic analysis of potential benefits, but often by close and more direct relations with

stakeholders (as compared to large companies), combined with strong embeddedness in local communities.

26. This analysis is based on the quantitative methodology of text analysis, whereby the frequency of use of certain key words is a key measure. The contextual aspect of the use of the words brings a slightly new dimension to the big picture of the corporate process of identity-building.

27. To determine in more detail how synthetic key words may predict the identities of the companies a factor analysis, with OBLIMIN rotation was run separately for the sample of mission statements, reports and other formal corporate communication, and articles and market communications related to the firms' sample. In the case of mission statements only 13 factors, explaining in total 74.76 per cent of the variation, were proven to have an eigenvalue of more than one, and only those were included for further analysis. In the case of reports 12 factors explained 91.23 per cent of the variation and, based on the scree test, only eight were included for further analysis. In the case of articles 12 factors explained 82.41 per cent of the variation and eight were included for further analysis (please see Appendix, Tables and Figures A.4–A.6).

28. The same exercise was done on the sample of press articles related to the 150 biggest companies operating in Poland, returning eight factors which explain 82.41 per cent of the variation. However, before these factors are interpreted, some theoretical elaboration is needed. The first question is: what is it that the authors of those articles are saying and is it justifiable to assume that, as the same key words are being used and tested, they also convey the same message – that is, they give a mirror reflection of the sense-making processes to what the companies were saying in their communication? Given that, from the linguistic point of view, those two groups will probably differ in the pragmatic context of the key words used, it seems quite logical to examine the press articles in the context of the purpose of this type of communication. While organizations communicate explicitly for the purpose of conveying a specific type of vision of themselves – in order to create a certain impression or view about themselves in the market and, thus, appear emotionally engaged in relation to the message they create – analysts and professional business journalists serve to provide emotionally disengaged, accurate and objective analysis of the facts. Therefore, from the perspective of contemporary contextualism, the same set of key words used by the companies and by the analysts might have very different meanings, given that they are constructed not only in different contexts, but also with different aims.

29. This may also be looked at from the perspective of the analytical approach of the respondent, where, in the first case, a generic question about the scale of business responsibility calls upon the philosophical statements they internalize, while the question of the role stakeholders might play requires more specific insight into operational realities. Since cases of broad responsibility, coupled with the stakeholders treated as partners and co-designers of strategies, are not complemented by any stakeholder

prioritization exercise, one might say that companies with generic and philosophical attitudes have less capacity to transform them into strict operational activities, while the others remain more pragmatic.

30. Instead of analyzing the elements of theoretical strategies from the perspective of the process, I choose to call them 'strategic figures' as this notion seems to present the sense-making character of relation strategies much better than the 'process', which indicates almost a mechanistic approach. There is a paradox to be dealt with embedded in the description of the communication strategies model because of the fact that aspects such as defining KPI for the communication manager or defining the goal of the communication process or locating the decision-making process in the organizations derive purely from the way in which a firm is being organized – that is, from basic management functions. In contrast to this, definition of the role of stakeholders inevitably involves making certain assumptions based on situational analysis and, as such, is a sense-making activity, which can later become the foundation for the planning function. In a sense, the role of stakeholders by definition precedes the other three features of the strategies. For this reason, it does not seem justified to treat the role of stakeholders and the other three features under one common denominator, as they fundamentally differ in their nature. Instead, the notion of 'strategic figures' allows a much better indication of the descriptive role they play in defining the strategies, not reducing them merely to the mechanical aspect of organizing and defining the processes.

31. The direction of causality remains one of the key questions in this research; however, given the impossibility of verifying it statistically, certain conceptual assumptions were made, mostly based on managerial experience and participant observation results. In this particular case it was assumed that the mission statement would be the dependent variable. The logic of this assumption is based on the fact that, although it is debatable to what extent the corporate identity is formed prior to corporate strategies and determines them and to what extent it forms itself as the result of certain strategies, the mission statement which is used as the corporate identity proxy in this research is undoubtedly the derivative of the management decision-making process. In this context, corporate identity becomes an abstract and virtual concept which is projected by the company into its environment and gains real dimensions in the shape of mission statements as perceived by corporate informants.

32. The difference between donations and sponsorship resides in the scale and type of corporate investment. While donations relate to one-off investment in the building of a public utility or enhancing local infrastructure (roads, parks, etc.) and are likely to be part of ongoing cooperation between the company and public administration, sponsorship relates typically to local cooperation between the company and sport clubs, schools, hospitals, etc. The latter scenario is often given as an example of CSR activities by those organizations questioned.

33. The analysis of messages embedded in the texts (although it resembles simplistic quantitative research, as key words sets are used and frequencies calculated) is determined by assumptions deeply grounded in language studies. Following the ideas of contextualism, it is admitted that the meaning of the word changes according to the context in which it is used. The word obviously gains the meaning in the context of a whole sentence, but it is also conditioned by its social (i.e., pragmatic) context. So it is not only the formal connection between the notions (syntactic) or formal rules, with their attributed meanings (semantics), but also it is why the text is being written or the speech spoken and under what conditions. Following this logic, it needs to be concluded that if two different groups are compared against the same key word criteria and the message which emerges from this comparison is different, then, obviously, the goal of the speech or text was different as well. While the theoretical model of the text analysis in this part of the research assumed the perfect alignment of the syntactic and semantic being, the adaptation of the contextual perspective of language studies suggests that this is hardly ever the case. The contextual approach makes speech acts responsible for carrying meaningful contents, as opposed to words and the rules of their connections, seen as meaning holders by the line of thought called 'literalism'. This way, the background knowledge of the researcher is utilized in analysis in order to understand the full meaning of the message in common situations where the literal meaning diverges from the intentions of those constructing the message. Moreover, Recanati (2004) argues that the conflict between literal conditions and the speaker's meaning is illusionary, as 'what is said is nothing but an aspect of speaker's meaning', thus opening the gate for the sense-making analysis acknowledging the non-linear character of the stories, which, in their complexity, are generated by multiple authors in multiple conditions.

34. Statistically significant relations between age, gender and education of the respondent and their perception of the business responsibility appeared in Krakow sample only (the sample of 144 respondents randomly selected from the community). The other three local samples, as well as the overall sample of 564 respondents, did not return any significant results. Equally, perceptions of corporate mission were dependent on age or gender or education in some of the local communities, but no coherent pattern of such dependency could be defined in the total sample of local community respondents.

35. The locally embedded people are very emotionally tied to their communities, where they were usually born and educated and they build their personal careers on the basis of private contacts and deep understanding of local specifics and the problems of the local society. They get to know as many people as they can, in order to expand their network of contacts, and they do it consciously with the purpose of facilitating their own careers. The influence they exercise comes not from professional knowledge or expertise, but from 'whom they know' and it relates to the

fact that they have a deep understanding of local issues as compared to cosmopolitans, whose prized expertise and professional skills is of a solely generic nature. Cosmopolitans, therefore, might seem more educated and skilled technocratically, but they often lack the 'local touch' in their conduct.

36. The measurement of growth would be an important methodological issue in this context. For the sake of this research, the size of the company was measured by its number of employees; however, from the perspective of local and cosmopolitan orientation, the internationalization of operations seems a more proper measure.

37. Locally oriented people read less and they usually concentrate on the local press or one which gives a lot of local information. They also tend to look for an emotionally embedded way of conveying messages, while cosmopolitans prefer the wide scale of information, touching upon international issues and diverse aspects of life, while searching for unemotional, fact-focusing analytics and commentators.

38. This is not so much a question of the differences of perceptional characteristics in men and women (although they can be defined in research on effectiveness of marketing and promotional practices), but rather a question as to what extent gender remains an explanatory variable for social phenomena, including role definitions.

39. This result should be interpreted in the context of the local community of a given company rather than in the context of a geographical location. First, the test run for the whole sample did not return any significant result, which would allow the conclusion that the perception of mission statements depends on demographic variables. Second, and more importantly, respondents were questioned about the perception of mission statements in the context of the specific company; hence, it is possible to hypothesize that the intermediating reason for the polarization of those perceptions between men and women, and people with various degrees of education, may reside in the way the company appeals to its stakeholders, crafting a message which might be unintentionally more appealing for certain groups. To verify whether the mission perceptions are company environment-embedded or whether there is a pattern of demographic dependence across the country requires further research.

40. Please note that, in the case of the results shown in Tables A.24–A.27, MISSION (showing three possible values: becoming a leader, gaining trust or solving social problems) is coded adversely (1 – the most important, 3 – the less important); hence, coefficients with '–' in fact mean a positive correlation.

41. Organizations selected for the qualitative part of the research include organizations with number of employees exceeding 250, all declaring dialogue strategy in contacts with stakeholders, operating in the travel and hotel sector ('O'), glass production ('KHS'), 'OSM' and as a developer and constructor ('B').

42. In the case of this research, data triangulation was done by repeated coding of the texts – first, when key word frequencies were calculated and, second, accounting for the variety of contexts in which key words were used. The result of the second coding was the emergence of multiple identities as a consequence of an overlap of generic identities. Furthermore, the issue questions defined in the case studies description were defined on the basis of the same dataset which was used for the quantitative part of the research. Both these aspects make my approach slightly different to the case study methodology as proposed by R. Stake; after all, it is not a standard case study but an attempt to construct a narrative account of what seems to be a non-linear and concurrent experience of various organizational identities, whose multiple characters derive from an overlap of stories accounted by various stakeholders (insiders, local communities, press).

43. A good way to do this is to present the case to a panel of other researchers and to participate in various seminars and think tanks prior to preparing the final report.

44. A simplistic way of looking into this is to assume that, since two researchers never present exactly the same point of view, every time we employ multiple researchers theory triangulation takes place.

45. This is disputable as the data in this particular case is not very coherent. The fact is that the market-induced message does not reflect identity aspects directly, thus not allowing immediate conclusions to be drawn on its perception, but talks a lot about the company's relational problems. Hence, it is a case of 'unperceived' identity with neglected relational aspects, which backfires when there is an economic problem.

46. In February 2009 the application for bankruptcy filed by the company was formally reported in the press. This looks like a typical case of a victim of the economic crisis and foreign currency options, with the company first attempting to save the situation by implementing profound cost-cutting measures, including redundancies of more than 1,500 people, before it, finally, was led to bankruptcy. The impact of this, as always in the case of big companies embedded in their regions, was to stimulate a backlash effect in the local community. While it is not surprising that the company was criticized by employees who lost jobs and by the local administration, which needs to cope with a sudden rise in unemployment, the true lesson from this story relates to the long-term effects of negligence with regard to stakeholder dialogue (which, in this case, did not exist at all).

47. 'OSM' operates as a cooperative; therefore, by definition, its goals should be defined through the fulfillment of interests of individual constituencies.

48. The content analysis was run twice independently. First, it was done for texts related specifically to a particular company in 'B' group, but since this part returned ambiguous results, probably due to the fact that the company is part of the big capital group which operates under the same brand name, a second analysis was done on text relating to the

whole group. Such a procedure was elected for two reasons: while the formal communication of the company is designed by individual entities in the group and was made available on the individual websites, rather than on the site of the group, market perceptions of the company seem to be strongly related to brand awareness without distinguishing between individual entities.

49. For a more detailed description, see 'Local communities: the portrait'.

50. ROLE stands for the perception of the stakeholders' role and RESPONS stands for the perception of the scale of business responsibility towards various constituencies.

51. I refer to D. Boje's terminology of storytelling and antenarratives. Although I am using the framework of a case study to organize the discourse about the four companies analyzed in more detail and to order the presentation of conclusions, the conclusions themselves are speculative, dependent on the context in which they appear; hence, what is presented is not a coherent case study, giving final conclusions, but a free-flowing story. Second, the four stories presented are, in fact, pictures composed of various separate discourses – that is, two discourses of the company embedded in their mission statements and formal reports and a discourse of the market analysts and commentators, as presented in press articles, which are stories by themselves. We, thus, have two important conditions of an antenarrative: a speculative bet and a multiplicity of voices. Although the research presented in this book combines qualitative and quantitative methods and the storytelling aspect of it is based on text analyses backed by frequency of words calculation, which in fact makes it also a quantitative method, the theoretical framework defining the use of text analysis is deeply embedded in the definition of a story by Ricoeur: 'a story describes ... experiences done or undergone by a certain number of people, real or imaginary. These people are presented either in situations that change or as reacting to such change. In turn these changes reveal hidden aspects of the situation ... and engender a new predicament which calls for thought' (Ricoeur, 1984, after Boje, 2001).

52. The strongest relations exist between the importance of local administration and the frequency of relations with central government (0.51), importance of capital lenders and frequency of relations with central government (0.42), importance of local communities and frequency of relations with consumer associations (0.46) and importance of local administration and frequencies of relations with local communities (0.44).

53. Please note that the variables MISSION and MNGOBJ are coded adversely, therefore a positive coefficient means a negative correlation.

References

Alvesson, M. and Robertson, M. (2006) 'The best and the brightest: the construction, significance and effects of elite identities in consulting firms', *Organization*, 13, pp. 195–224.

Alvira, R. (2010) 'The dialectics of democracy: common-particular and public-private', in B. Fryzel and P. H. Dembinski (eds), *The Role of Large Enterprises in Democracy and Society*, Basingstoke: Palgrave Macmillan.

Amalric, F. and Hauser, J. (2004) *Micro-economic Foundations of Corporate Responsibility Activities*, CCRS University of Zurich working papers, no. 02/04.

Armstrong, R. W., Williams, R. J. and Barrett, J. D. (2004) 'The impact of banality, risky shift and escalating commitment on ethical decision making', *Journal of Business Ethics*, 53, pp. 365–70.

Axin, C. N., Blair, M. E., Thach, S. and Heorhiadi, A. (2004) 'Comparing ethical ideologies across cultures', *Journal of Business Ethics*, 54, pp. 103–19.

Balmer, J. M. T. (1998) 'Corporate identity and the advent of corporate marketing', *Journal of Marketing Management*, 14, pp. 63–96.

Balmer, J. M. T. (2001) 'Corporate identity, corporate branding and corporate marketing: seeing through the fog', *European Journal of Marketing*, 35, pp. 248–92.

Balmer, J. M. T. and Greyser, S. A. (2002) 'Managing the multiple identities of the organization', *California Management Review*, 44, pp. 72–86.

Balmer, J. M. T. and Greyser, S. A. (2003) *Revealing the Corporation: Perspectives on Identity, Image, Reputation, Corporate Branding and Corporate-Level Marketing*, London: Routledge.

Balmer, J. and Soenen, G. (1998) 'A new approach to corporate identity management', *International Centre for Corporate Identity Studies, Working Paper*, 1998/5.

Balmer, J. M. T. and Soenen, G. B. (1999) 'The acid test of corporate identity management', *Journal of Marketing Management*, 15, pp. 69–92.

Baron, D. (2001) 'Private politics, corporate social responsibility and integrated strategy', *Journal of Economics and Management Strategy*, 10, pp. 7–45.

Bart, C. K. (2001) 'Exploring the application of mission statements on the World Wide Web', *Internet Research*, 11(4), pp. 360–9.

Bart, C. K., Bontis, N. and Taggar, S. (2001) 'A model of the impact of mission statements on firm performance', *Management Decision*, 39(1), pp. 19–35.

Bass, B. and Rosenstein, E. (2005) 'Integration of industrial democracy and participative management: US and European perspectives', in B. King, S. Streufert and F. Fiedler (eds), *Managerial Control and Organizational Democracy*, Washington, DC: Winstons & Sons, pp. 1–17.

Basu, K. and Palazzo, G. (2008) 'Corporate social responsibility: a process model of sensemaking', *Academy of Management Review*, 33(1), pp. 122–36.

Bazerman, M. and Schoorman, D. (1983) 'A limited rationality model of interlocking directorates', *Academy of Management Review*, 8(2), pp. 206–71.

Beatty, R. and Zajac, E. (1994) 'Managerial incentives, monitoring and risk bearing: a study of executive compensation, ownership and board structures in initial public offerings', *Administrative Science Quarterly*, 39(2).

Bergman, J. (2001) 'Darwin's influence on ruthless laissez-faire capitalism', Impact, March, at www.icr.org/article/darwins-influence-ruthless-laissez-faire-capitalis/

Berle, A. and Means, G. (1932) *The Modern Corporation and Private Property*, New York: Macmillan.

Bessire, D. (2005) 'La quête de transparance au risque de l'anti-humanisme', *Finance and Common Good*, 22 (Summer 2005), pp. 54–62.

Bigley, G. and Wiersema, F. (2002) 'New CEOs and corporate strategic refocusing: how experience as heir apparent influences the use of power', *Administrative Science Quarterly*, 47(4), pp. 707–27.

Boje, D. (2001) *Narrative Methods for Organizational & Communication Research*, London: Sage.

Bolesta-Kukułka, K. (2003) *Decyzje menedżerskie*, Warsaw: Polskie Wydawnictwo Ekonomiczne.

Brandt, R. (2001) 'Ethical relativism', in P. L. Moser and T. L. Carson (eds), *Moral Relativism: A Reader*, Oxford: Oxford University Press.

Brass, D. (1984) 'Being in the right place: a structural analysis of individual influence in an organization', *Administrative Science Quarterly*, 29, pp. 519–39.

Brickson, S. (2005) 'Organizational identity orientation: forging a link between organizational identity and organization's relations with stakeholders, *Administrative Science Quarterly*, 50(4), pp. 576–609.

Brooke, M. (1983) 'Organizational democracy and the multi-national corporation', in C. Crouch and F. Heller (eds), *Organizational Democracy and Political Processes*, New York: John Wiley & Sons, pp. 33–47.

Buck, T., Filatotchev, I. and Wright, M. (1998) 'Agents, stakeholders, and corporate governance in Russian firms', *Journal of Management Studies*, 35, pp. 81–104.

Bunge, M. (1989) *Treatise in Basic Philosophy, vol. 8. Ethics: The Good and the Right*, Dordrecht: D. Reidel.

Burckhardt, M. and Brass, D. (1990), 'Changing patterns or patterns of change: the effects of the change in technology on social network structure and power', *Administrative Science Quarterly*, 35, pp. 104–27.

Business Week (2000) *Business Week* online, 11 September.

Butrynowski, A. (2003) 'Misja firmy jako deklaracja etyczna', in C. Sułkowski (ed.), *Gospodarka i społeczeństwo – funkcjonowanie i rozwój*, Zapol: Szczecin.

Carroll, A. B. (1979) 'A three dimensional conceptual model of corporate social performance', *Academy of Management Review*, 4, pp. 497–505.

Carroll, A. B. (1991) 'The pyramid of corporate social responsibility: toward the moral management of organizational stakeholders', *Business Horizons*, July–August 1991, pp. 39–48.

Carroll, W. K. (2004) *Corporate Power in a Globalizing World*, Toronto: Oxford University Press.

Carpenter, M. A. and Westphal, J. D. (2001) 'The strategic context of external network ties: examining the impact of director appointments on board involvement in strategic decision-making', *Academy of Management Journal*, 44, pp. 639–60.

Carson, T. L. and Moser, P. L. (2001) 'Introduction', in P. L. Moser and T. L. Carson (eds), *Moral Relativism: A Reader*, Oxford: Oxford University Press.

Charan, R. and Freeman, R. E. (1979) 'Stakeholder negotiations: building bridges with corporate consituents', *Management Review*, November 1979, pp. 8–13.

Christensen, L. T. and Cheney, G. (1994) 'Articulating identity in an organizational age', in S. A. Deetz (ed.), *Communication Yearbook*, vol. 17, Thousand Oaks, CA: Sage.

Clarkson, M. B. E. (1995) 'A stakeholder framework for analysing and evaluating corporate social performance', *Academy of Management Review*, 20(1), pp. 92–117.

Clegg, S. (1983) 'Organizational democracy, power and participation', in C. Crouch and F. Heller (eds), *Organizational Democracy and Political Processes*, New York, NY: John Wiley & Sons, pp. 48–9.

Cloke, K. and Goldsmith J. (2002) *The End of Management and the Rise of Organizational Democracy*, San Francisco, CA: John Wiley & Sons.

Coles, J. W., McWilliams, V. B. and Sen, N. (2001) 'An examination of the relationship of governance mechanisms to performance', *Journal of Management*, 27 (1), pp. 23–50.

Corley, K. G. and Gioia, D. A. (2004) 'Identity ambiguity and change in the wake of a corporate spin-off', Administrative Science Quarterly, 49(2), pp. 173–208.

Corley, K., Harquail, C., Pratt, M., Glynn, M., Fiol, C. and Hatch, M. (2006) 'Guiding organizational identity through aged adolescence', *Journal of Management Inquiry*, 15, pp. 85–99.

Cornelissen, J. P. (2002) 'On the "organizational identity" metaphor', *British Journal of Management*, 13(3), pp. 259–68.

Cornelissen, J. P. (2003) 'Metaphor as a method in the domain of marketing', *Psychology & Marketing*, 20(3), pp. 209–25.

Cornelissen, J. P. (2005) 'Beyond compare: metaphor in organization theory', *Academy of Management Review*, 30(4), pp. 751–64.

Cornelissen, J. P. (2006) 'Metaphor and the dynamics of knowledge in organization theory: a case study of the organizational identity metaphor', *Journal of Management Studies*, 43(4).

Cornelissen, J. P. and Elving, W. J. L. (2003), 'Managing corporate identity: an integrative framework of dimensions and determinants', *Corporate Communications: An International Journal*, 8(2), pp. 114–20.

Cornelissen, J. P., Haslam, S. A. and Balmer, J. M. T. (2007) 'Social identity, organizational identity and corporate identity: towards an integrated understanding of processes, patternings and products, *British Journal of Management*, 18, pp. s1–s16.

Cunningham, S. Cornwell, T. B. and Coote, L. V. (2009) 'Expressing identity and shaping image: the relationship between corporate mission and corporate sponsorship', *Journal of Sport Management*, 23, pp. 65–86.

Czarniawska, B. (1997) *Narrating the Organization: Dramas of Institutional Identity*, Chicago, IL: University of Chicago Press.

Czarniawska-Joerges, B. and Jacobsson, B. (1995) 'Political organizations and commedia dell'arte', *Organization Studies*, 16(3), pp. 375–94.

Dahl, R. (1957) 'The concept of power', *Behavioural Science*, 2, pp. 201–15.

Davies, B. and Harre, R. (1991) 'Positioning: the discursive production of selves', *Journal for the Theory of Social Behaviour*, 20(1), pp. 46–63.

De George, R. T. (1993) *Competing with Integrity in International Business*, Oxford/New York: Oxford University Press, pp. 45–56.

Dembinski, P. H. (2010) 'Economic power and social responsibility of very big enterprises: facts and challenges', in B. Fryzel and P. H. Dembinski (eds), *The Role of Large Enterprises in Democracy and Society*, Basingstoke: Palgrave Macmillan.

Domhoff, W. (1998) *Who Rules America? Power and Politics in the Year 2000*, Mountain View, CA: Mayfield.

Donaldson, T. (1989) *The Ethics of International Business*, Oxford/New York: Oxford University Press, pp. 181–6.

Donaldson, T. and Preston, L. (1995) 'The stakeholder theory of the corporation: concepts, evidence and implications', *Academy of Management Review*, 20(1), pp. 65–91.

Dukerich, J. M., Golden, B. R. and Shortell, S. M. (2002) 'Beauty is in the eye of the beholder: the impact of organizational identification, identity, and image on the cooperative behaviors of physicians', *Administrative Science Quarterly*, 47, pp. 507–33.

Dunham, L., Freeman, R. E. and Liedtka, J. (2006) 'Enhancing stakeholder practice: a particularized exploration of community', *Business Ethics Quarterly*, 16(1), pp. 23–42.

Durkheim, E. (1982) *The Rules of Sociological Method*, London: Macmillan.

Dutton, J. E. and Dukerich, J. M. (1991) 'Keeping an eye on the mirror: image and identity in organizational adaptation', *Academy of Management Journal*, 34, pp. 517–54.

Dutton, J. E., Dukerich, J. M. and Harquail, C. V. (1994) 'Organizational images and member identification', *Administrative Science Quarterly*, 39, pp. 239–63.

Earle, J., Kucsera, C. and Telegdy, A.(2005) 'Ownership concentration and corporate performance on the Budapest stock exchange: do too many cooks spoil the goulash?', *Corporate Governance*, 2(13).

Elsbach, K. D. (1999) 'An expanded model of organizational identification', in B. M. Staw and R. I. Sutton (eds), *Research in Organizational Behavior*, 21, pp. 163–200.

Elsbach, K. D. and R. D. Kramer (1996) 'Members' responses to organizational identity threats: encountering and countering the Business Week rankings', *Administrative Science Quarterly*, 41, pp. 442–76.

Enz, C. (1988) 'The role of value congruity in intraorganizational power', *Administrative Science Quarterly*, 33(2), pp. 284–304.

Epstein, E. M. (1973) 'Dimensions of corporate power', *California Management Review*, 16(2).

Falkenberg, A. W. (2004) 'When in Rome ... moral maturity and ethics for international economic organizations', *Journal of Business Ethics*, 54, pp. 17–32.

Fama, E. (1980) 'Agency problem and the theory of the firm', *Journal of Political Economy*, 88, pp. 288–306.

Fama, E. and Jensen, M. (1983) 'The separation of ownership and control', *Journal of Law and Economics*, 26, pp. 301–25.

Farnsworth, K. (2004) *Corporate Power and Social Policy in a Global Economy*, London: Policy Press.

Feddersen, T. and Gilligan, T. (2001) 'Saints and markets: activists and the supply of credence goods', *Journal of Economics and Management Strategy*, 10, pp. 149–71.

Filatotchev, I., Kapelyushnikov, R., Dyomina, N. and Aukutsionek, S. (2001) 'The effects of ownership concentration on investment and performance in privatized firms in Russia', *Managerial & Decision Economics*, 22(6), pp. 299–313.

Forsyth, D. R. (1980) 'A taxonomy of ethical ideologies', *Journal of Personality and Social Psychology*, 39, pp. 175–84.

Foucault, M. (1997) *Il faut défendre la société: Cours au Collège de France (1975–76)*, ed. by M. Bertani and A. Fontana, Paris: Gallimard, Seuil.

Frederick, W. C. (1998) 'Creatures, corporations, communities, chaos, complexity', *Business and Society*, 37, pp. 358–89.

Freeman, R. E. (1984) *Strategic Management: A Stakeholder Approach*, Boston, MA: Pitman.

Freeman, R. E. (1994) 'The politics of stakeholder theory: some future directions', *Business Ethics Quarterly*, 4, pp. 409–21.

Frooman, J. (1999) 'Stakeholder influence strategies', *Academy of Management Review*, 24(2), pp. 191–205.

Fryzel, B. (2005) 'Governance of corporate power networks', *Observatoire de la Finance*, 23.

Fryzel, B. (2009) 'Globalization', in C. Wankel (ed.), *Encyclopedia of Business in Today's World*, Thousand Oaks, CA: Sage.

Fukuyama, F. (2000) *Wielki Wstrząs: Natura ludzka a odbudowa porządku społecznego*, Warsaw: Politeja.

Fulop, G., Hisrich, R. D. and Szegedi, K. (2000) 'Business ethics and social responsibility in transition economies', *Journal of Management Development*, 19(1), pp. 5–31.

Gabrielsson, J. and Huse, M. (2004) 'Context, behavior and evolution: challenges in research on boards and governance', *International Studies of Management and Organization*, 34(2), pp. 11–36.

Galaskiewicz, J. (1985) 'Interorganizational relations', *Annual Review of Sociology*, Palo Alto, CA: Annual Reviews, 11, pp. 281–304.

Galbraith, J. K. (1985) *The Anatomy of Power*, London: Corgi.

Gasparski, W. (2009), 'Ethical Infrastructure of Business with Special Emphasis on Poland: designing for the common good', in H.-C. de Bettingnies and F. Lépineux (eds), *Business, Globalization and the Common Good*, Bern, Peter Lang.

Gioia, D. A. (1998) 'From individual to organizational identity', in D. Whetten and P. Godfrey (eds), *Identity in Organizations: Building Theory Through Conversations*, Thousands Oaks, CA: Sage.

Gioia, D. A. and Thomas, J. B. (1996) 'Identity, image and issue interpretation: sensemaking during strategic change in academia', *Administrative Science Quarterly*, 41, pp. 370–403.

Gioia, D. A., Schultz, M. and Corley, K. G. (2000) 'Organizational identity, image and adaptive instability', *Academy of Management Review*, 25,
pp. 63–81.

Gioia, D. A., Schultz, M. and Corley, K. G. (2002) 'On celebrating the
organizational identity metaphor: a rejoinder to Cornelissen', *British Journal
of Management*, 13, pp. 269–75.

Goffman, E. (1981) *Forms of Talk*, Oxford: Basil Blackwell.

Golden, B. and Zajac, E. (2001) 'When will boards influence strategy?
Inclination x power = strategic change, *Strategic Management Journal*, 22(12),
pp. 1087–111.

Gourevitch, P. A. and Shinn, J. J. (2005) *Political Power and Corporate Control:
The New Global Politics of Corporate Governance*, Princeton, NJ: Princeton
University Press.

Gowri, A. (2004) 'When responsibility can't do it', *Journal of Business Ethics*,
54, pp. 33–50.

Granovetter, M. (1985) 'Economic action and social structure: the problem of
embeddedness', *American Journal of Sociology*, 91, pp. 481–510.

Gray, E. R. and Balmer, J. M. T. (1998) 'Managing corporate image and corporate reputation', *Long Range Planning*, 31, pp. 695–702.

Guzik, R. (2004) 'Przestrzenne zróznicowanie potencjału innowacyjnego w
Polsce', in Górzański, M. and Woodward, R. (eds), *Innowacyjność polskiej
gospodarki*, Zeszyty Innowacyjne 2 CASE.

Hart, S. (1997) 'A natural resource-based view of the firm', *Academy of
Management Review*, 20(4), pp. 986–1014.

Haslam, A. S., Postmes, T. and Ellemers, N. (2003) 'More than a metaphor:
organizational identity makes organizational life possible', *British Journal of
Management*, 14, pp. 357–69.

Hatch, M. J. and Schultz, M. (2001) 'Are the strategic stars aligned for your
corporate brand?', *Harvard Business Review*, pp. 128–35.

Hatch, M. J. and Schultz, M. (2002) 'The dynamics of organizational identity',
Human Relations, 55, pp. 989–1018.

Hathaway, L. (2010) 'Profits, but no jobs', *The Economist*, 8 July.

He, H. W. and Balmer, J. M. T. (2007) 'Perceived corporate identity/strategy dis-
sonance: triggers and managerial responses', *Journal of General Management*,
33(1), pp. 71–91.

Henisz, W. and Story, J. (2003) 'Corporate risk assessment and business strategy', in P. Cornelius and B. Kogut (eds), *Corporate Governance and Capital
Flows in a Global Economy*, New York, NY: Oxford University Press.

Herman, E. S. (1981) *Corporate Control, Corporate Power*, New York, NY:
Cambridge University Press, pp. 194–230.

Hertz, N. (2001a) www.thirdworldtraveler.com/Global_Economy/Silent_
Takeover_Part2.html.

Hertz, N. (2001b) www.thirdworldtraveler.com/Global_Economy/Silent_
Takeover_Part3.html.

Hertz, N. (2002) *The Silent Takeover, Global Capitalism and the Death of
Democracy*, London: Arrow Books.

Herzberg, F. (1959) *The Motivation to Work*, New York, NY: John Wiley & Sons.

Hickson, D. and McCullogh, A. (1980) 'Power in organizations', in G. Salaman and K. Thompson (eds), *Control and Ideology in Organizations*, Cambridge, MA: MIT Press, pp. 27–56.

Hilferding, R. (1981) *Finance Capital*, London: Routledge & Kegan Paul.

Hill, R. P. and Cassill, D. L. (2004) 'The naturological view of the corporation and its social responsibility: an extension of the Frederick model of corporation–community relationships', *Business and Society Review*, 109(3), pp. 281–96.

Hillman, A. and Keim, G. (2001) 'Shareholder value, stakeholder management and social issues: what's the bottom line?', *Strategic Management Journal*, 22(2), pp. 125–39.

Hindess, B. (1999) *Filozofowie władzy: Od Hobbesa do Foucaulta*, Warsaw: PWN.

Huang, Y. (2004) 'Is symmetrical communication ethical and effective?', *Journal of Business Ethics*, 53, pp. 333–52.

Hughes, P. and Demetrious, K. (2006) 'Engaging with stakeholders or constructing them?', *Journal of Corporate Citizenship*, Autumn 2006(2), pp. 93–101.

Huse, M. and Rindova, V. (2001) 'Stakeholders' expectation to boards of directors: the case of subsidiary boards', *Journal of Management and Governance*, 5, pp. 153–78.

Igalens, J. and Gond, J. P. (2005) 'Measuring corporate social performance in France: a critical and empirical analysis of ARESE data', *Journal of Business Ethics*, 56, pp. 131–48.

Industrial Democracy in Europe (IDE) (1981) International Research Group, Oxford: Clarendon Press.

Industrial Democracy in Europe Revisited (1993) Oxford: Oxford University Press.

Insch, G. S., Moore, J. E. and Murphy, L. D. (1997) 'Content analysis in leadership research: examples, procedures and suggestions for future use', *The Leadership Quarterly*, 8(1), pp. 1–25.

Jensen, E. C. (1989) 'Eclipse of the public corporation', *Harvard Business Review*, 67.

Jones, M. T., (2005) 'The transnational corporation, corporate social responsibility and the "outsourcing" debate', *The Journal of American Academy of Business*, 2 November, Cambridge.

Jones, T. and Wicks, A. (1999) 'Convergent stakeholder theory', *Academy of Management Review*, 24(2) , pp. 206–21.

Kemelgor, B. (1976) 'Power and the power process: linkage concepts', *Academy of Management Review*, 1(4).

Klein, G., Moon, B. and Hoffman R. F. (2006a) 'Making sense of sensemaking I: alternative perspectives', *IEEE Intelligent Systems*, 21(4).

Klein, G., Moon, B. and Hoffman R. F. (2006b) 'Making sense of sensemaking II: a macrocognitive model', *IEEE Intelligent Systems*, 21(5).

Klose, A. (1999) *Społeczna odpowiedzialność dzisiaj*, Krakow: Wydawnictwo Naukowe PAT.

Konecki, K. (2002) 'Tożsamość organizacyjna', in K. Konecki and P. Tonera (eds), *Szkice z socjologii zarządzania*, Lodz: Uniwersytetu Łódzkiego.

Kostera, M. (1996) *Postmodernizm w zarządzaniu*, Warsaw: PWE.

KPMG (2009) *Corporate and Indirect Tax Rate Survey*, KMPG.

Krackhardt, D. (1990) 'Assessing the political landscape: structure, cognition and power in organizations', *Administrative Science Quarterly*, 35(2), pp. 342–69.

Kula, V. (2005) 'The impact of the roles, structure and process of boards on firm performance: evidence from Turkey', *Corporate Governance*, 13(2).

Lee, M. Y., Fairhurst, A. and Wesley, S. (2009) 'Corporate social responsibility: a review of the top 100 US retailers', *Corporate Reputation Review*, 12(2), pp. 140–58.

Lorenzi, P. (2004) 'Managing for the common good: prosocial leadership', *Organizational Dynamics*, 33(3), pp. 282–91.

Lukes, S. (1974) *Power: A Radical View*, New York, NY: Macmillan.

Marcuse, H. (1991) *One-dimensional Man: Studies in the Ideology of Advanced Industrial Society*, London: Routledge.

Margolis, J. and Walsh, J. (2001) *People and Profits? The Search for a Link Between a Company's Social and Financial Performance*, Mahwah, NJ: Lawrence Erlbaum Associates.

Martin, S. and Parker, D. (1999) *The Impact of Privatisation: Ownership and Corporate Performance in the UK*, New York, NY: Routledge.

McDonald, G. and Nijhof, A. (1999) 'Beyond codes of ethics: an integrated framework for stimulating morally responsible behavior in organizations', *Leadership & Organization Development Journal*, 20(3), pp. 133–46.

McGregor, D. (2006) *The Human Side of Enterprise*, New York, NY: McGraw-Hill.

McWilliams, A. and Siegel, D. (2001) 'Corporate social responsibility: a theory of the firm perspective', *Academy of Management Review*, 26(1), pp. 117–27.

McWilliams, A. and Siegel, D. (2002) 'Additional reflections on the strategic implications of corporate social responsibility', *Academy of Management Review*, 27(1), pp. 15–16.

McWilliams, A., Van Fleet, D. D. and Cory, K. (2002) 'Raising rivals' costs: an application of resource-based theory', *Journal of Management Studies*, 39(5), pp. 707–23.

Melewar, T. C. and Jenkins, E. (2002) 'Defining the corporate identity construct', *Corporate Reputation Review*, 5(1), pp. 76–90.

Melich, A. (2010) 'European transparency initiative: monitoring Brussels lobbying', in B. Fryzel and P. H. Dembinski (eds), *The Role of Large Enterprises in Democracy and Society*, Basingstoke: Palgrave Macmillan.

Merton, R (1968) *Social Theory and Social Structure*, New York, NY: Free Press.

Mills, C. (1961) *Elita władzy*, Warsaw: Książka i Wiedza.

Mintzberg, H. (1983) *Power In and Around Organizations*, Englewood Cliffs, NJ: Prentice-Hall.

Miroński, J. (2000) *Władza i polityka w przedsiębiorstwie*, Warsaw: Difin.

Mizruchi, M. (2004) 'Berle and Means revisited: the governance and power of large US corporations', *Theory and Society*, 33, pp. 579–617.

Mizruchi, M. and Schwartz, M. (1987) (eds) *Intercorporate Relations: The Structural Analysis of Business*, Cambridge and New York: Cambridge University Press.

Morck, R., Shleifer, A. and Vishny, R. (1988) 'Management ownership and market evaluation', *Journal of Financial Economics*, 20(1/2), pp. 293–315.

Morgan, G. (1997) *Images of Organizations*, Thousands Oaks, CA: Sage.

Morsing, M. and Schultz, M. (2006) 'Corporate social responsibility communication: stakeholder information, response and involvement strategies', *Business Ethics: A European Review*, 15(4), pp. 323–38.

Moynihan, R. and Cassels, A. (2005) *Selling Sickness: How Drug Companies Are Turning Us All into Patients*, Vancouver: Greystone.

Napel, S. and Widgren, M. (2004) 'Power measurement and sensitivity analysis', *Journal of Theoretical Politics*, 16(4), pp. 517–38.

Negandhi, A. (1984) 'Interaction between multinational corporations and host countries: power, conflict and democratization in decision-making', in B. Wilpert and A. Sorge (eds), *International Perspectives in Organizational Democracy*, New York, NY: John Wiley, pp. 17–23.

Nestor, S. (2005) 'Falling between the cracks: privatisation and corporate governance in the European telecom industry', *Corporate Governance: An International Review*, 13(2), pp. 137–55.

Newman, K. (1986) *The Selling of British Telecom*, Eastbourne: Holt, Rinehart & Wilson.

Nijhof, A. and Jeurissen, R. (2006) 'Editorial: a sensemaking perspective on corporate social responsibility: introduction to the special issue', *Business Ethics: A European Review*, 15(4), pp. 316–22.

O'Dwyer, B. (2004) 'Stakeholder democracy: challenges and contributions from accountancy', *Research Paper Series, International Centre for Corporate Social Responsibility*, Nottingham University Business School.

OECD (2004) *Principles of Corporate Governance*, OECD.

OECD (2008) *Growing Unequal? Income Distribution and Poverty in OECD Countries*, OECD.

O'Riordan, L. and Fairbrass, J. (2008) 'Corporate social responsibility (CSR): models and theories in stakeholder dialogue', *Journal of Business Ethics*, 83, pp. 745–58.

Orlitzky, M., Schmidts, F. and Rynes, S. (2003) 'Corporate social performance and financial performance: a meta-analysis', *Organization Studies*, 24(3), pp. 408–41.

Parkinson, J. E. (1993), *Corporate Power and Responsibility: Issues in the Theory of Company Law*, Oxford: Clarendon Press, pp. 3–41.

Parsons, T. (1963) 'On the concept of political power', *Proceedings of the American Philosophical Society*, 107, pp. 232–62.

Pateman, C. (1983) 'Some reflections on participation and democratic theory', in C. Crouch and F. Heller (eds), *Organizational Democracy and Political Processes*, New York, NY: John Wiley.

Perkins, J. (2004) *Confessions of an Economic Hitman*, San Francisco, CA: Berrett & Koehler.

Perrini, F., Russo, A. and Tencati, A. (2007) 'CSR strategies of SMEs and large firms: evidence from Italy', *Journal of Business Ethics*, 74, pp. 285–300.

Petersen, M. (2008) *Our Daily Meds*, New York, NY: Sarah Crichton.

Pfeffer, J. (1972) 'Size and composition of corporate boards of directors: the organization and its environment', *Administrative Science Quarterly*, 17(1), pp. 218–28.

Pfeffer, J. (1981) *Power in Organizations*, Boston, MA: Pitman.

Pfeffer, J. (1992) *Managing with Power*, Boston, MA: Harvard Business School Press.

Pfeffer, J. and Salancik, G. (1978) *The External Control of Organizations*, New York, NY: Harper & Row.

Pfeffer, J. and Salancik, G. (2003) *The External Control of Organizations: A Resource Dependent Perspective*, Stanford, CA: Stanford University Press.

Porter, M. and Kramer, M. (2006) 'Strategy and society: the link between competitive advantage and corporate social responsibility', *Harvard Business Review*, 84(12), pp. 78–92.

Rampell, C. (2010) 'Corporate profits near pre-recession peak', *The New York Times* (27 August, online version).

Recanati, F. (2004) *Literal Meaning*, New York, NY: Cambridge University Press.

Ricoeur, P. (1984) *Time and Narrative, vol. 1*, Chicago, IL: University of Chicago Press.

Riesman, D. (1953) *The Lonely Crowd*, Garden City, NY: Anchor.

Rodriguez, P., Siegel, D., Hillman, A. and Eden, L. (2006) 'Three lenses on the multinational enterprise: politics, corruption and corporate social responsibility', *Rensselaer Working Papers in Economics*, April.

Roe, M. J. (1994) *Strong Managers, Weak Owners*, Princeton, NJ: Princeton University Press.

Russo, A. and Tencati, A. (2008) 'Formal vs informal CSR strategies: evidence from Italian micro-, small, medium-sized and large firms', *Journal of Business Ethics*, 85, pp. 339–53.

Russo, M. and Fouts, P. (1997) 'A resource-based perspective on corporate environmental performance and profitability', *Academy of Management Journal*, 40(3), pp. 534–59.

Salaman, G. and Thompson, K. (eds), (1980) *Control and Ideology in Organizations*, Cambridge, MA: MIT Press, pp. 27–56.

Salancik, G. and Pfeffer, J. (1974) 'The bases and use of power in organizational decision making: the case of university', *Administrative Science Quarterly*, 19(4), pp. 453–73.

Schein, E. H. (1985) *Organizational Culture and Leadership*, San Francisco, CA: Jossey-Bass. Schleifer, A. and Vishny, R., (1997) 'A survey of corporate governance', *Journal of Finance*, 52(2), pp. 737–83.

Scott, S. G. and Lane, V. R. (2000) 'A stakeholder approach to organizational identity', *Academy of Management Review*, 25, pp. 43–62.

Shah, A. (2010) Poverty Around the World, www.globalissues.org (accessed 29 October 2010).

Shore, C. and Wright, S. (1997) 'Policy: a new field of anthropology', in C. Shore and S. Wright (eds), *Anthropology of Policy: Critical Perspectives on Governance and Power*, New York, NY: Routledge.

Smith Hilmann, V. and Scott, A. (2010) 'Economic power: competition law, economic evaluation and policy implications', in B. Fryzel and P. H. Dembinski (eds), *The Role of Large Enterprises in Democracy and Society*, Basingstoke: Palgrave Macmillan.

Soenen, G. and Moingeon, B. (2002a), *Corporate and Organizational Identities: Integrating Strategy, Marketing, Communication and Organizational Perspective*, New York, NY: Routledge.

Soenen, G. and Moingeon, B. (2002b), 'The five facets of collective identities: integrating corporate and organizational identity', in G. Soenen and B. Moingeon (eds), *Corporate and Organizational Identities: Integrating Strategy, Marketing, Communication and Organizational Perspective*, New York, NY: Routledge.

Stake, R. E. (1995) *The Art of Case Study Research*, New York, NY: Sage.

Starkey, K. and Crane, A. (2003) 'Towards green narrative: management and the evolutionary epic', *Academy of Management Review*, 28(2), pp. 220–37.

Sternberg, E. (1998) *Czysty biznes, etyka biznesu w działaniu*, Warsaw: PWN.

Stiles, P. (2001) 'The impact of the board on strategy: an empirical examination', *Journal of Management Studies*, 5 pp. 627–51.

Strauss, G. (1982) 'Workers participation in management: an international perspective', *Research in Organizational Behaviour*, 4, pp. 173–265.

Strauss, G. and Rosenstein, E. (1970) 'Workers' participation: a critical view', *Industrial Relations*, 9(2), pp. 197–214.

Sułkowski, Ł. (2006) 'Dualizm w epistemologii nauk o zarządzaniu', in M. Przybyła (ed.), *Metody Badawcze w Zarządzaniu: Aspekt Teoretyczny i Praktyczny*, Wroclaw: Akademii Ekonomicznej im. Oskara Lanego we Wrocławiu.

Turek, D. (2010) 'Corporate social responsibility vs employee behavior: empirical findings', in D. Lewicka (ed.), *Organization Managemen:. Competitiveness, Social Responsibility, Human Capital*, Krakow: AGH University of Science and Technology Press.

Uzzi, B. (1997) 'Social structure and competition in interfirm networks: the paradox of embeddedness', *Administrative Science Quarterly*, 42, pp. 35–67.

Van der Voerd, F. and van den Brink, T. (2004) 'Feasibility of a responsive business scorecard: a pilot study', *Journal of Business Ethics*, 55, pp. 173–86.

Von Wright, G. H. (1971) *Explanation and Understanding*, Ithaca, NY: Cornell University Press.

Waddock, S. and Graves, S. (1997) 'The corporate social performance: financial performance link', *Strategic Management Journal*, 18(4), pp. 303–19.

Walsh, J. and Seward, J. (1990) 'On the efficiency of the internal and external corporate control mechanisms', *Academy of Management Review*, 15, pp. 421–58.

Walti, S., Kubler, D. and Papadopoulos, Y. (2004) 'How democratic is "governance"? Lessons from Swiss drug policy', *Governance: An International Journal of Policy, Administration and Institutions*, 17(1), pp. 83–113.

Wan, D. and Ong, C. H. (2005) 'Board structure, process and performance: evidence from public listed companies in Singapore', *Corporate Governance*, 13(2).

Wartick, S. L. and Cochran, P. L. (1985) 'The evolution of the corporate social performance model', *Academy of Management Review*, 10(4), pp. 758–69.

WBCSD (2006) *From Challenge to Opportunity: The Role of Business in Tomorrow's Society*, World Business Council for Sustainable Development.

Weber, M. (1978) *Economy and Society*, Berkeley and Los Angeles, CA: University of California Press.

Weber, M. (2002) *Gospodarka i społeczeństwo. Zarys Socjologii Rozumiejącej*, Warsaw: PWN.

Weick, K. E. (1995) *Sensemaking in Organizations*, Thousand Oaks and London: Sage.

Westphal, J. D. (1998) 'Board games: how CEOs adapt to increases in structural board independence from management', *Administrative Science Quarterly*, 43, pp. 511–37.

Westphal, J. D. and Zajac, E. J. (1995) 'Accounting for the explanations of CEO compensation: substance and symbolism', *Administrative Science Quarterly*, 40, pp. 283–308.

Williams, L. (2008) 'The mission statement: a corporate reporting tool with a past, present and future', *Journal of Business Communication*, 45(2), pp. 94–119.

Wood, D. J. (1991) 'Corporate social performance revisited', *Academy of Management Review*, 16(4), pp. 691–718.

World Income Inequality Database (2008) www.wider.unu.edu

World Investment Report (2007) *Transnational Corporations, Extractive Industries and Development*, United Nations Conference on Trade and Development.

Wright, P. and Ferris, S. (1997) 'Agency conflict and corporate strategy: the effect of divestment on corporate value', *Strategic Management Journal*, 18(1), pp. 77–83.

Zajac, E. (1990) 'CEO selection, succession, compensation, and firm performance: a theoretical integration and empirical analysis', *Strategic Management Journal*, 11(3), pp. 217–30.

Zajac, E. and Westphal, J. (1996) 'Who shall succeed? How CEO/board preferences and power affect the choice of new CEOs', *Academy of Management Journal*, 39.

www.forbes.com

www.monbiot.com

www.corporatewatch.org

Appendix

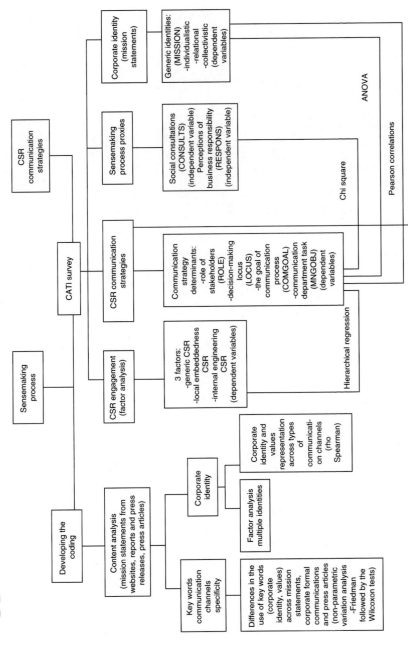

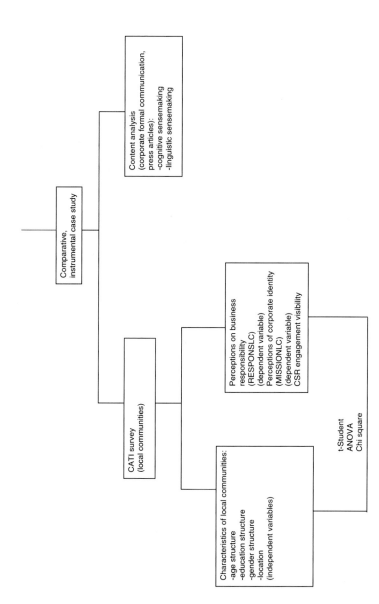

Figure A.1 Scheme of analysis

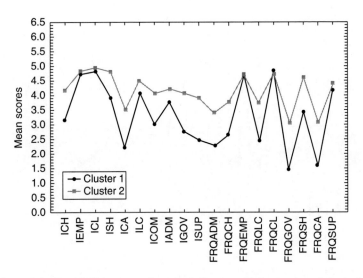

Figure A.2 Best Polish enterprises: importance and frequency of contacts with stakeholders

Table A.1 Variables summary

ICH	Importance of capital holders
IEMP	Importance of employees
ICL	Importance of clients
ISH	Importance of shareholders
ICA	Importance of consumer associations
ILC	Importance of local communities
ICOM	Importance of competitors
IADM	Importance of local public administration
IGOV	Importance of government
ISUP	Importance of suppliers
FRQADM	Frequency of contacts with local public administration
FRQCH	Frequency of contacts with capital holders
FRQEMP	Frequency of contacts with employees
FRQLC	Frequency of contacts with local communities
FRQCL	Frequency of contacts with clients
FRQGOV	Frequency of contacts with government
FRQSH	Frequency of contacts with shareholders
FRQCA	Frequency of contacts with consumer associations
FRQSUP	Frequency of contacts with suppliers
COMGOAL	Goal of the communication process
MNGOBJ	Key objective of the communication/PR manager
RESPONS	Scope of business responsibility
COMPSIZE	Size of the company
MISSION	Mission statement

(continued)

Table A.1 Continued

LOKUSDEC	Decision-making locus
ROLE	Role of stakeholders
Revenue	
Revenue dynamics	
(% y-o-y)	
CONSULTS	Social consultations
RESPONSLC	Perception of business responsibility in the local communities
MISSIONLC	Perception of corporate identities in the local communities

Table A.2a Scope of business responsibility in the local community in Krakow (chi square)

		Gender				Total	
		F		M			
		N	%	N	%	N	%
What should companies be responsible for? (RESPONSLC)	For generating profits for shareholders only	2	2.13	5	10.87	7	5.00
	For generating profits and fulfilling the expectations of clients and employees	28	29.79	18	39.13	46	32.86
	For generating profits and fulfilling the expectations of clients and employees and other stake-holder groups	64	68.09	23	50.00	87	62.14
	Total	94	100.00	46	100.00	140	100.00

Note: $chi^2(2) = 7.17$; $p = 0.028$.

Table A.2b Scope of business responsibility in the local community in Krakow (ANOVA)
Mean, standard deviations and analysis of variance for differences between the groups

	Mean			Standard deviation			Difference between the groups
	1	2	3	1	2	3	
Age	3.43	2.50	2.39	0.79	1.01	1.00	1 from 2, 1 from 3
Education	7.00	6.20	7.11	2.38	2.19	1.96	2 from 3

(continued)

Table A.2b   Continued

Analysis of variance

	F(2. 137)	P
Age	3.53	.032
Education	3.04	.051

Table A.3a   Relation between the mode of decision-making in the organization and the importance attributed to stakeholder groups (ANOVA)
Mean and standard deviation in the groups

	LOKUSDEC						Post-hoc REGW-F
	Mean			Standard deviation			
	1	2	3	1	2	3	
ICH	3.43	3.32	3.96	1.25	1.31	1.07	3 from 2, 3 from 1
IEMP	4.62	4.89	4.80	0.74	0.31	0.64	
ICL	4.85	4.85	4.91	0.47	0.62	0.55	
ISH	4.57	3.96	4.49	0.71	1.32	0.96	2 from 3, 2 from 1
ICA	2.61	2.95	3.02	1.04	1.48	1.30	
ILC	3.34	3.79	3.73	1.22	1.02	1.14	
ICOM	4.02	3.74	4.07	0.79	0.99	0.84	
IADM	3.13	3.32	3.76	1.10	1.30	0.94	3 from 1, 3 from 2
IGOV	2.79	3.15	3.61	1.18	1.30	1.17	1 from 3

Note: LOKUSDEC 1: only management decides upon the CSR focus; LOKUSDEC 2: management decides upon CSR focus on the basis of the research; LOKUSDEC 3: management decides on the CSR focus with participation of the key stakeholders in a decision-making process.

ANOVA

	F	df_B	df_W	P
ICH	4.04	2	140	.020
IEMP	2.64	2	147	.075
ICL	.21	2	147	.814
ISH	5.08	2	145	.007
ICA	1.41	2	141	.247
ILC	2.23	2	147	.111
ICOM	1.99	2	146	.140
IADM	4.42	2	146	.014
IGOV	5.84	2	144	.004

Table A.3b Relation between corporate identity, communication objectives and the importance attributed to the stakeholder groups (Pearson correlations)

	MISSION: become market leader	MISSION: gain trust	MISSION: solve social problems	MNGOBJ: design appealing message	MNGOBJ: identify stakeholder groups	MNGOBJ: build relations
ICH	-0.04	0.12	-0.09	0.05	-0.09	0.05
IEMP	0.12	-0.09	-0.07	-0.03	0.04	-0.01
ICL	-0.03	-0.02	0.07	0.01	0.03	-0.04
ISH	0.03	0.01	-0.06	-0.10	0.09	0.00
ICA	0.07	0.00	-0.12	0.01	-0.01	0.00
ILC	0.18*	-0.03	-0.25**	0.04	0.06	-0.09
ICOM	0.05	0.02	-0.09	-0.05	0.09	-0.04
IADM	0.06	0.05	-0.16	-0.06	-0.10	0.16*
IGOV	0.07	-0.04	-0.06	0.05	-0.09	0.04

Note: *: $p < 0.05$; **: $p < 0.01$.

Table A.4–A.6 Analysis of the key words in the mission statements, reports and articles (factor analysis with OBLIMIN rotation)

Table A.4a Mission statements
Eigenvalues and the percentage of the variance explained

Factor	Eigenvalue	% of variance explained	% cumulated of the variance explained
1	8.55	19.00	19.00
2	4.57	10.15	29.15
3	3.38	7.50	36.65
4	2.83	6.28	42.93
5	2.26	5.02	47.96
6	1.96	4.35	52.30
7	1.85	4.11	56.42
8	1.70	3.77	60.19
9	1.58	3.50	63.69
10	1.39	3.09	66.78
11	1.29	2.87	69.65
12	1.20	2.67	72.32
13	1.10	2.44	74.76

Note: 13 factors explain 74.76% of the variation. Based on the scree test (Figure A.4a), six factors were chosen for further analysis.

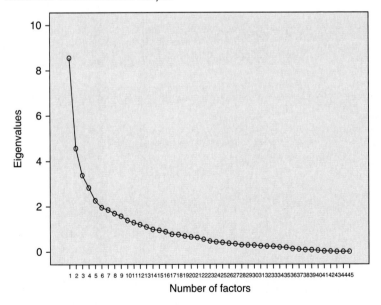

Figure A.4a Eigenvalues

Table A.4 Factor loadings

	Factors					
	1	**2**	**3**	**4**	**5**	**6**
Economic development	0.98					
Citizenship	0.98					
Leadership	0.96					
Help	0.85					
Diversity	0.85					
Science	0.52					
Information		0.79				
Obligations		0.78				
Compliance		0.75				
Social problems			−0.96			
Life quality			−0.82			
Society			−0.79			
Respect			−0.55			
Teamwork			−0.52			
The best			−0.52			
Experts				−0.68		
Market leader				−0.65		
Competition/competitors				−0.64		
Coherence				−0.53		
Product quality					0.79	
Security/safety					0.74	
Excellence					0.71	
Rights					0.51	
Employees					0.50	
Responsibility						0.88
Economy						0.53
Value						0.52
Ethics						0.50

Table A.5a Reports
Eigenvalues and the percentage of the variance explained

Factors	**Eigenvalues**	**% of variance explained**	**% cumulated of variance explained**
1	19.16	39.91	39.91
2	3.84	8.00	47.91
3	3.43	7.15	55.07
4	3.03	6.31	61.38

(*continued*)

Table A.5a Continued

Factors	Eigenvalues	% of variance explained	% cumulated of variance explained
5	2.58	5.38	66.76
6	2.38	4.96	71.72
7	1.96	4.08	75.80
8	1.76	3.67	79.47
9	1.48	3.07	82.54
10	1.45	3.02	85.56
11	1.40	2.91	88.47
12	1.32	2.75	91.23

Note: 12 factors explained 91.23% of the variation. Based on the scree test (Figure A.5a), eight factors were chosen for further analysis.

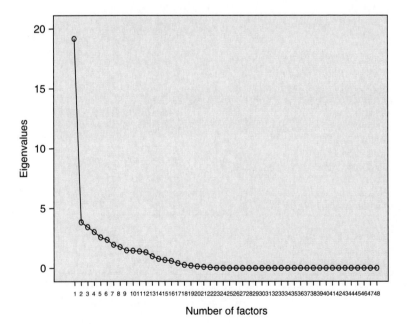

Figure A.5a Eigenvalues

Table A.5b Factor loadings

	Factors							
	1	2	3	4	5	6	7	8
Jobs	0.99							
Success	0.76							
Employees	0.69							
Report	0.59							
Social problems		0.99						
Coherence		0.97						
The best		0.55						
Community			0.84					
Dialogue			0.72					
Competition/competitors			0.52					
Diversity			0.51					
Economic development				0.96				
Economy				0.60				
Security/safety				0.44				
Penalties					0.98			
Sanctions					0.95			
Confidentiality						−0.94		
Ethics						−0.49		
Science						−0.47		
Economics						−0.44		
Responsibility						−0.40		
Obligations							0.68	
Teamwork							0.55	
Research							0.52	
Rights							0.42	
Relations							0.42	
Leadership								0.99
Market leader								0.78
Society								0.41

Table A.6a Articles
Eigenvalues and the percentage of the variance explained

Factor	Eigenvalue	% of variance explained	% cumulated of variance explained
1	16.44	34.25	34.25
2	4.04	8.41	42.67
3	3.31	6.90	49.57
4	2.79	5.80	55.37
5	2.25	4.69	60.06

(*continued*)

Table A.6a   Continued

Factor	Eigenvalue	% of variance explained	% cumulated of variance explained
6	2.04	4.24	64.30
7	1.92	4.00	68.30
8	1.57	3.27	71.57
9	1.54	3.20	74.77
10	1.31	2.72	77.49
11	1.28	2.67	80.16
12	1.08	2.25	82.41

Note: 12 factors explained 82.41% of the variation. Based on the scree test (Figure A.6a), eight factors were chosen for further analysis.

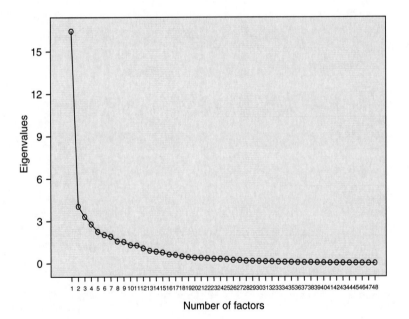

Figure A.6a   Eigenvalues

Table A.6b Factor loadings

	1	2	3	4	5	6	7	8
Economic growth	0.84							
Economic development	0.82							
Life quality	0.76							
Help	0.73							
Economics	0.71							
Report	0.70							
GDP	0.69							
Science	0.65							
Trust	0.61							
Society	0.52							
Economy	0.48							
Leadership		1.02						
Relations		0.89						
Security/safety		0.82						
Responsibility		0.77						
Success		0.55						
Experts		0.52						
Diversity			0.91					
Compliance			0.81					
GDP per capita				0.80				
Obligations				0.67				
Rights				0.65				
Innovations					−0.90			
Excellence					−0.55			
Research					−0.50			
Unemployment						0.93		
Sanctions						0.90		
Community							0.86	
Value							0.70	
Product quality							0.54	
The best							0.49	
Respect								0.78
Employees								0.54
Code of conduct								0.51

Table A.7 Differences between mission statements, reports and articles (non–parametric variation analysis, Friedman)

	chi^2 Friedman (2)	p
Success	14.07	0.001
Product quality	75.72	<0.001
Competition/competitors	74.50	<0.001
Value	4.21	0.122

(*continued*)

	chi² Friedman (2)	p
The best	29.82	<0.001
Ethics	9.46	0.009
Diversity	1.53	0.465
Help	21.50	<0.001
Employees	29.26	<0.001
Responsibility	3.17	0.205
Life quality	1.50	0.472
Market leader	31.69	<0.001
Trust	3.60	0.166
Society	0.65	0.723
Social problems	0.00	0.999
Relations	4.00	0.135
Expectations fulfillment	47.15	<0.001
Dialogue	1.12	0.570
Information	84.69	<0.001
Community	6.33	0.042
Obligations	17.58	<0.001
Rights	43.44	<0.001
Sanctions	1.14	0.565
Compliance	2.10	0.349
Confidentiality	2.00	0.368
Penalties	28.35	<0.001
Code of conduct	6.13	0.047
Science	5.52	0.063
Experts	44.39	<0.001
Research	18.83	<0.001
Analysis	16.06	<0.001
Report	39.43	<0.001
Jobs	33.57	<0.001
Economic growth	12.00	0.002
Unemployment	4.55	0.103
GDP per capita	6.00	0.050
Economic development	11.94	0.003
Economics	41.58	<0.001
Economy	74.55	<0.001
GDP	20.00	<0.001
Excellence	35.74	<0.001
Coherence	0.29	0.867
Respect	0.78	0.678
Innovations	6.61	0.037
Leadership	0.50	0.779
Diversity	2.00	0.368
Teamwork	5.64	0.060
Security/safety	9.26	0.010
Citizenship	1.00	0.607
Individualistic	71.96	<0.001
Partner	46.52	<0.001
Collectivistic	6.85	0.033

Table A.8 Differences between reports and mission statements (Wilcoxon tests)

	Means		Standard deviation		Wilcoxon test	
	Report	Mission	Report	Mission	Z	p
Success	0.23	0.29	1.05	0.69	−1.80	0.072
Product quality	0.79	2.30	2.70	3.02	−5.76	<0.001
Innovations	0.22	0.30	0.87	0.72	−1.21	0.225
Competition/ competitors	0.09	0.24	0.48	0.60	−2.52	0.012
Value	0.28	0.32	1.18	0.90	−1.10	0.271
The best	0.08	0.11	0.38	0.48	−0.38	0.701
Ethics	0.25	0.04	0.91	0.23	−2.80	0.005
Diversity	0.05	0.07	0.34	0.39	−0.37	0.715
Help	0.35	0.03	2.02	0.21	−2.07	0.038
Employees	1.59	1.07	6.82	1.69	−2.07	0.038
Responsibility	1.36	0.25	4.58	0.74	−2.32	0.021
Life quality	0.07	0.05	0.43	0.32	−0.16	0.876
Market leader	0.15	0.45	0.67	0.78	−4.15	<0.001
Trust	0.11	0.15	0.46	0.41	−0.52	0.603
Society	0.55	0.23	2.01	1.06	−1.79	0.073
Social problems	0.01	0.01	0.16	0.08	−0.45	0.655
Relations	0.12	0.15	0.57	0.48	−0.71	0.479
Expectations fulfillment	0.11	0.50	0.54	0.92	−4.56	<0.001
Dialogue	0.07	0.03	0.34	0.21	−1.15	0.248
Information	0.18	0.11	0.65	0.45	−1.29	0.198
Community	0.02	0.00	0.18	0.00	−1.34	0.180
Obligations	0.11	0.16	0.60	0.61	−1.06	0.291
Rights	0.35	0.20	1.19	0.56	−1.35	0.176
Sanctions	0.03	0.01	0.20	0.08	−1.13	0.257
Compliance	0.09	0.07	0.44	0.32	−0.49	0.623
Confidentiality	0.01	0.00	0.16	0.00	−1.00	0.317
Penalties	0.01	0.00	0.08	0.00	−1.00	0.317
Code of conduct	0.15	0.05	0.65	0.32	−1.64	0.102
Science	0.10	0.03	0.46	0.16	−1.85	0.065
Experts	0.09	0.03	0.38	0.16	−2.00	0.046
Research	0.39	0.37	1.86	1.11	−1.05	0.294
Analysis	0.08	0.18	0.34	0.54	−1.98	0.047
Report	0.13	0.01	0.74	0.12	−2.20	0.028
Jobs	0.07	0.01	0.51	0.08	−1.63	0.104
Economic growth	0.00	0.00	0.00	0.00	0.00	0.999
Unemployment	0.02	0.02	0.14	0.14	0.00	0.999
GDP per capita	0.00	0.00	0.00	0.00	0.00	−0.999

(*continued*)

Table A.8   Continued

	Means		Standard deviation		Wilcoxon test	
	Report	Mission	Report	Mission	Z	p
Economic development	0.13	0.01	0.63	0.16	−2.09	0.037
Economics	0.11	0.06	0.47	0.26	−1.18	0.239
Economy	0.24	0.07	1.29	0.30	−1.32	0.187
GDP	0.00	0.00	0.00	0.00	0.00	0.999
Excellence	0.28	0.65	1.00	1.36	−3.18	0.001
Coherence	0.03	0.02	0.26	0.14	0.00	0.999
Respect	0.06	0.07	0.33	0.30	−0.30	0.768
Innovations	0.22	0.29	0.87	0.69	−1.22	0.222
Leadership	0.01	0.04	0.08	0.42	−0.82	0.414
Diversity	0.05	0.07	0.34	0.39	−0.37	0.715
Responsibility	1.25	0.25	4.42	0.74	−2.12	0.034
Teamwork	0.05	0.04	0.27	0.20	−0.28	0.776
Security/safety	0.73	0.82	2.10	2.01	−0.58	0.559
Citizenship	0.01	0.01	0.08	0.16	−0.45	0.655
Individualistic	0.25	0.54	0.77	0.58	−5.49	<0.001
Partner	0.48	0.47	1.94	0.61	−3.74	<0.001
Collectivistic	0.30	0.10	1.02	0.28	−0.28	0.782

Table A.9   Differences between articles and mission statements (Wilcoxon tests)

	Means		Standard deviation		Wilcoxon test	
	Articles	Mission	Articles	Mission	Z	p
Success	0.75	0.29	2.29	0.69	−1.85	0.064
Product quality	0.95	2.30	2.31	3.02	−4.93	<0.001
Innovations	1.09	0.30	4.49	0.72	−0.60	0.551
Competition/ competitors	2.27	0.24	4.51	0.60	−6.44	<0.001
Value	0.21	0.32	0.74	0.90	−1.51	0.130
The best	0.59	0.11	1.49	0.48	−3.86	<0.001
Ethics	0.05	0.04	0.27	0.23	−0.27	0.791
Diversity	0.03	0.07	0.18	0.39	−1.00	0.317
Help	0.52	0.03	1.80	0.21	−4.34	<0.001
Employees	2.77	1.07	6.56	1.69	−1.64	0.101
Responsibility	0.48	0.25	1.46	0.74	−1.86	0.063
Life quality	0.02	0.05	0.18	0.32	−1.03	0.301
Market leader	0.86	0.45	1.91	0.78	−1.58	0.114
Trust	0.26	0.15	0.94	0.41	−0.74	0.458
Society	0.29	0.23	0.88	1.06	−1.06	0.289
Social problems	0.01	0.01	0.08	0.08	0.00	0.999

(continued)

Table A.9 Continued

	Means		Standard deviation		Wilcoxon test	
	Articles	Mission	Articles	Mission	Z	p
Relations	0.08	0.15	0.39	0.48	–1.70	0.089
Expectations fulfillment	0.12	0.50	0.40	0.92	–4.31	<0.001
Dialogue	0.06	0.03	0.29	0.21	–0.92	0.357
Information	2.83	0.11	7.13	0.45	–6.81	<0.001
Community	0.04	0.00	0.23	0.00	–2.12	0.034
Obligations	0.83	0.16	2.49	0.61	–3.60	<0.001
Rights	2.69	0.20	7.36	0.56	–5.95	<0.001
Sanctions	0.03	0.01	0.20	0.08	–1.13	0.257
Compliance	0.05	0.07	0.35	0.32	–0.88	0.378
Confidentiality	0.00	0.00	0.00	0.00	0.00	0.999
Penalties	0.34	0.00	1.52	0.00	–3.59	<0.001
Code of conduct	0.01	0.05	0.12	0.32	–1.40	0.161
Science	0.28	0.03	1.29	0.16	–2.80	0.005
Experts	0.91	0.03	2.60	0.16	–5.14	<0.001
Research	1.35	0.37	3.45	1.11	–3.51	<0.001
Analysis	0.71	0.18	2.06	0.54	–3.21	0.001
Report	0.99	0.01	3.26	0.12	–4.94	<0.001
Jobs	0.46	0.01	1.52	0.08	–4.35	<0.001
Economic growth	0.06	0.00	0.33	0.00	–2.26	0.024
Unemployment	0.11	0.02	0.60	0.14	–2.14	0.032
GDP per capita	0.02	0.00	0.14	0.00	–1.73	0.083
Economic development	0.16	0.01	0.73	0.16	–3.23	0.001
Economics	0.59	0.06	1.47	0.26	–4.87	<0.001
Economy	2.03	0.07	4.69	0.30	–6.44	<0.001
GDP	0.14	0.00	0.62	0.00	–2.84	0.005
Excellence	0.19	0.65	0.64	1.36	–4.17	<0.001
Coherence	0.01	0.02	0.12	0.14	–0.45	0.655
Respect	0.05	0.07	0.29	0.30	–0.79	0.430
Innovations	1.09	0.29	4.49	0.69	–0.52	0.600
Leadership	0.01	0.04	0.08	0.42	–0.82	0.414
Diversity	0.03	0.07	0.16	0.39	–1.29	0.197
Responsibility	0.48	0.25	1.46	0.74	–1.86	0.063
Teamwork	0.00	0.04	0.00	0.20	–2.45	0.014
Security/safety	1.31	0.82	4.54	2.01	–1.11	0.269
Citizenship	0.00	0.01	0.00	0.16	–1.00	0.317
Individualistic	1.33	0.54	2.55	0.58	–2.08	0.038
Partner	0.81	0.47	1.84	0.61	–0.17	0.865
Collectivistic	0.17	0.10	0.45	0.28	–1.29	0.197

Table A.10   Differences between articles and reports (Wilcoxon tests)

	Means		Standard deviation		Wilcoxon test	
	Articles	Report	Articles	Report	Z	p
Success	0.75	0.23	2.29	1.05	–3.19	0.001
Product quality	0.95	0.79	2.31	2.70	–1.21	0.226
Innovations	1.09	0.22	4.49	0.87	–1.66	0.097
Competition/ competitors	2.27	0.09	4.51	0.48	–6.86	<0.001
Value	0.21	0.28	0.74	1.18	–0.18	0.854
The best	0.59	0.08	1.49	0.38	–4.17	<0.001
Ethics	0.05	0.25	0.27	0.91	–2.53	0.011
Diversity	0.03	0.05	0.18	0.34	–0.61	0.541
Help	0.52	0.35	1.80	2.02	–1.92	0.055
Employees	2.77	1.59	6.56	6.82	–3.14	0.002
Responsibility	0.48	1.36	1.46	4.58	–0.97	0.330
Life quality	0.02	0.07	0.18	0.43	–1.12	0.263
Market leader	0.86	0.15	1.91	0.67	–4.58	<0.001
Trust	0.26	0.11	0.94	0.46	–1.29	0.197
Society	0.29	0.55	0.88	2.01	–0.76	0.446
Social problems	0.01	0.01	0.08	0.16	–0.45	0.655
Relations	0.08	0.12	0.39	0.57	–0.77	0.440
Expectations fulfillment	0.12	0.11	0.40	0.54	–0.54	0 .587
Dialogue	0.06	0.07	0.29	0.34	–0.07	0.948
Information	2.83	0.18	7.13	0.65	–6.37	<0.001
Community	0.04	0.02	0.23	0.18	–1.34	0.180
Obligations	0.83	0.11	2.49	0.60	–3.97	<0.001
Rights	2.69	0.35	7.36	1.19	–5.06	<0.001
Sanctions	0.03	0.03	0.20	0.20	0.00	0.999
Compliance	0.05	0.09	0.35	0.44	–1.31	0.191
Confidentiality	0.00	0.01	0.00	0.16	–1.00	0.317
Penalties	0.34	0.01	1.52	0.08	–3.44	0.001
Code of conduct	0.01	0.15	0.12	0.65	–2.55	0.011
Science	0.28	0.10	1.29	0.46	–1.13	0.257
Experts	0.91	0.09	2.60	0.38	–4.62	<0.001
Research	1.35	0.39	3.45	1.86	–3.56	<0.001
Analysis	0.71	0.08	2.06	0.34	–4.00	<0.001
Report	0.99	0.13	3.26	0.74	–3.75	<0.001
Jobs	0.46	0.07	1.52	0.51	–3.24	0.001
Economic growth	0.06	0.00	0.33	0.00	–2.26	0.024
Unemployment	0.11	0.02	0.60	0.14	–2.05	0.041
GDP per capita	0.02	0.00	0.14	0.00	–1.73	0.083

(*continued*)

Table A.10   Continued

	Means		Standard deviation		Wilcoxon test	
	Articles	Report	Articles	Report	Z	p
Economic development	0.16	0.13	0.73	0.63	−0.48	0.629
Economics	0.59	0.11	1.47	0.47	−3.98	<0.001
Economy	2.03	0.24	4.69	1.29	−5.70	<0.001
GDP	0.14	0.00	0.62	0.00	−2.84	0.005
Excellence	0.19	0.28	0.64	1.00	−0.69	0.491
Coherence	0.01	0.03	0.12	0.26	−0.38	0.705
Respect	0.05	0.06	0.29	0.33	−0.42	0.676
Innovations	1.09	0.22	4.49	0.87	−1.66	0.097
Leadership	0.01	0.01	0.08	0.08	0.00	0.999
Diversity	0.03	0.05	0.16	0.34	−0.86	0.388
Responsibility	0.48	1.25	1.46	4.42	−0.75	0.454
Teamwork	0.00	0.05	0.00	0.27	−2.07	0.038
Security/safety	1.31	0.73	4.54	2.10	−1.47	0.141
Citizenship	0.00	0.01	0.00	0.08	−1.00	0.317
Individualistic	1.33	0.25	2.55	0.77	−5.99	<0.001
Partner	0.81	0.48	1.84	1.94	−3.18	0.001
Collectivistic	0.17	0.30	0.45	1.02	−0.22	0.829

Table A.11   Relation between scope of business responsibility and social consultations

| | | Are decisions about CSR involvement made in consultations with representatives of stakeholder groups? (CONSULTS) | | | | Total | |
| | | Yes | | No | | | |
		N	%	N	%	N	%
	For generating profits for shareholders only	2	1.79	0	0.00	2	1,33
What should the companies be responsible for? (RESPONS)	For generating profits and fulfilling the expectations of the clients and employees	50	44.64	15	39.47	65	43,33
	For generating profits and fulfilling the expectations of the clients and employees and other stakeholder groups	60	53.57	23	60.53	83	55,33
Total		112	100.00	38	100.00	150	100.00

Note: $chi^2(2) = 9.19$; $p = 0.010$.

Table A.12 Relation between scope of business responsibility and the importance attributed to the stakeholder groups (t-student tests)

	Scope of responsibility						t	df	P
	Means		Standard deviation		N				
	2	3	2	3	2	3			
ICH	3.72	3.40	1.23	1.23	78	63	1.55	139	0.124
IEMP	4.75	4.83	0.64	0.52	83	65	–0.86	146	0.393
ICL	4.83	4.92	0.68	0.32	83	65	–1.01	146	0.316
ISH	4.40	4.27	1.05	1.07	83	63	0.72	144	0.470
ICA	3.10	2.57	1.32	1.20	79	63	2.48	140	0.014
ILC	3.76	3.48	1.07	1.23	83	65	1.50	146	0.137
ICOM	3.96	3.95	0.91	0.86	82	65	0.07	145	0.948
IADM	3.66	3.12	1.09	1.15	82	65	2.88	145	0.005
IGOV	3.44	2.84	1.27	1.13	81	64	2.96	143	0.004

Note: RESPONS 1: For generating profits for shareholders only (not included in the analysis due to the marginal rate of responses); RESPONS 2: For generating profits and fulfilling the expectations of the clients and employees; RESPONS 3: For generating profits and fulfilling the expectations of the clients and employees and other stakeholder groups.

Table A.13 Relation between scope of business responsibility and the frequency of relations with the stakeholder groups (t-student tests)

	Means		Standard deviation		N		T	df	p
	2	3	2	3	2	3			
FRQADM	3.10	2.62	1.197	1.170	80	63	2.41	141	0.017
FRQCH	3.41	2.82	1.285	1.112	75	60	2.84	133	0.005
FRQEMP	4.75	4.63	0.514	0.747	83	63	1.07	144	0.285
FRQLC	3.32	2.79	1.076	1.080	82	63	2.90	143	0.004
FRQCL	4.82	4.77	0.608	0.636	83	64	0.52	145	0.604
FRQGOV	2.56	1.84	1.297	1.036	82	61	3.59	141	<0.001
FRQSH	4.14	3.79	1.191	1.332	81	62	1.63	141	0.105
FRQCA	2.59	1.95	1.189	1.096	78	60	3.24	136	0.001

Table A.14 Relation between the scope of responsibility of business and the perception of the role of stakeholders

		For generating profits and fulfilling the expectations of clients and employees		For generating profits and fulfilling the expectations of clients and employees and other stakeholder groups		Total	
		N	%	N	%	N	%
How are the stakeholders perceived by the company? (ROLE)	As the end receivers of corporate communications	33	50.77	28	33.73	61	41.22
	As potential opposition to be neutralized	9	13.85	3	3.61	12	8.11
	As co-designers of the corporate CSR strategy	23	35.38	52	62.65	75	50.68
	Total	65	100.00	83	100.00	148	100.00

Note: chi^2(2) = 12.62; p = 0.002.

Table A.15 Perception of stakeholders' role and the objective of communication (ANOVA)

	Mean			Standard deviation		
	ROLE 1	**ROLE 2**	**ROLE 3**	**ROLE 1**	**ROLE 2**	**ROLE 3**
COMGOAL: provide information	1.68	1.42	1.84	0.76	0.51	0.78
COMGOAL: prove the fulfillment of expectations	2.24	2.50	2.29	0.80	0.80	0.78
COMGOAL: build dialogue	2.08	2.08	1.87	0.80	0.79	0.82
MNGOBJ: design appealing message	2.47	2.42	2.54	0.65	0.79	0.62
MNGOBJ: identify stakeholder groups	2.24	1.75	2.11	0.67	0.75	0.66
MNGOBJ: build relations	1.29	1.83	1.36	0.61	0.83	0.69

Note: Role 1: stakeholders perceived as neutral end receivers of corporate communication; Role 2: stakeholders perceived as active opposition; Role 3: stakeholders perceived as co-designers of CSR strategies.

Test post-hoc REGW - F: (Ryan–Einot–Gabriel–Welsch test)
ANOVA

	$F_{(2, 147)}$	**p**
COMGOAL: provide information	1.99	0.140
COMGOAL: prove the fulfillment of expectations	0.54	0.586
COMGOAL: build dialogue	1.30	0.277
MNGOBJ: design appealing message	0.32	0.727
MNGOBJ: identify stakeholder groups	2.81	0.063
MNGOBJ: build relations	3.33	0.038

Table A.16   Perception of stakeholders' role and the mission statement (ANOVA)

Mean and standard deviation in the groups

	Mean			Standard deviation		
	ROLE 1	ROLE 2	ROLE 3	ROLE 1	ROLE 2	ROLE 3
MISSION: become market leader	1.79	1.75	1.62	0.60	0.75	0.67
MISSION: gain trust	1.32	1.42	1.54	0.47	0.51	0.53
MISSION: solve social problems	2.89	2.83	2.84	0.37	0.39	0.46

Note: Role 1: stakeholders perceived as neutral end receivers of corporate communication; Role 2: stakeholders perceived as active opposition; Role 3: stakeholders perceived as co-designers of CSR strategies.

Test post-hoc REGW - F: (Ryan–Einot–Gabriel–Welsch test)

Analysis of variance (ANOVA)

	$F_{(2, 147)}$	p
MISSION: become market leader	1.23	0.297
MISSION: gain trust	3.18	0.045
MISSION: solve social problems	0.22	0.801

Table A.17 Intercorrelations for factor analysis on CSR engagement (variables MNGOBJ, COMGOAL and MISSION are coded adversely: higher number means lower value of variable)

	COMGOAL: provide information	COMGOAL: prove the fulfillment of expectations	COMGOAL: build dialogue	MISSION: become the market leader	MISSION: gain trust	MISSION: solve social problems	MNGOBJ: design appealing message	MNGOBJ: identify stakeholder groups	MNGOBJ: build relations
COMGOAL: prove the fulfillment of expectations	-0.45**								
COMGOAL: build dialogue	-0.50**	-0.54**							
MISSION: become the market leader	0.11	0.14	-0.24**						
MISSION: gain trust	-0.10	-0.02	0.11	-0.77**					
MISSION: solve social problems	-0.05	-0.20*	0.25**	-0.62**	-0.02				
MNGOBJ: design appealing message	-0.01	-0.01	0.01	-0.02	0.06	-0.04			
MNGOBJ: identify stakeholder groups	0.03	-0.06	0.03	0.03	-0.09	0.07	-0.47**		
MNGOBJ: build relations	-0.02	0.07	-0.04	-0.01	0.03	-0.03	-0.47**	-0.55**	
COMPSIZE	-0.11	0.26**	-0.15	0.04	0.04	-0.12	-0.01	0.02	-0.01

Note: *: $p < 0.05$; **: $p < 0.001$.

Table A.18   Social consultations and size of the company

		COMPSIZE (employment)						Total	
		1–50		51–250		above 250			
		N	%	N	%	N	%	N	%
Are decisions about CSR involvement made in consultation with representatives of stakeholder groups? (CONSULTS)	Yes	5	41.67	40	76.92	66	77.65	111	74.50
	No	7	58.33	12	23.08	19	22.35	38	25.50
Total		12	100.00	52	100.00	85	100.00	149	100.00

Note: $chi^2(2) = 7.41$; $p = 0.025$.

Table A.19 Predictors of local embeddedness CSR
Percentage of variance explained and statistical significance of prediction

Variables entered	R	R^2	R^2_{sk}	F	p
COMPSIZE	0.25	0.06	0.06	9.86	0.002
Other predictors	0.34	0.11	0.07	2.57	0.016

Regression coefficients and statistical significance of predictors

Variables entered	Predictor	B	Beta	t	p
COMPSIZE	Constant	1.31		3.06	0.003
	Employment	-0.38	-0.25	-3.14	0.002
Other predictors	Constant	1.87		1.49	0.139
	Employment	-0.36	-0.24	-2.94	0.004
	COMGOAL: provide information	-0.14	-0.11	-1.22	0.223
	COMGOAL: prove the fulfillment of expectations	-0.09	-0.07	-0.76	0.450
	MISSION: become the market leader	-0.26	-0.17	-1.63	0.106
	MISSION: solve social problems	-0.10	-0.04	-0.39	0.697
	MNGOBJ: design appealing message	0.14	0.09	0.99	0.325
	MNGOBJ: build relations	0.17	0.12	1.28	0.203

Note: RESPONSLC – perception of business responsibility in the local communities
MISSIONLC – perception of corporate identities in the local communities

Table A.20 The role of stakeholders and types of CSR engagements (ANOVA)

	Mean			Standard deviation			N			Total
	ROLE 1	ROLE 2	ROLE 3	ROLE 1	ROLE 2	ROLE 3	ROLE 1	ROLE 2	ROLE 3	
Generic	0.16	0.17	−0.15	0.92	0.81	1.07	62	12	76	150
Local embeddedness	−0.12	0.65	0.00	0.90	0.93	1.06	62	12	76	150
Internal engineering	−0.03	−0.04	0.03	0.98	0.90	1.04	62	12	76	150

Note: Role 1: stakeholders perceived as neutral end receivers of corporate communication; Role 2: stakeholders perceived as potentially active opposition; Role 3: stakeholders perceived as co-designers of CSR strategies.

	F	df_B	df_w	p
Generic	1.85	2	147	0.161
Local embeddedness	3.07	2	147	0.049
Internal engineering	0.08	2	147	0.924

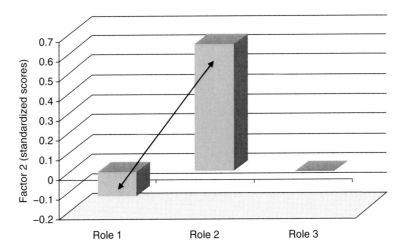

Figure A.20 The role of stakeholders and local embeddedness CSR

Table A.21 Internal engineering CSR and goal of communication

Percentage of the variance explained and statistical significance of prediction

Variables entered	R	R^2	R^2_{sk}	F	p
COMPSIZE	0.10	0.01	0.00	1.53	0.218
Other predictors	0.30	0.09	0.04	1.99	*0.061*

Regression coefficients and statistical significance of predictors

Variables entered	Predictor	B	Beta	t	p
COMPSIZE	Constant	0.53		1.21	0.228
	Employment	−0.15	−0.10	−1.24	0.218
	Constant	2.05		1.60	0.112
	Employment	−0.07	−0.05	−0.55	0.584
	COMGOAL: provide information	−0.04	−0.03	−0.32	0.746
Other predictors	COMGOAL: prove the fulfillment of expectations	−0.36	−0.28	−2.97	0.004
	MISSION: become the market leader	0.07	0.05	0.44	0.662
	MISSION: solve social problems	−0.30	−0.12	−1.12	0.264
	MNGOBJ: design appealing message	−0.03	−0.02	−0.24	0.808
	MNGOBJ: build relations	−0.07	−0.05	−0.49	0.623

Table A.22 Views on the scale of corporate responsibility among enterprises and local communities

What should companies be responsible for? (RESPONS)	Enterprises		Local communities		Total	
	N	%	N	%	N	%
For generating profits for shareholders only	2	1.33	20	3.55	22	3.08
For generating profits and fulfilling expectations of clients and employees	65	43.33	161	28.55	226	31.65
For generating profits and fulfilling expectations of clients and employees and other stakeholder groups	83	55.33	383	67.91	466	65.27
Total	150	100.00	564	100.00	714	100.00

Note: chi²(2) = 12.94; p = 0.002.

Table A.23 Relation between donations and company revenue (t-student tests)

	Mean		Standard deviation		N		t	df	p
	Donating	Not donating	Donating	Not donating	Donating	Not donating			
Revenue	296163,69	393360,14	265652,10	786979,11	62	72	−0,93	132	0,355
Revenue dynamics	116,80	126,02	20,97	30,10	61	72	−2,01	131	0,046

Table A.24   Gender and the perception of corporate mission (t-student tests), (Piatnica)

	Mean		Standard deviation		Number		t	df	p
	F	M	F	M	F	M			
Become a leader	2.14	1.80	0.83	0.85	85	55	2.35	138	0.020
Gain trust	1.47	1.73	0.68	0.68	85	55	−2.18	138	0.031
Solve social problems	2.39	2.47	0.64	0.72	85	55	−0.73	138	0.467

Table A.25   Gender and the perception of corporate mission (t-student tests), (Warsaw)

	Mean		Standard deviation		Number		t	df	p
	F	M	K	M	K	M			
Become a leader	2.07	1.85	0.73	0.77	69	75	1.75	142	0.082
Gain trust	1.33	1.60	0.56	0.68	69	75	−2.56	142	0.011
Solve social problems	2.59	2.55	0.60	0.70	69	75	0.43	142	0.665

Table A.26   Age and education in perceiving corporate mission (Pearson correlations)

Company		Age	Education
'B'	Become a leader	0.11	−0.21*
	Gain trust	−0.03	0.05
	Solve social problems	−0.08	0.17
'KSH'	Become a leader	0.16	0.26**
	Gain trust	0.00	0.27**
	Solve social problems	−0.19*	0.04
'OSM'	Become a leader	−0.06	−0.04
	Gain trust	0.13	0.08
	Solve social problems	−0.06	−0.04
'O'	Become a leader	0.01	−0.18*
	Gain trust	−0.08	0.00
	Solve social problems	0.06	0.21*

Note: *: $p < 0.05$; **: $p < 0.01$.

Table A.27 Corporate identities (MISSION) and communication strategy elements (Pearson correlations)

	MISSION: become market leader	MISSION: gain trust	MISSION: solve social problems
COMGOAL: provide information	0.11	–0.10	–0.05
COMGOAL: prove the fulfillment of expectations	0.14	–0.02	–0.20*
COMGOAL: create dialogue	–0.24**	0.11	0.25**
MNGOBJ: design appealing message	–0.02	0.06	–0.04
MNGOBJ: identify stakeholders groups	0.03	–0.09	0.07
MNGOBJ: build relations	–0.01	0.03	–0.03

Note: *: $p < 0.05$; **: $p < 0.01$.

Index

Key: **bold** = extended discussion; f = figure; n = endnote; t = table.